The
Problem
of
Being
Human

Lloyd J. Averill

The Problem of Being Human

Judson Press, Valley Forge

THE PROBLEM OF BEING HUMAN

Bible quotations in this volume are in accordance with the Revised Standard Version of the Bible, copyright 1946 and 1952 by the Division of Christian Education of the National Council of the Churches of Christ in the United States of America, and are used by permission.

Permission is hereby gratefully acknowledged for use of material which first appeared as articles in the following issues of *The Christian Century:*

Chapter 3, January 12, 1972, Copyright 1972, Christian Century Foundation.
Chapter 7, August 12, 1964, Copyright 1964, Christian Century Foundation.
Chapter 9, October 2, 1963, Copyright 1963, Christian Century Foundation.

Library of Congress Cataloging in Publication Data
Averill, Lloyd James, 1923-
The problem of being human.

Includes bibliographical references.
1. Man. 2. History—Philosophy. I. Title.
BD450.A9   128   73-15211
ISBN 0-8170-0617-6

Printed in the U.S.A.

To Carol

Acknowledgments

Some of the ideas expressed in this book were first tried out in campus lectureships, and I am glad to record here my sense of the honor conferred by the appointments and my appreciation for the hospitality of my official hosts: to President Durwood Fleming of Southwestern University, Georgetown, Texas, on the occasion of the Willson Lectures; to President John D. Moseley and Chaplain Allen Smith of Austin College, Sherman, Texas, on the occasion of the Willson-Nichols Lectures; to the late President James Laurie and Chaplain Raymond Judd of Trinity University, San Antonio, Texas, on the occasion of the David and Roxanne Willson Lectures; and to Chaplain David Bremer of Muhlenberg College on the occasion of the Institute of Faith lectures.

It gives me pleasure to recall the enthusiasm expressed for this project by my friend, Dr. Douglas Oldenburg, minister of the Covenant Presbyterian Church, Charlotte, North Carolina, which renewed my efforts to press on to its eventual publication.

My colleague, Dr. Larry L. Rose, has been an incisive and constructive critic of these pages. Although he will not approve of everything which has survived to the final draft, his probing questions helped me to draw the statement into rhetorically tighter and intellectually tougher form.

Carol Anne Averill was the first auditor of most of the ideas written here, and she paid me the ultimate compliment of taking them seriously. The writing is clearer for the hours we spent in conversation about them. She also participated substantially in the preparation of the typescript. Throughout the project, and indeed in everything we have done together, her gifts of warmth and encouragement have buoyed my flagging spirits and renewed my own problematic humanity at important points. To her the book is affectionately dedicated.

Contents

Part I. Presuppositions for a Diatribe

Chapter One: A Problematic Ambience   13
Chapter Two: Historicity and Humanhood   23
Chapter Three: An Autobiographical Excursus: 31
                Apologia pro vita mea

Part II. History as Fate

Chapter Four: How "New" Is Modern Man?   45
Chapter Five: Revolutionaries and Other Romantics: 61
                The Escape from Fate

Part III. History as Freedom

Chapter Six: The Coordinates of Man   85
Chapter Seven: Political Fundamentalists
                and Other Reactionaries: 103
                The Escape from Freedom

Part IV. History as Relation

Chapter Eight: The Matrix of Man   127
Chapter Nine: Crisis in Sexuality: The Loss of the Other   151

Part V. History and the Transhistorical

Chapter Ten: The Inexpugnably Personal   179
Chapter Eleven: History over Our Heads: 203
                  The Recovery of Hope

Notes   217

Part I
Presuppositions
for a Diatribe

Chapter One

A
Problematic
Ambience

AN UNFAMILIAR WORLD

If, in any period of history, human life deserves to be designated problematic, it is surely our own.

Writing in *The Meaning of the Twentieth Century*, the distinguished social scientist Kenneth Boulding has said, "Our precious little planet, this blue-green cradle of life with its rosy mantle, is in one of the most critical stages, perhaps the most critical stage, of its whole existence." [1] This is not the clever ploy of a social scientist, who might like the world to appear as desperate as possible for the fun of saving it. What Boulding observes is widely affirmed intuitively as well as empirically. Existence "on the boundary"—awareness at once of the stubbornness and of the fragility of human life, of the possibility of an expanded humanness and humaneness beyond all our dreams, and yet of the possibility, too, of a dehumanization beyond all our nightmares— this boundary-line situation is probably the most pervasive theme of our present culture. It finds literary delineation in the works of Nathaniel West and Faulkner, of Conrad and Joyce and Eliot, of Kafka and Celine, of Camus and Becket. It has been dramatized in the "theater of the absurd" and the so-called "living theater." It is analyzed in the existential psychology of Frankl, Fromm, and May;

in the existential philosophy of Heidegger and Marcel; and in the existential theology of Tillich and Bultmann. And it is frighteningly exemplified in the struggle between the totalitarian and the libertarian which seems now, in America, to be reaching a new intensity.

There can be little doubt that our current perplexities have their roots, in part at least, in certain massive intellectual achievements, all of which appeared before World War I but whose full force and effect were reserved for this century's midpoint. With *The Communist Manifesto*, Marx and Lenin set in motion a seismic shudder of social upheaval which has split the world and initiated more than a century of uncertain conflict about the relationship between man and his institutions.

In *Origin of Species*, Charles Darwin gave empirical force to the vision of a great chain of being throughout the organic world, awesomely if often frighteningly moved by a drive for survival and preserved by natural powers of selection and adaptation. Darwin dislocated man from his special place in creation and let loose upon the world a category—evolution—which has had powerful influence upon our interpretations of man's social as well as of his biological development. Darwinian evolutionary theory exposed the problematic nature not only of man's origins but also of his ends.

In the work of Sigmund Freud, the liberal optimism with respect to man's nature, which had been the legacy of the nineteenth century to the twentieth, was permanently traumatized by the dark turbulence and the restless energies of the unconscious. If Marx had set man against the hostile forces in his social environment and Darwin against the hostile forces in his natural environment, Freud set man against the hostile forces within himself.

In the work of Albert Einstein, the fixity and universality of such qualities as time and extension were challenged, and in their place was put the view that such reality is relative to the system in which it is perceived. Einstein's technical work has not been widely appropriated by the popular culture and may therefore appear to be less influential in a direct shaping of our mid-century ethos. Yet there can be little doubt that it has appeared popularly to confer a kind of cosmic confirmation upon the historical and moral relativisms which are so prevalent among us and which deepen the human experience of tentativeness in the twentieth century.

Each of these intellectual achievements has brought about a radically new perception of ourselves and our world. Any one of them alone would have been enough for any generation to cope with, but it has been reserved to our own time to struggle with all of them at once. It is no criticism of our own generation to observe that the outcome of that struggle is still very much in doubt.

EVENTS THAT PERPLEX

But the problematic nature of life in our times is the product of more than intellectual influences. It has been dramatically shaped by concrete historical events. Who can doubt that a decade of undeclared war in Southeast Asia, regardless of its political and military justification, has created moral trauma? Half a world away it may have been, but its influence was morally palpable in the American heartland. How could it have been otherwise? As President Wilson once said, "To fight, you must be brutal and ruthless, and the spirit of ruthless brutality will enter into the very fiber of our national life, infecting Congress, the courts, the policeman on the beat, the man in the street." The trauma, indeed, has been worldwide. Eric Sevareid has commented that in Vietnam American military power was misused on a massive scale for the first time.[2] There can be no doubt that it has shaken confidence, at home and abroad, in American righteousness and restraint; and, even more importantly, it has opened up a debate about the justification of war as an instrument of national policy whose consequences may alter the future of warfare.

There are, in the American society today, new and broader sanctions for morally capricious behavior—created by the indiscriminate slaughter in Indochina, the actions of police and National Guardsmen in urban riots and campus disorders, the dangerous excesses of certain civil rights leaders in a cause whose rightness seemed to them to render any means acceptable, the celebration of sadism in the mass media, the depiction of deviance as normal in popular pornography, and the growth of an ethical solipsism. To be sure, our behavior itself is not greatly different from that of earlier generations, who indulged in it but with a bad conscience. The broader public sanctions which support morally capricious behavior today make it possible to indulge but with a good conscience, which creates quite a different moral equation and not a little moral confusion.

Surely it is no coincidence that, at such a time, our national mood is marked by an element of arrogance, since arrogance commonly fills the vacuum, and supplies a substitute if demonic energy, when moral sensibilities take flight. There have been two kinds of arrogance virtually at war with each other in recent years. One has been practiced by radical activists who called for "power to the people," when that turned out in translation to mean "power to *my* kind of people, up against the wall with all the rest!"; who appropriated for themselves the property of others and blithely excused their larceny by calling it "liberation"; whose contempt for their adversaries has been so deep that they would not accord them the most common of decencies; and who disrupted and destroyed quite without apparent moral scruple.

The other has been practiced by public officials who called for "law and order" while practicing their own forms of selective observance of law, who have preferred the arbitrary exercise of power to public debate on the issues, who have practiced deceit as a matter of official policy, and who have been unreachable and unresponsive in the presence of moral appeal. I cannot escape the conviction that, while both forms of arrogance are morally culpable, the latter must bear primary moral responsibility for the former. Official arrogance provides a plausible sanction for an answering arrogance. Should we be surprised, when official power is manipulative or beyond reach, that those who are left powerless should betake themselves either to resignation or to rage? Rage has clearly been ascendant and, even with the end of our Vietnam involvement, it is by no means clear that it has yet reached its zenith. There will be more of it before our current domestic political misadventures play themselves out.

Vietnam, with its military overkill and its moral fallout, has not been the only complex event with which Americans have lately had to come to terms. Racial equality—human equity—is clearly an idea whose time has come, and it is one of the major events of the century. McGeorge Bundy seems to be right: that the last college generation thought of racial equality as logical, while the present generation thinks of it as natural. And the change seems all but irreversible, in spite of desperate and sometimes violent rearguard action to prevent it. Yet even those who support the change are finding that it thrusts them into a world they had not quite bargained for, with demands from newly emancipated segments of society which appear arrogant and unreasoning, and with a radical restructuring needed in established social institutions to overcome the caste and class biases to which even men and women of goodwill have become so well accommodated. There has been no one more perplexed than the white liberal, who worked all his life for integration, only to be charged in these new times with being an assimilationist—an epithet which has replaced segregationist—because he finds it difficult to adjust to the separatist demands of black militants. All of which is to say that, if those who oppose the change in our pattern of human relations are discomfited by the loss of a familiar social order, those who support the change are discomfited at the discovery that the new order is not as familiar as they had expected it to be. And we seem destined to live this unfamiliar and disconcerting existence for some time to come.

Our lives are complicated in more ways than we know by the fact that we live in the midst of a knowledge revolution. The several fields of knowledge are growing so rapidly that the ordinary practitioner lives daily with the apprehension that he may very quickly be left behind. So, ironically, fear of ignorance is one of the enervating effects of our knowledgeableness. More than that, electronic information storage and retrieval means that contemporary men and women have more facts stored up and instantly accessible than any previous generation in the history of the world. While this accumulated knowledge is an incredible boon to human life—in the diagnosis and treatment of physical disorders, to name only a single application of the new information science— it also induces a certain sense of bewilderment. For even under the best of circumstances, we literally have more facts than we know what to do with. That is because facts are not the same as wisdom. Facts are increasing exponentially, but a disposing wisdom does not grow by quantum leaps. Lacking an adequate disposition, ordinary men and women are increasingly disoriented by the clutter of indisposed facts, and there has seemed to be only one way to cope. Says George Morgan:

The individual man, feeling unable to gain a valid perspective of the world and of himself, is forced to regard both as consisting of innumerable isolated parts to be relinquished, for knowledge and control, to a legion of experts. [3]

Yet resort even to the expert is, as it turns out, a frail dependence. After the East Coast experienced an extensive power blackout a few years ago, a member of the Federal Power Commission commented that only five people in the entire country had a knowledge of the computer system which controlled the distribution of power in that region which could have made it possible for them to figure out what had gone wrong, and those five didn't know. So, again ironically, human understanding remains problematic even while human knowledge grows.

We have also reached, in this country at least, a critical demographic event: the time when more than 40 percent of the American population is under the age of twenty-five. Surely it can be no coincidence that one of the most intense experiences of moral self-searching this nation has ever undergone—witness both Vietnam and the racial revolution—has occurred at that particular moment in our demographic history. I am persuaded that Franklin Ford, then Dean of the Faculty of Arts and Sciences at Harvard, was right when he wrote that the "torments of our day have hit thoughtful young people with peculiar force.... Youth is a time of extreme vulnerability to grief and frustration, as well as a time of impatient, generous sympathy." [4] So the restless energy of young idealism has probed and protested, with greater force than ever before in America, the negations and contradictions of our society.

When we complain, as middle-aged Americans are likely to do, that the protest of the young are not accompanied by any positive, constructive program, that complaint displays a sad ignorance of the convictional vacuum into which the American young have been thrust. No one is born with convictions; one learns what it means to hold convictions in the presence of convictional models. But middle-class America has been described by Norman Cousins as "the bland leading the bland." If convictional adult models are not available or, though available, are singularly lacking in moral passion, the young experience a moral vacuum. And since this is a vacuum which idealistic adolescence abhors, adolescents tend to be attracted to passion where it is both visible and vocal, even if it is not principled, since that may be a discrimination they cannot afford. They may not be able to afford it because nothing less than their self-identity is at stake. Self-identity is the product of conflict—of the ability to mark one's self off from other selves—as Edgar Friedenberg and others have shown. Healthy self-identity emerges out of an environment which has convictional distinctiveness, in which the maturing self has access to a wide range of clear and competing values, and where the competition serves to sharpen and enliven the options rather than to subjugate or to obliterate them. But when the adult culture, by its own convictional shapelessness, fails to provide for the young that environment of healthy clash and clarity—as it has failed to do in our own years—then the young must create conflicts of their own, whether on estimable grounds or not, as a matter of literal self-survival. And since the adult culture does not show signs of sudden conversion to a new sense of its own values, we may expect to live with this conflict in one form or another for the foreseeable future.

So the problematic character of events in our time ranges from the macrocosmic to the microcosmic, from the ironies and tragedies of emerging peoples to the struggles of the emergent self.

A CALL TO AFFIRMATION

If, in the light of what I have written above, there is a nub to the problematic character of our contemporary ambience, it can perhaps be expressed in this way: *We do not yet know what kind of man will emerge out of the upheavals of our time—or indeed whether anything recognizably human will emerge at all.* This is the pressing consideration which has led me to conclude that to keep silent—not to speak now in behalf of problematic man—would be to acquiesce in all that is most menacing in what besets him.

It is therefore appropriate that these chapters are written in an *adversary* mood. I use that term as it is used in law, where an adversary proceeding is the quite partisan means by which each man who sues for justice is assured of the fullest and most favorable statement of his case. History has not retained me as the advocate for twentieth-century man, but I have written in the conviction that man can use every *amicus curiae* who can be found.

Taken together, therefore, this book comprises a diatribe. That ancient and once honorable word, now fallen upon evil connotation, deserves to be renovated. As the Greeks coined it, it meant literally "to rub through." This is to say, then, that the ideas here are deliberately abrasive—not in the sense that they are merely designed to irritate (though some readers will surely experience that sensation), and certainly not in the sense that they are intended to exacerbate the problematic situation; but in the sense that they are meant to rub through the problematic and to find the man who is in danger of being overwhelmed, obscured, and finally lost beneath the debris of a fragmented time. So I intend these chapters as a modest contribution to a critical need for which Archibald MacLeish has issued an urgent and eloquent call:

> Centuries ago in a world of gods and mysteries and monsters when man's creativity, his immense creative powers, had been, as Berdyaev put it, "paralyzed by the Middle Ages"—when men had been diminished in their own eyes by the demeaning dogma of the Fall—centuries ago the university conceived an intellectual and spiritual position which released mankind into a new beginning, a rebirth, a Renaissance. What is demanded of us now in a new age of gods and mysteries and monsters, not without dogmas and superstitions of its own, is a second humanism that will free us from our new paralysis of soul as the earlier humanism freed us from that other . . . belief in man—a return to a belief in man—is the reality on which a new age can be built.[5]

While I share what I take to be the essential spirit of this manifesto, and while I delight to make common cause with it, there are two points at which I must differ from it. For one thing, though it is quite right to say that some medieval and Reformation doctrines of the Fall did indeed demean man, it is quite wrong to insist that when we take seriously man's self-regarding proclivity, we promulgate an inherently demeaning view. A realistic doctrine of sin is, rather, an essential check against that waywardness which distorts the human not because it settles for too little, but because it claims too much. And the latter is no less paralyzing of human powers than the former. Exaggerated claims for man—claims on which no man could possibly make good—are one of the sources of our present predicament. We are excessively impressed, on the one hand, with our own unprecedented cleverness, but we are bewildered, on the other, by the durability of such ancient enemies as greed and hate, whose powers cleverness has scarcely diminished at all. The belief in man which our times require must be strong enough to stand the full awareness that man literally delights to do evil even as he rejoices to do good, and to derive man's surpassing importance from *both* of these paradoxical truths about him.

My second disclaimer is from MacLeish's view that we need a "second" humanism—though here there is some ambiguity in his statement, for a few lines later he invites us to a "return" to a belief in man. In my own view, the affirmation of man we need will be both old and new. It will be old in the sense that it will be an affirmation of human dignities which were man's glory in ancient times no less than in modern, and which were indeed sometimes more evident then than now. But it will be new in the moral imagination it will require to affirm, give effect to, and sustain those dignities within the peculiar complex of intellectual and social forms and of historical conditions which have never existed before.

Chapter Two

Historicity
and
Humanhood

THE LOSS OF DIMENSION

Intellectual movements which are shaking the foundations and historical events which seem larger than life conspire to confer upon our times their peculiar sense of crisis. Yet something is happening to us which is more subtle than broad movements or discrete events, something pervasively problematic which is more important than ideology or activism because it discloses their larger significance. It is what Archibald MacLeish has called "the diminishment of man"—"the long diminishment, the progressive diminution, of value put upon man, upon the idea of man, in modern society. . . ." It has been a long time in coming, the poet has written; but in our own generation we have become "aware of a flatness in human life, a loss of depth as though a dimension had somehow dropped from the world—as though our human shadows had deserted us."[1]

Efforts to simplify man have been common in history—attempts to reduce him to manageable proportion, to flatten out his threatening multi-dimensionality, to make him more pliable and predictable. Such efforts have sometimes taken the form of intellectual schemes which view man as an essentially monochrome figure: as rational or as spiritual or as animal, as subordinate to all law or as subject to none. This flattening has sometimes occurred in subtle social processes, like the American "melting pot" which sought the total assimilation of all "alien" differences in a community in which everyone was expected, in the end, to look, act, and think alike. Sometimes the social process has been blatant, like the institution of American slavery which deliberately and systematically divested African blacks of all the cultural carriers of their identity as men—language, kinship, marriage, social organization; or like brainwashing, which seeks total abject compliance with a mastering will. Organized warfare and guerrilla terrorism alike seek to deal ruthlessly with men either as killers or as victims; while at the other end of the spectrum of human passion, reductionism takes the form of that clinical detachment illustrated by a professor of psychology at a major state university, who declared that he was "only interested in the stimulus which goes into the meat and the response which comes out of the meat."

Such efforts to simplify man have not only been common but commonly disastrous; for man simplified is *reductio ad absurdum et nullum*. A man is a complex event. His character is marked by chemistry and by art, by sameness and by singularity, by guilelessness and by guilt, by misery and by grandeur, by the disarmingly obvious and by the elusively mysterious.

Man is *homo ambiguus!*

But a tolerance for ambiguity is not one of the virtues of our time. The problematic in man is complicated not so much by external influences themselves as by an unwillingness on the part of men to accept their ambiguous, and hence problematic, nature. Life at its most effective can be lived only where men find the courage to affirm *all* of the varied dimensions of their humanhood: fate, freedom, relation, and transcendent mystery. Attempts, rather, to escape from one or another of these dimensions are the source of our most pressing problems now, as in the long history of man they have often been. It is precisely the denial of one or another of these vital dimensions which has led, as Archibald MacLeish noted, to that flatness in human life which makes it seem "as though our human shadows had deserted us."

Before we look at the peculiar historical forms this escape or denial is taking in our own times, we need to examine more closely these human dimensions themselves, since they represent the primary anthropological terms within which is set all that follows.

HISTORICITY: LOCUS OF THE PROBLEM

To be a man is to have a history. That is, manhood is not subject to *radical* redefinition with the appearance of each individual man. If it were, history as a discipline of inquiry would be impossible. We are able to make sense out of our reading of ancient records precisely because there is a continuity between the humanness of the contemporary historian and the humanness of the men whose story those ancient records tell. Continuity here does not mean relation on an evolutionary scale, as if in looking back we saw the record of a more childish race now, in our time, grown to greater maturity. Earlier in this century, confidence in the omnicompetence of the category of evolution, applied to social as well as to biological development, led some scholars to that mistaken conclusion. It was widely asserted that, when the biblical documents were arranged chronologically, from the earliest fragment about 1500 B.C. to the last about A.D. 100, they disclosed a steady development from theological territorialism to theological universalism, from ethical crudity to ethical elevation, from the simple and simplistic to the complex and sophisticated. More recent scholarship, possessed of better means to date the biblical documents, has shown how mistaken that evolutionary conclusion was. It was only possible in the first place because those evolution-oriented scholars filled in the considerable gaps in their knowledge of documentary dating *on the assumption that the ideas in the documents would move developmentally.* Thus what purported to be a chronological arrangement was dictated as much by the evolutionary bias of the scholars as by the biblical material itself. The more accurate dating which is now possible points to a different conclusion: that, no less in ancient times than in our own, the parochial and the universal, the crude and the elevated, the simplistic and the sophisticated, *coexist in the same historical period,* and indeed sometimes coexist in the same historical personage. So the continuity between ourselves and our ancient forebears is not simply one in which we might undertake to instruct them from the vantage point of a supposedly more advanced age, but also one in which at points they may be at least as advanced as we. Thus the study of history bears more than antiquarian significance.

It has not been popular among anthropologists, of late, to admit to any universal terms in the definition of human nature. Yet it seems to me that anthropology as a discipline would be impossible, were there no continuities among human cultures. Anthropological activity itself seems to me to demonstrate that, at the practical level, anthropologists regularly assume what, at the theoretical level, they are sometimes disposed to deny. If indeed the humanity of the anthropologist were "wholly other" than the humanity of those who people the cultures he studies, there would be no point of contact between him and them, and thus no point of entry whatever for his anthropological work. In order to have any confidence in the reliability of the scientific enterprise, the natural scientist must assume that there is a correspondence between the scientific mind and the scientific phenomena upon which that mind works its inquiry; the laws of thought must be kin to the laws of high energy physics. Were man himself not continuous with the order of nature upon which he fixes his scientific scrutiny, that would be an "egocentric predicament" indeed, from which no objectively warranted conclusions about the nature of the world beyond the inquirer could be expected. If the analogy is not exact, it is nevertheless instructive; for in a similar way, without the continuity of his own humanity with that of the peoples he studies—without the assumption of some things that are universally human—the anthropologist would also be caught in an "egocentric predicament" from which arbitrary observation but no behavioral science could be expected.

This is by no means to say that all men everywhere think and act in precisely the same ways, but it is to say that thinking and acting in one culture bear paradigmatic relationship to thinking and acting in other cultures. If it appears to be a common moral demand that all men should do the larger good, there is by no means a common understanding among all men as to what that larger good is. If it appears to be a common persuasion that men are subject to numinous powers which they neither create nor control, there is by no means a common persuasion about the character and intent of those powers. If to be a man at all is to be able to speak, that does not require us to overlook the special rhythm and cadence, the nuance and music, which distinguish one tongue from another. So an insistence on continuities in our larger humanity does not deny the rich and peculiar ways in which men shape their own smaller worlds.

To be a man is to have a history: this means, then, that the human is a vast brotherhood, and that it is both perilous and pretentious when a man sets himself against it or apart from it. But it means something else as well: *to have a history is to have a past.* It means that, even from the moment of his conception, each man inherits a past—both biologically and culturally—which he does not will and later may not welcome. And it also means that, as he lives, he acquires his own past to add to that inherited history, and the two—the past inherited and the past lived—become an organic whole.

To speak of "having a past" is to speak of events as irreversible and indelible. "History is only where there is irrevocable change," as the physicist C. F. von Weizsäcker has asserted. "The Second Law of thermodynamics" is, in von Weizsäcker's view, also "the law of the historic character of nature," namely, that "events in nature are fundamentally irreversible and incapable of repetition."[2] It is not man alone who is historical; historicity marks the whole vast process of which man is but a part. But there is, as von Weizsäcker notes, something distinctive about man's historicity:

> Nature undergoes history, but she does not experience it. She is history but does not have history, because she does not know that she is history. And why does man have a conscious, experienced history? Because he alone has consciousness and experience. And so it does seem to me meaningful after all to see man's distinction not in his historic existence as such, but *in his awareness of his historic existence.*[3]

Man's awareness of his past, and what is sometimes the burden of that awareness, is one of his most persistent problems. He is not free to decide whether or not he shall have a past, nor is he free to wish or wipe out of existence what is past. To be sure, he remembers and forgets selectively, but he is not immune to the unconscious influence of what he has thus "forgotten." He is only free to take a position toward his past, to decide what attitude he will take toward it, and what he will make of it, in the present. So what Omar Khayyám wrote is only partly true:

> The Moving Finger writes; and, having writ,
> Moves on; nor all your Piety nor Wit
> Shall lure it back to cancel half a Line,
> Nor all your Tears wash out a Word of it.

The other part of the truth is contained in words Ellis Arnall put into the mouth of a character in his novel *The Shore Dimly Seen:*

"You know what I think? I think that everything you do today, or I do, affects not only what is going to happen but what already has happened, years and centuries ago. Maybe you can't change what has passed, but you can change all the meaning of what has passed. You can even take all the meaning away. That is why men have to be careful. . . ."[4]

One of the problems with having a history is that the meaning of the events which make it up cannot be read off the surface of those events. It appears to be necessary for men to ask the question of the meaning of their own existence—that is one of the universal characteristics of men under whatever circumstance they may be found—but there are no necessary meanings to which they must give their consent. Meanings change, or appear to change, with time and location. Forced, then, by their human constitution to ask, but deprived of self-evident or permanently satisfying answers, men live constantly in a problematic situation. One's autobiography is never complete with respect to events past but is always in the process of revision and reinterpretation, of devaluation and revaluation. Peter Berger notes that "we have as many lives as we have points of views. We keep reinterpreting our biography very much as the Stalinists kept rewriting the Soviet Encyclopedia, calling forth some events into decisive importance as others were banished to ignominious oblivion." With Berger, I am prepared to assume that "this process of reshaping the past . . . probably is inherent in the very fact of language itself." In any case, it is as old as man himself, with "Every rite of passage . . . an act of historical interpretation and every wise old man . . . a theorist of historical development."[5]

Berger also notes that change in either geographical or social position induces fresh activity in the reinterpretation of our past experience, since change provides us with fresh vantage points from which to view and value the past anew. And if, as in the present period of history, there is an acceleration of the rates at which men change both their geographical and social positions—

moving from one part of the world to another, moving up or down the socioeconomic ladder, changing jobs or mates—we should also expect the reinterpretation of the past to reach a critical stage, since the demand for reinterpretation may exceed a man's ability to find new and at least temporarily satisfying significance. The result in some who experience this problem is identity crisis, a sense of dislocation and *anomie*.

THE TERMS OF OUR EXISTENCE

Man's historicity confers upon him, then, a certain fate: fate in the sense of a basic constitution whose terms he cannot change; fate in the sense of a heritage he did not choose; fate in the sense of a lived past which cannot be revoked at the level of event but can only be reworked at the level of significance. This fateful aspect of our humanness will be the main concern of Part II.

Historicity also means freedom, a seeming, but only a seeming, paradox, since freedom is a constituent of man's basic constitution. It is also a part of his fate: he is "condemned to be free," as the Sartreian existentialists would have it. If man has a basic constitution, he has also virtually an infinite variety of ways of combining and of utilizing what that constitution confers, and an almost infinite variety of ways of valuing it. Thus in spite of his fate, man still determines in large measure what he will make of himself. *Historicity means that manhood is always in process,* and that, in spite of his fate, his nature is not fixed. That is why, in chapter 6, I have felt it more appropriate to attempt to locate man by means of coordinates in a dynamic system, rather than in terms of morphology which arrests and thus falsifies man's historical— i.e., processive—character.

Historicity means relation. To "have" a history, as von Weizsäcker noted, is to be aware of having a history, and awareness is both created and communicated by language. Since language must be learned from those who already know it, the history of individual man is no private, lonely affair, but is rather a social history. Self and society, language and history, are thus all terms of corelative importance, each entailing all of the others. In determining what attitude to take toward his own history, man never begins *de novo,* as if he were the first man; he begins, rather, with the attitudes which are given to him in that continuing conversation out of which his selfhood emerges and within which it is sustained, as Part IV attempts to make clear.

Finally, *historicity means participation in the transhistorical*. If, as a result of his historicity, man is driven to ask the question of his own existence, not many men have found in history itself a sufficient resource in supplying the answers to that questioning. This may be, as Augustine believed, because of man's astonishing capacity to transcend both historical process and his own selfhood—to step outside of them, as it were, in order to take an attitude toward them; for this transcendence (as Reinhold Niebuhr described Augustine's view) points to the conclusion that "the limits of the self lie finally outside the self." Augustine concluded, said Niebuhr, "that the power of transcendence places [man] so much outside of everything else that he can find a home only in God."[6] In describing his own very similar position, Niebuhr wrote: "Human life points beyond itself. But it must not make itself into that beyond. . . . It can, therefore, understand the total dimension in which it stands only by making faith the presupposition of its understanding."[7] Thus the historical is finally fulfilled only in the transhistorical, as Part V concludes.

The locus of the problematic in man is primarily, then, his historicity. He is not merely the victim of autonomous, external events which thrust him, willy-nilly, into a problematic ambience. Ambiguity and ambivalence there are, indeed, in the historical events which play around and upon him; but ambiguity and ambivalence are also, as we have seen, permanent dimensions of the self-as-history. It is the interaction of outer and inner histories which weaves the problematic, now one generating the urgency and now the other.

Human life is thus *inherently problematic;* whether it is also *ultimately problematic* is a different order of question, to which I shall address myself in the last part of this volume.

Chapter Three

An Autobiographical Excursus:
Apologia pro vita mea

THE POINT OF VIEW

In protesting the dehumanizing influences of our times, it would be ironic indeed if I were to consent in what I have written to the submergence of my own history and humanity. That these adversary essays are written from a distinctive human location will very quickly become clear in what follows, and I gladly acknowledge in advance some of the influences which shape that view. I am by confession a Christian of Protestant heritage, by profession a theologian, and by opportunity a teacher and administrator for two decades in colleges of the liberal arts and sciences. Each of these has formed to some degree the angle of my vision, the places and ways in which I have experienced the problematic myself, the aspects of it which have laid an imperative grasp upon me, and the responses I propose to make to them.

The style and content of these chapters are strongly influenced by my primarily theological bent. It is, in fact, possible to say both that I have attempted here to do my theological work from a secular perspective, and that I have attempted to do my secular work from a theological perspective. In spite of the currency, even notoriety, of books with the word "secular" in their titles in recent years, there is still no assurance that the word itself is accurately understood, particularly by the self-consciously religious among us. It is reported that when three churchmen were asked by their pastor to define "secular," the first replied that it referred to the differences among denominations, the second said that it had to do with the division between the North and the South, and the third stuttered with embarrassment that it had to do with relations between men and women. The truth is, of course, that the "secular" is simply the world of time and sense. And that leads, for some, to difficulty in bringing together the words "secular" and "theology," since it is a popular notion, outside the churches as well as among them, that such a combination would be a disjunction if not an outright contradiction. They simply do not go together, on this view, because worldliness is a different order of things from faith. For all its popularity, however, that view has been mistaken, at the very least since the Fourth Evangelist first announced that "the Word became flesh and dwelt among us."

Perhaps my intention will become clearer if I say that what I have attempted here is a kind of *situational theology*, in which the Christian consciousness addresses itself to some pressing reality in the world, in the hope of bringing clarity out of, and persuasion in behalf of, a Christian world view. Any theological work may do that, of course, but it is ordinarily expected to bring a problem into direct contact with the special biblical and technical language which distinguishes Christian from other kinds of discourse, and with those special events whose significance Christian discourse has traditionally probed and explicated. A situational theology is different. In it the Christian consciousness engages itself with man's experienced demand for responsible action in the face of some pressing moral choice; the Christian imagination plays upon man's awareness of a depth beneath the surface of his daily life. Thus situational theology tests the extraordinary possibilities of very ordinary discourse; it looks for transparency in the continuities of life rather than in those singularities for which the claim of special revelation is sometimes made. *And it does these things without feeling obliged to remind the world at every turn of just how Christian the whole process is.*

In this regard, then, what I have written is a reflection of the way Christian theology is being done these days, at least by some theologians. Roger Hazelton has commented that "any honest faith in what the Christian past called God" arises for our own time out of "an exploration and examination of our mysterious humanness," most particularly "in those experiences of transcending or being transcended. . . ."[1] In this sense, at least, the chapters which follow represent Christian advocacy—or so I hope—and I have found it necessary neither to obscure nor to belabor the point.

LOCATING A LIBERAL

Ideologically, the other term which must be added to my identification as a Christian is that I am a liberal. I realize that some readers will find that a quaint confession at best, and the book which results a kind of old-fashioned document. Worse, in the mouths of some of our contemporaries the epithet "liberal" has become a term of angry reproach. To be a liberal at this juncture of American history is to be cordially despised by the hard-liners of the Right for being allegedly soft on disorder and lawlessness, and to be despised with something less than cordiality by the hard-liners of the Left for continuing to believe that any good may yet come out of existing institutions and due process. David Riesman has recently observed that, in the view of the American undergraduate these days, "if you are a radical you must be ready to kill and if you are not then you are a liberal (which in their vocabulary is a swear word). And this bitter choice has had a paralyzing effect, for the students don't want to kill nor do they want to be liberals."[2]

For some time I considered choosing another term to describe my ideological position, not to escape the reproaches, which have a certain bracing quality, but to avoid misunderstanding. There is much in what has been denominated "liberalism" in the past quarter-century which I too reject. But the other terms I might have chosen—humanist, personalist—while less political, are scarcely less subject to misreading. I have therefore decided simply to live with being a liberal and to try to say as clearly as I can what I think it means to be so. Part of that definition I shall give here, but the more important parts will emerge as I work through the issues which preoccupy the chapters which follow.

Liberal, as I intend the term, means location with elasticity. One of the chief problems any man faces is that of finding a posture for life which will permit him to be a respondent rather than a victim. To be a respondent means having a steady and steadying base from which to respond, sometimes adding the weight of that base to the momentum for social change, sometimes using it to resist when change moves in undesirable directions. But to be a respondent means, as well, finding the kind of base which permits what historian Herbert Butterfield has called "the maximum elasticity" for response—a base that enables rather than enslaves.

What locates a liberal is that he gives priority to human—that is to say, personal—values over intellectual, institutional, property, or any other kinds of values. I do not mean to suggest that personal values bear no relation at all to the others. The danger with those other values, when we permit them to become isolated and to claim inordinate attention, is that they seize on one aspect of the human while depreciating or ignoring the others, and thus succeed in reducing man to a one-dimensional being. The liberal insistence on personal holism is an attempt to understand the complexity of man and a determination to resist the reductionism of special interests and the tyranny of limited values. The liberal is pledged to take seriously all the interests which support and enlarge human life and to hold the sometimes competing and imperialist claims of those interests in creative tension, which is as risky as it is essential to a fully human integrity.

It is precisely this humanism which gives the liberal elasticity for his location. Through centuries of experience, man has had a common identity, men participate in a continuing humanity, such that the latest arrivals on the human scene can mark their similarity to the earliest. If, in reading the records of ancient peoples, we find much that is strange, the more remarkable thing is that so much is familiar; and what is familiar is precisely our common *humanitas*.

Yet, in spite of the strains which mark us all, the human cannot be crowded into some all-comprehending system, cannot be exhaustively explained or even exhaustively described. Man cannot be confidently predicted. He will be what he will be, not necessarily all that he was, and we do not know fully what he will make of himself until he appears and acts.

Here, then, in this liberal humanism is what it takes to be a respondent to life: location with elasticity, identity with freedom.

Unlike the fundamentalist, whether political or religious, the liberal need not be suspicious of the future; and unlike the radical, he need not be contemptuous of the past. Unlike the fundamentalist, the liberal need not absolutize what is merely the prudential wisdom of the ages and fear the innovative; and unlike the radical, he need not absolutize the innovative and despise the old.

LIBERALISM IN PROFILE

Liberal means a rejection of incivility and outrage in dealing with one's opponents. Incivility, when it becomes a way of life, is a form of social treason: it subverts the society by dissolving an essential ingredient in the mortar that holds society together. Civility makes possible the peaceful coexistence of differences—in other words, it makes a society possible—because it assumes, often mistakenly but in the long run usefully, that differences among men are matters of good faith. Civility is probably the best guarantee that, though ideas may be despised, men can still win some measure of respect and thus a social order can be preserved. Incivility as a way of life becomes viciously *ad hominem,* attacks men rather than their persuasions, and thereby falls readily into that nonnegotiability which is the enemy of every social order.

Liberal means confidence in a process of compromise and consensus as the best means of approximating that very complex human arrangement we call social justice.

Liberal means a commitment to complicate life rather than to simplicize it; not a commitment to entangle or obscure, nor a delight in theoretical or structural elaboration for their own sake, but rather an appreciation of the organic complexity of all life, in which the whole is entailed in every part and the influence of each part reaches even to the remotest perimeter of the whole. Thus the liberal knows that to despise any man is to indulge in self-hatred.

Liberal means a sense of moral subtlety which refuses to embrace change as if change were always progress; which declines to agree that more is always better; and which refuses to consent to the popular demand that, because a thing *can* be done, it *ought* to be done. Jacques Ellul seems to be right: "Everything which is technique is necessarily used as soon as it is available, without distinction of good or evil. This is the principal law of our age."[3] The liberal means to repeal that law. A Christian liberal will agree with D. T. Niles that our urgent task is "the discovery of what brilliantly successful methods must now be discarded because they are not faithful to the gospel of Jesus Christ."

Liberal means a sense of intellectual subtlety which is not content with monolithic descriptions (treating, say, communism and Roman Catholicism as if they were undifferentiated entities, as some of the simple-minded critics continue to do even at this late date); which refuses to credit the reality of monads (the pretense, for instance, that there is any such thing as a "self-made man," or that there is a natural harmony of interests which justifies the selfishness of individuals); and which repudiates claims to univocal meaning (as if there were only a single self-evidently right way to read history).

And finally, *liberal means an attempt to be both tenacious and tentative.* In a report on my book *American Theology in the Liberal Tradition,*[4] a reviewer in a conservative journal wrote that, considering the criticisms of liberalism which the book contains, "one wonders why the author still wants to regard himself as a liberal." What that reviewer failed to understand—and he has had lots of company in recent years, including some so-called liberals—is that liberalism can engage in the process of self-criticism and of reformation without hasty abandonment or ritual self-hatred. Indeed, when the liberal no longer experiences the tension between the value of old formulas and the need for new formulations—when he no longer holds his absolutes provisionally—he ceases in that moment to be a liberal and forsakes the risks of elasticity for the spurious safety of a fixed location.

Somehow we have the notion that one cannot be fully serious about a proposal made *for the time being.* Serious proposals, we have usually thought, must be absolute, timeless. Once they are seriously put forward, we feel bound to defend them long after their human usefulness is at an end. That, I am persuaded, is a misunderstanding which had got men and societies into difficulty as far back as memory can reach. Intellectual conflicts, political struggles, and military battles have raged for no other reason than to perpetuate ideas, even ideals, whose time has quite properly run out.

We have seen this happening all around us. The New Left, critical of the bankruptcy which it thought had befallen the traditional liberal statement of American ideals, proclaimed a new absolutism with virtually no recognition that time itself would soon enough change New Left into Old Obsolescence. Conservatives in the Congress regularly frustrate legislation intended to ease the frightful stresses of our national transition to a thoroughly urbanized society, because they mistake agrarian impulses—quite at home in an earlier generation—for immutable moral law which they think ought to be at home in every generation. And in Vietnam, men on both sides died in senseless numbers because an arrangement intended a decade before to serve very limited political and military ends was tragically translated into the eternal myth of the struggle of good with evil.

By way of contrast, the strategy of the liberal must be *serious, but for the time being.* It is not only that perceptions themselves have a limited validity; it is also a matter of historical priorities. When man undervalues man, he must be called to a higher level; when man goes wild with deific pretension, he must be reduced to life-size. To shift the emphasis from one historical moment to another is not to lack conviction; it is rather to be *expedient* in the best sense: *proper under the circumstances.* A man who was a nonpacifist on August 5, 1945, and a pacifist on August 7, 1945, did not lack moral seriousness. Rather he was struggling to take seriously a new order which burst with the brilliance of a thousand suns over Hiroshima on August 6, 1945. I am quite prepared to insist that anyone who could take the *same* view of power after August, 1945, that he took before it had simply lost his grip on history. Even a decade ago I would not have stated the human stakes or the issues as I do today. I may think it mistaken or unnecessary to do so a decade hence. I see no alternative to stating them as I do now.

"Liberal" assuredly does *not* mean "gifted with prophetic powers," but I hazard the prediction that a re-formed liberalism is the most likely direction for the diffused and almost instinctive humanism of many Americans—particularly the young—to take in the immediate future. Current anger directed against liberalism is, in some, clearly revulsion; in others it is, rather, a lover's quarrel, and the possibility of reconciliation seems to me very good indeed. The student radicals who reject political murder do so out of a humanism which also marks liberalism at its best; and unless a really new radical ideology appears which can "get it together" for humanists who populate much of the radical movement largely by default—a development which I seriously doubt—the repristinization of liberalism is likely to seem a more and more attractive enterprise. Radical spokesman Jack Newfield has called for a return to "the old Populist passion for participation and decentralization" in order to offer "the post-linear kids something inside their own nation with which to identify, so they won't have to import exotic fantasy notions of revolution from North Korea or Bolivia."[5] Newfield refuses to call his "new Populism" liberal; liberalism, he asserts, is dead. But the same influences which make possible a "new Populism" are improving the chances for a new liberalism, for at the base of both there is a passion for human dignity. Liberal humanism now has the prospect of shaking off the unimaginativeness and dogmatism into which a certain kind of success—the capture by the liberals of the major centers of power— has beguiled and betrayed it, and of recovering something of its essential genius.

THE RELIGION OF A LIBERAL

Rather than leaving my description of liberalism principled but unspecified, something more by way of preliminary specification may be in order as a means of disclosing the nature of that humanism which is in and under the chapters which follow. To be a *liberal Christian* means, in my view, that faith subsists primarily in personal loyalty rather than in loyalties defined on institutional or creedal grounds. This is neither a pietistic nor a docetic view. It requires intellectual structure in order to achieve intelligibility, and social structure in order to achieve relevance. But structures tend toward fixity and imperialism and must be constantly reminded of their derivative and dependent character in order to inculcate a proper modesty. Let me return to the remark of historian Herbert Butterfield, which I cited earlier, but this time I shall supply the fuller context of the remark, Butterfield wrote:

> There are times when we can never meet the future with sufficient elasticity of mind, especially if we are locked in the contemporary systems of thought. We can do worse than remember a principle which both gives us a firm Rock and leaves us the maximum elasticity for our minds: the principle: Hold to Christ, and for the rest be totally uncommitted.[6]

For the liberal Christian, faith subsists primarily in loyalty to the person of Jesus as the Christ, and no requirement may be placed upon the life of faith which does not spring from that loyalty.

And what does spring from it? Two things at least. One has to do with a certain style. A man is what he does. The significance of the historical person of Jesus as the Christ is to be discerned in his action; to hold fast in loyalty to him means to commit myself to his style. That style is in no doubt. If we call it "love," we must nevertheless recognize that, in acting it out, he gave new effect to that old term. His style of love is the reconciliation which seeks to overcome the enmities and lonelinesses of life, whether chosen or imposed. It is the compassion which cares for another's hurt. It is the service which participates in another's good. And those to whom he directed his love were not simply those whom he could identify in the popular and narrow sense as "his kind" but included the whole of humankind. To hold fast in loyalty to Jesus as the Christ is to commit myself to his style: therefore to choose Jesus is to choose every man.

The other thing which springs from that loyalty is faith that personality is the key to reality. If Jesus as the Christ valued persons, that was because he experienced God as the Supreme Person, addressing him in the most intimate of personal terms. In spite of the difficulties which it entails, I see no satisfactory alternative to asserting unequivocally that God is Person, unless it be to say with Paul Tillich that God is the *ground* of the personal. If more than personal attribution must be made to God, nothing less can be made. No ultimate explanation of the universe will do which is less than personal; for if such explanation were less than personal, then the very least among us would be a more ultimate fact than the supposed ultimate. So God must include in himself our own kind of personal reality even as he transcends it.

As a theologian who has passed his fortieth birthday, it might be assumed that I am facing a crisis in identity—not mine but God's. It is from my age group that Christian theologians have come in recent years to announce the death of God, though their influence at this writing is in marked and—in my view—both proper and predictable decline. I want to make it clear that I do not believe God is dead. That is not to say that nothing affecting our experience of God has happened at all. Something has indeed happened, but it is not in the first instance an inability any longer to experience the divine; rather it is our inability to experience the human. We live in a depersonalized moment of time when men are increasingly swallowed up in masses and when bureaucratic and technical values often take precedence over human ones. Roman Catholic scholar Michael Novak spoke for me when he wrote:

> Religion can thrive only in a personal universe; religious faith, hope, and love are personal responses to a personal God. But how can the immense question of a personal God even be posed and made relevant when fundamental questions about the meaning and limits of personal existence are evaded? [7]

Then I, for one, cannot escape Novak's conclusion: "God, if there is a God, is not dead. He will come back . . . when man comes back." [8]

THE POLITICS OF A LIBERAL

Political liberalism aims at maintaining an open society. What the liberal wants society open for is dialogue. To live in a monologue world is to be condemned to a peculiar kind of tyranny—the tyranny of self-limitation. Those who insist on telling it "like it is" while deafening themselves to the witness of those who see things differently have not seized freedom; they have renounced it. Freedom exists, not in isolation, but in the midst of conflicting and competing ideas, where each challenges and corrects, and is in turn challenged and corrected by, the others; where the limitations of each are supplemented by the insights of all. Which is really to say, though to some it will seem strange to say it, that freedom exists only where dialogue makes compromise possible.

One of the most sensitive indices of any society's political regard for man, and of its determination to guard the integrity of man, is the degree to which the individual citizen is secure in his person against the arbitrary and excessive curiosity of his neighbors, his employers, and the state. One of the most ominous and still popularly underrated threats to the open society in this country is the steady invasion of privacy. Government data banks store up an incredible amount of the most intimate kinds of information—and misinformation—about very ordinary citizens. Military intelligence has conducted unauthorized and constitutionally inappropriate surveillance of civilian activities; and the Federal Bureau of Investigation, with presidential connivance but with the same constitutional impropriety, has interested itself in all manner of perfectly legal activities of private citizens. And what may, in the end, be equally as bad as this official snooping is a prospering and profitable "eavesdropping industry" which recognizes no man's right to be alone.

The open society is one which respects the rights of the wrong and which determines to restore the rights of the wronged. In an open society, an idea which is unpopular may not, for that reason alone, be considered true. An open society must care more for justice than it does for its own convenience; and it cannot afford the luxury of polarization by political anathema, of which the slogan "America, love it or leave it!" is one of the most arrogant and reprehensible examples. There is no better statement of the liberal faith in an open order than that written by Judge Learned Hand:

> Risk for risk, for myself I had rather take my chance that some traitors will escape detection than spread abroad a spirit of general suspicion and distrust. . . . That community is already in process of dissolution where each man begins to eye his neighbor as a possible enemy; where nonconformity with the accepted creed, political as well as religious, is a mark of disaffection; where denunciation, without specification or backing, takes the place of evidence; where orthodoxy chokes the freedom of dissent; where faith in the eventual supremacy of reason has become too timid that we dare not enter our convictions in the open lists, to win or lose. Such fears as these are a solvent which can eat out the cement that binds the stones together; they may in the end subject us to a despotism as evil as any that we dread.[9]

The human and historical location from which these chapters are written, then, is Christian and liberal, and the predilections which I have exposed in discussing these two terms above are the themes and variations which are woven into all that follows.

Part II
History
as Fate

/

Chapter Four

How "New" Is Modern Man?

A UNIVERSE ON THE MOVE

Astronomers tell us that we are living in an expanding universe. The notion, once confidently held, that those points of light which pierce our diurnal darkness are forever fixed has been given up long since, and instead we peer wonderingly out into a space whose frontiers are continually being pushed further into the infinite unknown. Once upon a time the star was our most persuasive metaphor for changeless reality, for dependability. After all, do we not take our direction from it and set our clocks by it? But that was before a more sophisticated astronomy revealed that some objects which we thought belonged to our own star system are, instead, massive independent systems of stars so distant from our own system that crude observation mistook them for single stars. Changeless and dependable they may be when measured by our own momentary time and place, by our cosmic myopia; but when taken in their own cosmic measure, it now appears that they are not fixed but fugitive.

The fact seems to be that everything in the universe is on the move. A simple illustration helps us to understand how that fact was arrived at. When I sit in my car at a grade crossing waiting for a train, the whistle of the speeding engine is high-pitched as it approaches where I sit; but immediately after it passes me, the pitch of the whistle seems to drop. The pitch of sound is related to the length of the waves that transmit it. As the train approaches, those waves are shortened, piling up on each other, as it were; but as the train passes and disappears, the waves are lengthened out, lowering the pitch of the sound. Scientists call this the Doppler effect, and it can be applied to moving light as well as to moving sound. As a light source approaches the observer, the light waves are shortened, moving toward the blue end of the spectrum; but as the light recedes, the waves are lengthened and move toward the red end of the spectrum. The greater the distance of the receding light, the more marked is the shift toward the red on the spectrum.

When the light from the great star systems of the universe was analyzed, the shift toward the red suggested that each system was apparently rushing away from every other system with a speed which increased with its distance. The picture of the universe which emerges from this observation is almost incredible. There are perhaps 100 million galaxies, or star systems, within the range of our telescopes, and each of them is moving away from all the others like particles from the center of an explosion, with the most distant of them traveling at perhaps 200 million miles an hour.

However much the fact of an accelerating universe may intrigue us, or momentarily move us by its awesome mystery, it is not likely to have any direct effect on the way in which we face the decisions of the next twenty-four hours, or even the choices which will shape a lifetime. If an expanding universe temporarily humbles us, its implications are much too remote to touch us in any permanent way. We may react like the student who heard a lecturer predict that our sun will eventually grow hotter and life will disappear from our planet. In great agitation, the student raised his hand and asked, "How soon did you say this will happen?" "Perhaps in ten billion years," replied the lecturer. "Oh," said the student with evident relief, "I thought you said ten million!"

But the fact is that acceleration cannot simply be dismissed as "out there," awesome but irrelevant. The observation that everything in the universe is on the move seems to apply as well to man's social life on this planet as it does to cosmic evolution, and the rush of history toward undetermined ends is the human analog of the haste of the stars. Even in the nineteenth century the

quickening pace of things human was becoming clear. So James
Russell Lowell could insist that

> New occasions teach new duties;
> Time makes ancient good uncouth;
> They must upward still, and onward,
>   Who would keep abreast of Truth.[1]

And Alfred Lord Tennyson could remind us that

> Our little systems have their day;
> They have their day and cease to be. . . . [2]

Simply consider, for example, how much more of the world is
immediately accessible to us than ever before. Wireless telegraphy
began with Marconi's first experiments just before the turn of the
century, and wireless telephony followed not long after 1900 with
the work of Fessenden, Fleming, and DeForest. Commercial
broadcasts began in the 1920s. It was in the 1930s, during the
Spanish Civil War, that battlefield sounds were first relayed by
radio to audiences thousands of miles behind the lines; but in
recent years, for those who dared to look, television satellites
brought almost instantaneously into our homes the specter of
death methodically dealt out by "search and destroy" operations in
an Asian nation half a world away. Few Americans have the
opportunity to attend a national political convention, but
millions of us have felt our political pulses quickened and our
interests sharpened by television coverage which gives those
watching at home a broader experience of the event than is
available to the official delegate who sits on the convention floor.
Perhaps most incredible of all, 125 million Americans—to say
nothing of the millions in other countries who watched by satellite
transmission and delayed telecast—saw the first two earth men at
the moment they set foot upon the moon.

Not only television but travel has accelerated the rate at which
we experience the world. Already we are able to travel so fast by
commercial aircraft that it takes hours, if not days, for our bodies to
adjust to the change; and what we do today at subsonic speeds we
shall shortly do at supersonic.

Nor is it simply that our experience grows at a quickened pace.
Formal knowledge seems to increase at a geometrical rate. It is
confidently estimated that in some technical and professional
fields, half of what a man will need to know ten years from now in

order to do his work competently is not even known at this time.

IS THERE A NEW MAN TO MATCH THE NEW WORLD?

It would scarcely be surprising, then, if we concluded that our own time is different from earlier times not simply in degree but in kind. And there is a sense in which that is true. Simply consider the power available to us for destructive purposes. Ever since the invention of gunpowder, men have been devising cleverer and more efficient ways to increase the degree of its destructiveness. And when gunpowder was made obsolete by the invention of nitroglycerin and TNT, that degree was raised to an even higher power. But in 1945 something utterly, shudderingly new burst upon the world. Nuclear devices are not simple chemical reactions like nitro and TNT. Rather they represent a totally different kind of power. They do not merely raise the degree of our destructiveness; they create a whole new kind of destructiveness. It is new in the almost cosmic intensity of its power; new in the indiscriminate rain of invisible death carried by the winds and dropped capriciously on the helpless and hapless anywhere in the world; new in the uncontrollable side effects it generates; new in its lingering presence in the winds and in the genes for generations.

It is a new world in the possibility of total genocide and global destruction, at least; not simply in degree, but a new kind of world which has not appeared before. But is it *a new man* who now lives in this new world? The wrong answer to that question can create a vast amount of mischief. If there is a new man to match the new world, then failure to make a total break with the old man will only frustrate and postpone and in the end defeat our ability to cope with a totally new situation. If, on the other hand, it is not man but the potency of his tools which has changed—not the human condition but the environment with which that condition must now cope—then to pretend that we are "new" men will give us a false confidence in inner resources we do not, in fact, possess. It will only delay the process by which our ancient human problems and possibilities are adapted to a new environment. And in an accelerating world, delay may be fatal.

There are many who tell us now that we *are* "new" men—men at last "come of age," grown beyond the childhood and adolescence which marked our earlier historical eras, able for the first time to declare our independence from oppressive notions of human limitation and to work out our own salvation with the same imaginative and inventive genius which created the laser and first sent a manned satellite hurtling into space. Those who hail a "new" man tell us that he can be recognized by these new powers: by the unprecedented progress he has created; by his ability to accept scientific explanation without recourse to the metaphors and mythologies traditionally supplied by religion; and by his ability to live without the moral conventions of the past to guide him.

It is this view of the new man about which I want to record my own profound skepticism. It is not the vocation of the theologian to keep men perpetually enslaved by a pessimism about their own nature, but it is the vocation of the theologian to be skeptical about human pretentiousness. Christian theology does not depend on man's continual childishness, but it may contribute another meaning for maturity.

So I want to examine these marks of the alleged new man and to say what at least one Christian theologian sees in them.

THE CHANGING AND THE UNCHANGING

Does progress point to a new man? This is where my skepticism begins. Whenever there is talk of progress, the instances which come most readily to mind are the technical advances of our era in electronics, in space travel, in nuclear energy, and in medical discovery. And there can be no doubt at all that these are absolutely astonishing achievements which, a bare decade or two ago, seemed like so much science fiction.

But, someone might protest, these are not simply technical achievements; they are human achievements. What man makes also makes man. Then how is man being made by his achievements, and what is man making of them?

I can dream of the peaceful uses of nuclear energy harnessed for constructive and civilized ends; but I cannot shake off the awful picture of destruction which the bomb threatens, or the hypocrisy of scientific and military pronouncements about "clean" bombs, or—most important of all—the haunting memory that the nation which talks most about the peaceful uses of the atom was the first to unleash its dissolving fire upon human beings. "Preventive" war with nuclear weapons has been urged upon American presidents by influential military and political figures in the highest councils of state; but it is the survival of anything which passes for civilized life that such warfare would prevent.

I can bask in the warm feeling toward nature inspired by a growing conquest of man's oldest biological enemies; but I see no abatement of that common hypochondria in which men imagine malignancies which have their etiology not in microorganisms but in a profound malaise of the spirit, which drugs may dull but from which they cannot deliver us.

I am thrilled by direct transmissions from men on the moon; but I am sobered by the possibility, now assured by the technology which put men there, of satellites around our earth which will be able to conduct a surveillance of our behavior more searching than anything George Orwell could have predicted. Nor is there reason to be wholly reassured that the mad, or the near mad, may not some day attempt to hurl into orbit nuclear missile stations in a bold and brutal effort to intimidate and finally to subjugate the entire world.

I watch commercial television; and though I am sometimes instructed by what I see, I am also aware of the cultural, intellectual, and even technical poverty of much that is shown. And I am disturbed by its power to mold tastes and behavior.

Electronics have made our lives incredibly easier and more efficient, and I am mystified by the miniaturization which can reduce a complex circuit to barely visible dimensions; but I am distressed at my inability to carry on a successful correspondence with a computer which has charged me for purchases I did not make and seems programmed to prevent a correction of the account.

Still someone may rightly insist that our achievements are not only technical but social, and that in the social progress of our times there is evidence of man renewing himself. Only recall that in this century the divine right of kings has all but vanished, the United Nations gives promise that the world may yet be a community, and the movement for civil and human rights has raised a new generation dedicated to human equity.

To be sure, I too note with an approval inspired by my democratic bias the departure of the divine right of kings; but I must note with more than passing disapproval the claim to inexorable and unimpeachable right allegedly conferred by the dialectical movement of history, which has catapulted the Communist rulers into despotic and bloody control over vast areas of the world.

I am greatly heartened by the movement toward world community which the United Nations promises, even though that movement is inch by inch; but I am distressed by the many who are so ready to denounce and at every occasion to subvert its influence. There is some evidence, indeed, that we may be moving into a new era of nationalism in this country, to say nothing of the entrenched nationalisms of Asia and Africa, Europe and the Middle East.

I acknowledge with gratefulness the courage of a Martin Luther King in behalf not alone of Negro rights but of human rights; but I am still revolted by those in North and South alike, whether black or white, who spread the virus of racism. I am no more prepared to recognize Lester Maddox or George Wallace as the New Adam than I am Stokely Carmichael or Eldridge Cleaver.

There is more in all this than an attempt to strike some kind of balance sheet. With all man's knowledge and accomplishment, he still knows what it is to face a threatened and meaningless existence, an existence in which his gadgetry multiplies his fears and mocks his emptiness. It is still possible to ask, as one man phrased the desperate question to me: How is it possible to be so miserable in the midst of so much? In spite of unsurpassed knowledge and control over the world, men still know what it is to face powers within their own personal worlds which seem bent upon destroying them at the very source and center of their being.

So contemporary man is as new as Paul crying: "I do not do the good I want, but the evil I do not want is what I do. . . . Wretched man that I am! Who will deliver me from this body of death?" (Romans 7:19, 24). Or the rich young ruler crying from the midst of his wealth and power, "What must I do to be saved?"

SCIENCE AND MYSTERY

Then a second sign of man's newly achieved maturity, we are sometimes told, is his ability to accept scientific explanation without recourse to the metaphors and mythologies traditionally supplied by religion. Religion, on this view, has always fed on the credulous in men—on their eagerness to believe what cannot be demonstrated and to hope for what seems unlikely. Religion and science are thus as unlike as two things could be. Religion is speculative, mythic, and questionable; science is empirical, factual, and probable. Increasingly as science is able to demonstrate the way the world really is, mature men find they no longer have need of the speculative answers religion has supplied to their questioning. So the argument goes.

It is the kind of argument that the very modern man, Fred Hoyle, approves. Hoyle is a world-famous cosmologist and professor of astronomy at Cambridge University. In his popular book, *The Nature of the Universe*, Hoyle leaves no doubt about the matter. In a personal epilogue to the book, Hoyle writes:

> And now I should like to give some consideration to contemporary religious beliefs. There is a good deal of cosmology in the Bible. My impression of it is that it is a remarkable conception, considering the time when it was written. But I think it can hardly be denied that the cosmology of the ancient Hebrews is only the merest daub compared with the sweeping grandeur of the picture revealed by modern science. This leads me to ask the question: Is it in any way reasonable to suppose that it was given to the Hebrews to understand mysteries far deeper than anything we can comprehend, when it is quite clear that they were completely ignorant of many matters that seem commonplace to us? No, it seems to me that religion is but a desperate attempt to find an escape from the truly dreadful situation in which we find ourselves. Here we are in this wholly fantastic Universe with scarcely a clue as to whether our existence has any real significance. No wonder then that many people feel the need for some belief that gives them a sense of security, and no wonder that they become very angry with people like me who say that this security is illusory. But I do not like the situation any better than they do. The difference is that I cannot see how the smallest advantage is to be gained from deceiving myself. . . .[3]

Clear enough. Hoyle's point is quite simple: there is an impassible gap between the biblical and the scientific, and only those will repair to mythical categories of explanation who do not dare to live in this world of science.

Earlier in his book Hoyle discussed the concept of an expanding universe with which I began this essay. With all of the star systems in range of our telescopes rushing pell-mell toward the limits of our observation, it would seem to follow that gradually the total number of observable systems would be reduced. Hoyle doubts that this will be so. As galaxies disappear, he says, new ones will condense out of what he calls "the background material" so that the number of observable galaxies will remain what it is now. But will the "background material" eventually become exhausted and thus the number of galaxies finally reduced? Hoyle thinks not. Why? ". . . I find myself forced to assume that the nature of the Universe requires continuous creation—the perpetual bringing into being of new background material." Hoyle then asks himself the question you and I want to ask: Where does the created material come from? And he answers:

> It does not come from anywhere. Material simply appears—it is created. At one time the various atoms composing the material do not exist, and at a later time they do. This may seem a very strange idea and I agree that it is, but in science it does not matter how strange an idea may seem so long as it works—that is to say . . . so long as its consequences are found to be in agreement with observation. [4]

On the contrary, Professor Hoyle, I do not find this idea of matter created out of nothing strange and unfamiliar at all. I find it, in fact, in the book of Genesis, placed there out of the religious experience and speculation of the Hebrew people about whom, you have assured us, it is unreasonable to suppose that they understood "mysteries far deeper than anything we can comprehend, when it is quite clear that they were completely ignorant of many matters that seem commonplace to us." Ignorant they were indeed; but instead of leaving them in the primeval mists of history, this modern astronomer has, all unwittingly, found them at the frontier of an expanding universe.

> In the beginning God created the heavens and the earth. The earth was without form and void, and darkness was upon the face of the deep; and the Spirit of God was moving over the face of the waters. And God said, "Let there be light"; and there was light (Genesis 1:1-3).

Creatio ex nihilo—creation out of nothing—that is the way Genesis begins; and that mythic assertion has formed the beginning of all Jewish and Christian orthodoxy since Genesis. It should be clear that I am using the term "myth" here in the sense in which it is employed in current discussions of theology, the history of religions, and literature. Myth is not an arbitrarily constructed fairy tale indifferent to truth. It is, rather, the nonliteral language which is used to speak about mysteries which stand at the center of things. Myth speaks of a reality which appears to be discontinuous, even primal, and which therefore cannot be accounted for by invoking the usual causal categories of explanation. Myth casts an image rather than denoting an object and thus is able to catch truths no merely literal language can contain.

It is clear that, on this ground, when Professor Hoyle writes about creation out of nothing, he has left ordinary scientific explanation and has employed mythological language as surely as the Genesis writers and their theological descendants have done.

I have a suspicion that in retrospect Professor Hoyle saw that this was what had happened, and that, on the terms of his own argument about the dispensability of religion, he was understandably embarrassed about it. The statements cited above were from the first edition of his book, which appeared in 1950. In revising the book ten years later, the earlier language about the new matter not coming from anywhere—it "simply appears—it is created," he had said—is changed. This is the way Hoyle wrote that same passage in 1960:

> The most obvious question to ask about continuous creation is this: Where does the created material come from? At one time created atoms do not exist, at a later time they do. The creation arises from a field, which you must think of as generated by the matter that exists already. We are well used to the idea of matter giving rise to a gravitational field. Now we must think of it also giving rise to a creation field. Matter that already exists causes new matter to appear. Matter chases its own tail.[5]

And so, if I may say so, does the scientist. In an attempt to avoid the use of mythological language, Hoyle now tells us that the new matter is "caused" by the old, but clearly causation as he here employs it means something quite different from its ordinary meaning. Existing matter, he speculates, generates a "creation field," and out of that field—not, note, derivatively out of the old matter—new material emerges. Thus to say that "matter that already exists *causes* new matter to appear" stretches the notion of causation beyond admissible limits.

There is, in fact, some slight acknowledgment of the peculiarity of his argument when Hoyle tells us that continuous creation "is perhaps the most surprising of all the conceptions described in this book."[6] He leaves us quite uninstructed about this new concept of a "creation field," except by analogy to a gravitational field. Yet surely the analogy is largely verbal and not really very helpful in explicating Hoyle's meaning.

And no wonder. Talk of a "creation field" which brings previously nonexistent matter into being bears only a semantic difference from his statement a decade earlier that new matter "does not come from anywhere." "Creation field" is a myth, nonliteral language used to speak of a reality which appears to be discontinuous, even primal, and which therefore cannot be accounted for by invoking the usual causal categories of explanation. It is, in fact, strikingly like the myth of the "divine field" which is used by process theologians—John A. T. Robinson is one, and he writes about it at length in *Exploration into God*[7]—to describe the ways in which God influences events in nature and in history. The "creation field" of the astronomer is no less mythological than the "divine field" of the theologian and the *creatio ex nihilo* of the biblical writer.

So this is what our "new" man—our scientific man grown beyond the need for myth—comes to: full circle back to the book of Genesis!

The point here is not to criticize Professor Hoyle for what he has done, since in my view the religious response to experience is indelible rather than vestigial. Chapter ten will deal with this theme at some length. The point here is to criticize Professor Hoyle for pretending that he has not done what he has done. The same criticism, but on a massive scale, must be directed against the Soviet Union. Nowhere in history has there been such a deliberate and systematic attempt to root up and tear out all vestiges of religious practice. The Soviet authorities have attempted to give not only philosophical but also legal force and effect to the proposition that "man come of age," meaning scientific socialist man, has no need of religion in any form. Yet the ideology of the Soviet system would collapse, were it not for the religious apparatus its perpetrators have constructed to replace the ones they have suppressed. So official Soviet life has its rituals and holy days, its sacramental *rites de passage*, its creeds and inspired writings, and its saints whose relics are the objects of popular veneration. Like the Vatican, the Kremlin occasionally revises its authorized hagiography as former saints become nonpersons. And all this is done without the faintest glimmer of official recognition that supposedly scientific socialism is grounded in myth and cultus.

Religion is, indeed, reformable, and it regularly requires reformation; but it is not eradicable. Man *sans* religion would require a world *sans* mystery; but that would be an altogether different world from the one in which, without our consent and against all our contrary efforts, we are set. Perhaps what is discerned as mysterious in one religious tradition is not transferable to another religious tradition, as the humanist philosopher Ronald Hepburn has insisted.[8] But awareness of the mysterious in existence, of that which awakens in us a sense of awe, of dread, of succor, "can continue to occur even in agnosticism," as Hepburn admits; and he adds significantly, "They seem in this sense to be 'autonomous,' not belief-dependent, experiences."[9] Religions take their shape around the ways in which men respond to what they thus experience as "sacred." And when the attempt is made to criticize certain forms of religion—to call men away from mistaken mysteries, as, for example, the humanist may want to call away the Christian—"this work of criticism," as Hepburn quite properly notes, ". . . has itself a religious aspect. It is continuous with the religious task of overthrowing idols, of superseding inadequate notions of deity, with the quest for the 'God behind god.' . . . Even if we have no God behind god, we have form-of-life behind form-of-life, vision behind vision."[10]

Then, rather than disavowing and discrediting the religious, as Professor Hoyle invites us to do, we follow a more reliable guide in another very modern man, biologist Julian Huxley, who views religions quite indispensably as "the noetic organs of evolving man"—organs whose "special function concerns [man's] position and rôle in the universe, his relations to the rest of the cosmos, and in particular, his attitude to the powers or forces operating in it, including those in his own nature: or in the fewest possible words, with his attitude towards his destiny."[11] Or we may follow the scientific humanist Max C. Otto, who believed that it is better for a wise man to befriend mystery than to pretend that our technical knowledge can master and unmask it. "It seems to me better to admit," wrote Professor Otto,

that in things which matter most we are compelled to leave something at loose ends . . . . whether we admit it or not there is always an unexplored beyond, always mystery.

A conscious awareness of this mystery does healing work on the inward man. It is the healing work of acknowledged ignorance in the revered presence of that which eludes comprehension—the incomprehensible in each other, in the life we are called upon to live, in the great cosmic setting that reaches from our feet to the infinities.[12]

MORAL CONVICTIONS AND MORAL AMBIGUITY

Finally let us look at this third assertion: that the "new" man can be recognized by his ability to create his own moral precedents in a "new" world to which the moral experience of the past is no longer relevant. Here the argument seems to be that history today moves with such rapidity as to defy any permanently satisfying or universally applicable moral precepts; that modern life is so complex that the moral wisdom of earlier (i.e., simpler) periods of history provides no reliable guidance.

Now if this means that the availability of nuclear power, for example, has created weapons which are different from earlier arms not simply in degree but in kind; that our exploding world population is creating unprecedented problems for communication and for the equitable distribution of goods and services; that biochemical research is putting into our hands the power to imitate life in the laboratory and to shape human personality—if the argument is that these developments and others like them create incredibly tough problems for moral decision, then of course I want to agree. But I fear that the real point of the argument, as it finds popular expression and endorsement, is rather different. We are really being told that, in earlier periods of human history, life was more transparent and men were more credulous, and that under those conditions moral certainty was much easier to come by than it is today when life is opaque and men are terribly knowledgeable. If, then, at an earlier time it was possible to make a simple appeal to honesty in the relations of men and of nations, now it is more difficult than it ever was to know what the truth is. In a more face-to-face existence altruism may have seemed not only desirable but attainable, but in the impersonality of an urban-technical society altruism has no morally translatable meaning. In a less threatened world it may have been possible to weigh other values over self-preservation, but our own threatened times require a radical reassessment of that old ideal.

If this is the argument, then I want to insist that it represents a distorted reading of both the past and the present, and that it perpetrates a dangerous misunderstanding of our existence as men under the conditions of history.

It distorts the past because it imputes to it a simplicity of life which was not there. There was nothing simple about the problems which faced Jesus and his contemporaries in the economic sphere. The majority of the Palestinian population lived in grinding poverty, with few natural resources and almost no technology to create them. The distance between the "haves" and the "have-nots" was stark, shocking, and nearly hopeless. There was nothing simple about the attempt to win sustenance from the earth in order to overcome their perpetual hunger, so much were they at the mercy of a nature which they did not understand and over which they could exercise pitifully little control. There was nothing simple about their struggle to stay alive, in view of the ravages of disease which created a staggering rate of infant mortality and a tragically brief adult life span. And there was nothing simple about the political problems of a small and terribly vulnerable country which had been a pawn in the politics of the Near East for centuries.

Life was not simple then, and it is only the distortion of distance, intensified both by our pride and our self-pity, which makes it appear so. Our present problems are indeed unprecedented, in the sense that they require a technical knowledge both for their understanding and for their solution unlike any which have preceded them. But this surely does not mean that the *proportion* of moral difficulty with which they now face us is greater than men have ever faced before. Technology is morally ambivalent; at the same time that it creates problems, it also creates the resources for their solution. I seriously doubt—though I know of no way to measure it with precision—that there is any greater imbalance between our problems and our resources today than there has ever been.

And if we are inclined to impute to the past a simplicity of life which was not there, so we prefer to think that at earlier times men found less difficulty in arriving at the moral convictions which their difficulties required. Where was it, then, that men were once quite certain about those moral standards which seem so tenuous to some of our contemporaries? To what historical period should we go to find unquestioning acceptance of that moral wisdom which now seems to us problematic, if not outdated? I ask for information, because I do not know of any such place or period.

Everywhere I look in human history I find the same debate going on, indecisively, over the same issues. What is justice? What is truth? What is the good life? The problematic character of human morality is one of the chief themes of the Books of Moses, the dialogues of Plato, the Gospels and Epistles of the New Testament, and the confessions of Augustine and of Leo Tolstoy. Self-interested deception versus honesty, the one versus the many, survival values over social values: these are the historically permanent tensions within which men have sought to live the moral life. And everywhere I look in human history, I find men excusing moral confusion and indecision by saying that it is no longer possible to be as certain about the "old" standards as it once was.

The truth is, rather, that moral clarity and moral conviction are no harder, no more agonizing, now than they have ever been. Moral ambiguity is not a new fact of life; it is, rather, one of the permanent and ineradicable facts about existence under the conditions of history. Man's values have always been hazards which required imagination and courage.

A new man for a new time? No, I think not. Man came morally of age in the Garden when he discovered his nakedness.

Chapter Five

Revolutionaries and Other Romantics: The Escape from Fate

THE DISENCHANTMENT OF OUR TIMES

If one were to look for a single word in which to catch up the mood of many Americans these days—Americans who, with the exception that they share this common mood, often look very much *un*like each other—I think that word would have to be *disenchantment*.

The poor are disenchanted because, in the world's richest society, there appears to be no will to do what could be done if we willed it: the abolition of poverty. Affluent middle-class men and women are disenchanted at the discovery that "making it," or having it made for them, is such an unsatisfying point at which to arrive. The undereducated are disenchanted because they lack political and economic clout, while intellectuals are disenchanted because, for all their purported influence, they seem to be able to change so little. Radicals of the Left and radicals of the Right have been disenchanted—if for quite different reasons—with American performance in Southeast Asia during the last decade.

Men of all sorts and conditions wonder why, in a world where change accelerates, there seems to be so little of genuine progress. An age of technology has emphasized technique and driven out spirit, with the result that we are now able to accomplish an

61

incredible number of things, but we are not sure why one ought to be done rather than another. At a time when mass communications bring citizens closer than ever to the centers of political decision, the massive centralization and bureaucratization of government, and the dependence upon the technocrat for its management, create an unprecedented distance and popular sense of detachment. When institutions of higher education were at the height of their power and prestige in American life, they exhibited an astonishing incapacity to manage their own affairs and a strange confusion arose about their own proper role in society. And so the specification of disenchantment could go on.

Romanticism seems to be a standard refuge for the disenchanted. At the turn of the eighteenth century into the nineteenth, European disenchantment with a philosophical and religious reason ruled by formal logic led to a new quest for the free spirit; disenchantment with the priority given to life scientifically analyzed led to a new authority claimed for life subjectively experienced; disenchantment with an art dominated by geometry led to a fresh unleashing of the imagination. And in politics, disenchantment with monarchical mismanagement, insensitivity, and extravagance led to popular revolutionary movements on both sides of the Atlantic.

And in our own century, it was German disenchantment with military defeat, the humiliations imposed by the treaty that supposedly brought peace in 1919, fumbling attempts at shaping democratic institutions, and the economic ravages of uncontrolled inflation that led to the romantic idealizations of "blood and soil" in National Socialism.

Let it be said at once that romanticism—with its typical love of nature, its frank sensuality, its discontent with what is and its willingness to dream of what ought to be, its emphasis upon imagination and the unfettered spirit—is an indispensable element in our humanness. How much the poorer we should all be without the music of Mozart, Brahms, and Rachmaninoff; the literature of Blake, Hugo, and Melville; the philosophy of Schleiermacher and Emerson; the painting of Turner; and the political impulses toward popular government! But romanticism can also run riot, as it did in Germany from the Munich *putsch* of 1923 to Hitler's suicide in 1945. When romanticism, with its emphasis on natural virtue, feeling and intuition, and human autonomy, claims that these are the whole truth about man, then it simply offers an alternative form of blindness and tyranny to the ones it would replace. Taken alone, romanticism is a dangerous distortion of the human situation, because it is an effort to escape what I described in the preceding chapters as the *fate* of our existence under the conditions of history. It is dangerously mistaken in assuming that it can shape the future with little or no regard for the past, or that man can be changed simply by reconceiving him, or that elements in the human constitution— rationality, for example, or a sense of the transcendent—can be ignored with impunity in favor of other more romantically congenial elements, such as emotionality or total immersion in the sensory.

Two forms of romantic escape from fate have been particularly active in the period through which we have been passing. Some participate in both movements, others only in one or the other. One form is essentially political and involves a call to revolution. The other is essentially nonpolitical and involves a call to eroticization. Both result, I am persuaded, not in humanness recovered, as they insist, but rather in man diminished.

REVOLUTION AND THE ROMANTIC FLAW

There is one absolutely indispensable requirement for a successful revolution, and that is a proper understanding of the nature of man. The revolutionary ideology can be expected to work only if it is pretty savvy about the nature of human nature. The reason that some splendidly motivated revolutions have gone sour lies precisely, I think, in the fact that they mistook the nature of the human situation. And having discovered, after embarking upon their revolution, that things do not go quite as they had expected— that human nature does not react in the revolutionary situation quite as they had anticipated—the revolutionaries grow desperate, unwilling either to admit their error or to abort their revolution, and so they resort to any means available to keep a bad thing going, if for no other reason than to retain whatever power they may have seized. Thus a root error about the nature of human nature—not just an egregious error about the nature of the enemy but even about the nature of the revolutionary himself as a man—changes the careless rapture of revolutionary idealism into a desperate, naked, calculated struggle for survival.

The Russian revolution is a case in point. It was both profoundly moral and profoundly mistaken. It was moral in that it desired to give to every man a degree of economic equity which modern history has nowhere else provided. It was mistaken in its failure to understand that revolutionary leaders who are "temporarily" invested with absolute political authority in order to create the new society in a hurry—even when it is announced in advance that their authority will be transferred to the people once social justice has been achieved—will become so enamored of their power that they will never voluntarily relinquish it and will invent whatever historical and ideological fictions may be necessary to hold on. Thus, ironically and tragically, a revolution for social justice is transmuted by desperately mistaken men into one of history's more repressive regimes.

Reflections like these have given me pause in the presence of that recent crop of romantic American revolutionaries denominated the New Left, for I very much fear that their programs for needed social reform are fatally compromised by the profoundly flawed views of human nature which they appear to hold. More conservative voices among us have insisted, rather shrilly, that the New Left is simply fascism, 1933 style, in more benign disguise. I do not know whether that historical analogy will do in every detail, but I am impressed by the fact that many advocates of a new American revolution have shared, both with German National Socialism and with Soviet Communism, a romantic view of human nature which seems to me as wrong as it is beguiling. Revolutionary romanticism erred recently, as it has sometimes done in the past, by attributing to all men, or at least to some preferred group of men—the Aryan race, the proletarian class, the unestablished young, or the disestablished poor—more nobility, more wisdom, and more natural virtue than there is any warrant in history to claim. So romanticism may be expected to lead inevitably to disillusionment, disillusionment to desperation, with desperation finally evaporating whatever idealism is left, revealing at last an acid precipitant which burns and blights all who come in contact with it. This seems to be happening, at the present writing, in the demoralization—almost the demise—of the

New Left. But it is by no means entirely gone as a cultural and political force, and its influence is much too recent to ignore. And who can say that capricious political events may not yet reinvigorate it?

RECENT REVOLUTIONARIES AS ROMANTICS

The romanticism of our recent revolutionaries has lain in their notion that, in a state of nature, man is innocent and good, pure in ideal and uncorrupted in motive. In their peculiar rewriting of the narrative of man's Fall, the new radicals seemed to see the satanic creeping into their Eden, not in the temptation to be "like gods, knowing good and evil," as in the biblical story, but rather in the temptation to be like establishment men, knowing rules and regulations. Left to himself, man always does what the good requires, in this radical view. Men go wrong only when they permit their playground paradise to be turned into an institution. It is life in a socially organized mode which causes man to lose his innocence and dries up his goodness, which pollutes his ideals and corrupts his motives. Institutions are not only unnatural, in the radical view, but they also are actually contrary to nature, because they frustrate the uninhibited freedom which nature intended to confer upon every man. Institutions compel a man to give up doing "his own thing" and force attention upon a corporate will, which is to say that institutions rob man of his identity and warp his integrity. If so, the only way to recover true manhood is to tear down all social institutions, in the faith that Eden will be regained thereby, and innocence restored.

But there is, so one gathered from the professions of some of the younger radicals, a point of no return. There comes a time in life, apparently, when institutional discipline has so broken and domesticated a man that there is for him no way back to the innocent wildness of paradise, a time when he will actually prefer the comfortable slavery of Egypt to the stony openness of the Sinai. Some radicals seemed to fear that there is an age—and it pressed younger and younger—beyond which natural goodness is irretrievable, idealism irrecoverable. Perhaps that was one of the reasons for their haste: apprehension that, if they were not quick to cut the ties of institutional tyranny upon their own lives, they might themselves step across that continental divide and become hopelessly trapped in a system which grinds men into mulch.

Then I want to insist that it is always romantic to assert that men taken individually are good, but that institutions are evil; that there is no seed of corruptness in man's heart until it is placed there by the compromises and immoralities into which he is driven by the pressures of organized society upon him.

To put the matter in theological terms, the radical view is romantic because it denies the reality of original sin. If I understand that ancient doctrine correctly, it asserts that all his life long every man struggles with, and regularly succumbs to, the temptation to treat the universe as if its center were located precisely at the place where he stands, and not elsewhere; as if its topography were drawn to the contours he sees, and not otherwise; and as if its horizons were exactly where he measures them, no nearer, no farther. The wisdom of that doctrine in no way depends upon simpleminded interpretations of Eden as a place to be located on a map, of Adam and Eve as our literal first progenitors, and of our sin as the inherited result of their primal misdeed. Of course that is nonsense! Each man's own nature as a man is the sufficient explanation for his sometimes subtle, sometimes savage, attempts to remake the world in his own image. That desire is rooted deep in the excessive demands of his own esteem. If he cannot have life on his own terms, played by his own rules, he fears that he will be swallowed up in oblivion, that he will literally become a nonentity. If he cannot claim all importance, he fears that he will qualify for no importance at all. So each man is his own Adam, each woman her own Eve.

Nor is the wisdom of this doctrine in any way dependent upon outrageous notions of "total depravity" which have sometimes been associated with it, as if *all* man's effort were directly contrary to the good, the true, and the beautiful. Of course that is nonsense! Original sin does not deny that men achieve much that is good; rather, it insists that even the best we do is touched and tainted by our self-interestedness. It does not deny that men may possess truth about the absolute; rather, it refutes their claims to possess absolute truth. It does not deny man's discrimination of beauty; rather, it warns against his eagerness to profit from ugliness. It does not deny his capacity to love; rather, it discloses his readiness to idolize.

It is not difficult to understand why revolutionaries reject the doctrine of original sin and, indeed, are threatened by it. They reject it because they are engaged in all-out war, and wars are not won by generals and enlisted men who go off into battle beating their breasts and crying, *"Mea culpa!"* Wars are won only if warriors can be persuaded that their cause is absolutely right and the enemy is absolutely wrong. Reasonably normal men may perhaps learn to kill devils with a good conscience. But if the enemy should be seen simply as a man like ourselves, uncertain about the full rightness of either cause, it is infinitely harder to make that enemy out to be a demon dangerous enough to kill. And there is nothing more devastating than, having maimed or killed another man, to have to live with doubts about the moral justification of that act. So when wars are fought, mass hypnosis is aimed at relieving the soldier of any guilt and the enemy of any good. This is a part of what makes warfare immoral: it can be prosecuted successfully only if the real moral proportions of praise and blame, wisdom and folly, cause and effect, right and wrong are deliberately distorted.

The radicals quite understood that as it related to Vietnam, and they delighted to prick the balloon of American pretentiousness and self-righteousness at being the moral policeman of the world. What they had not the wit, nor even the humor, to see was that they were themselves pointed instances of precisely the way original sin works: they imitated in themselves what they professed to hate in the American presence in Vietnam; what was condemned as evil in their adversaries was adopted as virtue in themselves. So civil authorities became "pigs," and university authorities became monsters of repression upon whom the ordinary human courtesies of dignity or civility would be wasted. "Listen to me!" the radical demanded. "I have something to say which is worth hearing because I am uncorrupted, standing as I do outside the corrupt establishment."

At the same time the radical insisted, "I will not permit you to listen to him! He has nothing to say worth hearing, since no good can possibly emerge out of the establishment."

"Listen to me!" the radical persisted. "I am young and will therefore tell it, clear-eyed, like it is."

"I will not permit you to listen to him!" the radical repeated. "He passed the point of no return and has lost his vision."

So the instruments of mass hypnosis—chant and slogan, march and martyrdom, berating and burning—served the radical purpose of widening the polarities between their virtue and someone else's vice, between their truth and someone else's deception, between their innocence and someone else's establishment. Radicalization simply cannot permit the cry, *"Mea culpa!"* within its own ranks. It cannot admit uncertainty, complicity, or error, without becoming deradicalized. Admission of uncertainty, complicity, or error, is what communism calls "counter-revolutionary" activity. Since, therefore, the radicals' warfare is threatened by the idea of man's *universal* sinfulness, what cannot be domesticated must be denied. What they cannot do is annul the law of life, that those who reject the doctrine of original sin are condemned to illustrate the doctrine.

To insist that recent radicalism has suffered from a moral infection which is common to all of us is not to deny genuine moral excellence in the radical program. Today's radicals are, indeed, notable for what Professor Sidney Hook has called "high-mindedness."[1] They declare passionately for humanity and against brutalism, for freedom and against repression, for truth and against error. Nor is there any reason to doubt the sincerity of their declarations. There is ample reason to doubt both their intellectual consistency and their practical judgment. When jazz critic and novelist Nat Hentoff asked one of the radicals whether the new order had any place for due process, the man replied, "There are times when those of us preparing a revolutionary society must simply go ahead and do what's right because we understand what's right better than anyone else." Hentoff comments, "I saw the utter conviction with which he spoke and knew how sincere a jailer he could be."[2] Professor Herbert Marcuse made it quite clear that there would be limits to the tolerance of the revolutionary society which he envisioned and of which he became the chief philosophical architect. He spoke of "discriminative tolerance." He insisted that the new order cannot be expected to "protect false words and wrong deeds,"[3] that movements and ideas "which are obviously and objectively aggressive and destructive" will simply not be permitted when the radicals come to power. When asked what "objective" tests he would propose to use in detecting the false and wrong, the aggressive and destructive, Professor Marcuse replied, "The nature of such a movement would be clear."[4]

Few instruments in the hand of man are more dangerous than an excessively good conscience, nurtured by faith in one's own moral purity and infallibility. Such a conscience can create mischief without misgiving and justify the world's worst deeds with the world's best reasons. As Shailer Mathews, late dean of the University of Chicago Divinity School, wrote more than sixty years ago, "Agitators are indispensable, but an agitator mad with altruism is as dangerous as any other madman."[5]

So I want to associate myself with an observation made by George Kennan, former American ambassador to the Soviet Union, who has had a unique opportunity thus to assess the character and consequences of one historically recent form of revolutionary radicalism. Mr. Kennan writes:

> I have seen more harm done in this world by those who tried to storm the bastions of society in the name of utopian beliefs, who were determined to achieve the elimination of all evil and the realization of the millennium within their own time, than by all the humble efforts of those who have tried to create a little order and civility and affection within their own intimate entourage, even at the cost of tolerating a great deal of evil in the public domain. Behind this modesty, after all, there has been the recognition of a vitally important truth—a truth that the Marxists, among others, have never brought themselves to recognize—namely, that the decisive seat of evil in this world is not in social and political institutions, and not even, as a rule, in the will or iniquities of statesmen, but simply in the weakness and imperfection of the human soul itself, and by that I mean literally every soul, including my own and that of the student militant at the gates. For this reason, the success of a society may be said, like charity, to begin at home.[6]

LANGUAGE AND PROTEST

The view of revolutionaries is romantic, not only when it locates the source of evil exclusively in institutions rather than in men, but also when it believes that men can live most humanly apart from what it believes to be the enslavements of institutions. So the radical gospel asserted the self-sufficiency of individual men and affirmed their full completeness as men apart from the organized human community.

Those who held this distortion literally convicted themselves out of their own mouths. Were they the first men in history to be troubled by the tension between man and society? How far back beyond Socrates must we push to search out the origins of that issue? Were they the first men in history to espouse self-determination and profess hatred of tyranny? How far beyond Moses must we press to find that issue first appearing? If recent radicals have betrayed any innocence, perhaps it is simply that they are innocent of possessing any historical awareness. One wonders whether they could possibly know that they were merely appropriating, very late in the debate, words whose meanings have been refined by centuries of continuous and systematic philosophic examination. Could they possibly have been aware that they were repeating arguments which have appeared over and over in our social history? Did they know that they could not even speak of man and society, freedom and tyranny, were it not for the fact that such concepts have been preserved and transmitted by the oldest of man's institutions, the school and the state? Judging from the proprietary way they attempted to possess these ideas, it seems apparent that they did not know.

In an even more basic way they convicted themselves out of their own mouths. They did not invent the four-letter vulgarisms with which they hoped to offend middle-class sensibilities. Whether they knew it or not, some of their most valued verbal weapons are the most venerable of words, learned by succeeding generations from Old-English and Middle-English usage, and preserved by continual employment through these long centuries because of the unique monosyllabic thud with which they make their verbal impact.

The point is that the very language of protest against institutions is itself institutionalized communication. Indeed, uninstitutionalized, or deinstitutionalized, communication would be a contradiction in terms, since it would put nobody in touch with anybody. Words are not lonely inventions. If they were, there would be no communication but only moanings in the wind. Words are socially formed, socially recognized, socially sanctioned symbols, their meanings preserved through the organized memory of society. Words are used according to certain rules called grammar, and grammar is a convention, a social agreement, the regulation of our verbal behavior by certain social norms. If we care about being understood, we can defy those norms only within certain limits, like saying "ain't" or "we was." Total defiance of the social regulation of our verbal behavior would simply make the defiant one irrelevant. Such defiance would make protest quite harmless, since no one would have the least idea what was being protested, or indeed that the sounds uttered were to be understood as protest at all.

The phoniness of the radicals' indiscriminate rejection of all forms of institutionalization, then, is demonstrated in this: that radical protest against the institutionalisms which enslave men can only be effectively understood by society when the radical himself consents to the institutionalism which frees him for communication through the use of the social convention called language.

When we speak of "dumb animals," we commonly think of those forms of animal life which lack human intelligence, but something even more basic is at issue in the description. They lack man's intelligence in part because they are "dumb" in the sense of being unable to speak. A capacity for language marks the threshhold into the human, as I shall argue at some length in chapter eight. Our humanness is conferred by the *gift* of language: we do not create it; we must *learn* it from those who already know it, and who, in their turn, have been given it out of a funded human experience of incredible range and depth. Human individuality— the ability each of us has to mark himself off as different from the dumb world around him—is socially conferred. Far from being the natural enemy of our humanness, the institutionalization of experience is the absolutely indispensable precondition of our being human at all.

Having said that, I am under no necessity to defend *every* institution which men have produced as somehow beneficial to life. Of course institutions distort and corrupt, and when they do, they require reformation or replacement—*by other institutions;* for it is precisely by the institutionalization of experience that humanness is nurtured.

Then let us be quite clear about this: protest against the institutionalization of experience is simply protest against being human.

RHETORIC AS ACTION

Something more needs to be said just here about the problem of language and the recent revolutionary movement, in the light of a complaint commonly entered by the radicals against liberalism.

Paul Jacobs and Saul Landau, in their study, *The New Radicals,*
wrote:

> to The Movement it is the liberal way of life and frame of mind that represent evil
> in America. Those in The Movement feel that modern American liberals have
> substituted empty rhetoric for significant content, obscured the principles of
> justice by administrative bureaucracy, sacrificed human values for efficiency, and
> hypocritically justified a brutal attempt to establish American hegemony over the
> world with sterile anti-Communism.[7]

To all of that, liberals ought to have the candor and the moral
courage to plead "guilty as charged." I am not prepared, however,
to consent without vigorous reply to the familiar technique used
regularly by the New Left, which compared themselves at their best
with their adversaries—in this case the liberals—at their worst. If
meaningless rhetoric, accommodation to bureaucratic power, and
certain tragically misguided forms of anti-communism do, indeed,
mark the failures of liberalism in the last twenty-five years, I want
to insist that the liberal weakness lay more in wit and courage and
stamina and imagination than in aim.

Humanistic rhetoric is no substitute for other forms of action;
but it is a fatal mistake—to which the new radicals seemed
particularly vulnerable—not to understand that *rhetoric is a form
of action* which either reinforces or compromises other actions,
and that rhetoric which is careless or reckless may either frustrate
worthy ends or, by subtle transformation, make worthy ends less
worthy. Social strategists will ignore at the peril of their strategies
the power of self-fulfilling prophecy. The New Left seemed not to
have learned this, with the result that it was prepared to employ the
most brutal language in the supposed service of humane ideals.
The result, almost inevitably, is the increasing brutalization of the
ideals.

Willingness of liberals to adjust expectations by the requirements of their participation in bureaucratic power structures
has compromised the careless rapture of ideal ends; but when the
quality of life is at stake, to be indifferent to the requirements for
success—even indeed to small successes—is morally indefensible.
"The whole loaf or none" is a fine, round slogan for affluent
radicals who are not hungry. There is no social change apart from
willingness to participate in the structures of power which can
bring about change. Ironically, the new radicals discovered that;
for, in spite of their loathing for liberalism, they found no way to

survive apart from the financial support of liberals, and they found no way to get along without the political leverage which was exerted in their behalf by liberal friends in the establishment.

Anti-communism has become an apparently good excuse for doing some patently evil things, and no better example can be found than the doctrinaire anti-communism which was used to justify American involvement in Vietnam for over a decade. Yet, in spite of its unforgivable excesses, liberal anti-communism has its source in a refusal to tolerate tyrannies even when they allege a devotion to economic and racial justice. The New Left fatally jeopardized its future as a politically viable force in the American society precisely because it elected to replace the "sterile" anti-communism of the liberals with its own virulent and sometimes violent apology for such anti-democratic terrorists as Fidel Castro, Ho Chi Minh, and Mao Tse Tung.

Perhaps this radical failure to recognize that language is not *mere rhetoric* but is, rather, a form of action which has consequences was the result of a larger and more dangerous failure to recognize that any kind of action has consequences. There seemed to be, in many young radicals, a kind of innocence which believed that the most outrageous things could be done with impunity and immunity. Renata Adler, when she was movie critic for *The New York Times*, was the first to draw this odd fact and its possible origins to consciousness in a comment on Jean-Luc Godard's film *La Chinoise*. The aim of the Maoist heroine in the film is to blow up the Sorbonne, but not because she has any desire to build in its place a university nearer to her own ideal, for she is motivated by no substantive ideal. For her, revolution is theater—drama and style; the consequences of this revolutionary activity are of no interest to her. Miss Adler's comment on the situation seems to me so apt and ingenious that I want to quote it at length:

One wonders how much of the radical casualness toward where things *lead* is derived from a worldview created by movies—particularly cartoons—but movies in general. Where everything is reversible and can be undone. Where heroes are killed in one movie only to rise in the next. The same is true, of course, in theater but not to the same extent. You cannot, for example, run a theater reel backwards. And, more important, the stage does not encapsulate an actor for all time in celluloid. Movie actors survive physically on film long after their deaths. So do real events, conserved in documentaries. It is hard to sustain a traditional logic—an awareness of any sort of rational consequences—when a movie sensibility blurs even the terminal fact of mortality.[8]

THE REFUSAL TO HONOR THE PAST

The prospects of the recent revolutionary movement in America, even at its best, were unpromising, in part because the movement was built upon a distortion of the American experience which was both historical travesty and a peculiarly unfortunate form of self-hatred. Since the radicals insisted upon perpetrating and flaunting what was clearly travesty, and because they indulged the luxury of their peculiar masochism, they were unable to marshal the kind of popular support which could have given effect to some of their wholly admirable revolutionary ideals.

Driven to despair by what they took to be the present sickness of the American society, the new radicals turned their backs defiantly upon the American heritage. Unwilling to engage in such "irrelevances" as the actual reading of American history, they could only assume that the pathology of the present is directly traceable to polluted origins, and that only by complete quarantine of those origins can healthy growth begin. But since this historical renunciation involves not someone else's history but their own history, it was in fact a form of self-renunciation which has its own pathological consequences. Jack Newfield was only the first of the New Left spokesmen to realize that critical situation, and he warned that "no insurgent movement has ever succeeded that was rooted in hatred of its own country—a fatal mistake of which parts of the New Left (Weathermen, Yippies) are guilty." [9] As I noted in chapter three, Newfield is attempting to recover a new form of populism in order to "offer the post-linear kids something inside their own nation with which to identify, so they won't have to import exotic fantasy notions of revolution from North Korea or Bolivia." [10]

This is a lesson which some liberals, whose excessively bad conscience has led them to join the chorus of national self-hatred, would do well to learn. There is simply nothing to be gained from failing to acknowledge that, in some respects at least, the American experiment is absolutely unparalleled in the history of the world, both in its scope and in its implication. Historian Henry Bamford Parkes points out that, from the beginnings of colonization until the eve of the First World War, nearly sixty million people left their homes in Europe alone to reestablish themselves in this new world; and during that same period, some five to ten millions were brought here from Africa. "This," Parkes writes, "is by far the largest movement of peoples in all history. . . . Whether one judges it by the number of individuals involved in it or by its results and implications, it is the most important single factor in the recent history of the human race." [11]

Yet it is not simply the scope of the experiment which is unique but its influence as well. Parkes insists that the belief "that the average man can be trusted with freedom," though derived from European intellectual sources, was put to effective and successful test for the first time on the American continent, and that this experience has had a profound effect upon the subsequent political development of Europe:

> The revolutionary doctrine of equality, preached by European radicals but most fully exemplified in the American world, has been the chief provocation of European internal conflicts; and the inability of some European countries to make the necessary adaptation of their institutions has been the main underlying cause of twentieth-century totalitarianism. [12]

Parkes, Sheffield-born and Oxford-educated, is joined in his appraisal of American influence by Sir Denis Brogan, perhaps England's most knowledgeable observer and critic of American institutions. Professor Brogan is not given to political pieties, as I know from having sat regularly in his Cambridge lecture hall, and in his book *The American Character* he makes it quite clear that he is by no means an unmitigated partisan of things American. Still he can write that, when European intellectuals express alarm over the invasion of their culture by the products of an American mass culture, it tells us more about Europe than it does about America.

> [America] is the most democratic of cultures. It has to be banned, harassed, distorted, to prevent its sweeping even over and through the Iron Curtain. "What will come of it, knows God," as was said in another connection. But in a world prating of democracy, it is worth noting that it is this culture that, given a choice, the masses want. Even criticisms of the United States reveal this truth. For it is the burden of complaint that the United States puts up barriers at its doors, betrays the promise of the verses on the Statue of Liberty. . . . It [does], but what a change from a society that devotes far more energy to keeping people in than the United States does in keeping them out! [13]

Anyone who would be critical of the American society must—as a matter of simple historical justice—exercise that criticism in responsibile recognition of the unique role this society has played in the recent history of the world. Indeed, no criticism can be taken seriously which does not demonstrate its willingness to take that record with full seriousness. If we are sometimes embarrassed—as I, for one, am—by the brashness of American political self-congratulation and overstatement of the virtues of American life which occur particularly during quadrennial presidential campaigns when the whole world is tuned in, that should not prevent us from acknowledging that the whole world was tuned in to the American experiment long before communications satellites made that connection almost instantaneous. The words of English historical wisdom written by Parkes and Brogan may be an appropriate antidote, if not to our moral criticism of the inadequacies and unfulfilled promises of American life, at least to the moral overkill in which radicals and liberals alike have indulged themselves of late.

THE REFUSAL TO RESPECT THE FUTURE

In at least one other way the recent radical has romanticized and thus falsified the human situation. He assumed not only that he could dissociate himself from his own past with immunity—we see this in his effort to shake himself loose from the social history that has spawned him—but that he could also dissociate himself without penalty from his own future. To put the matter more directly, he failed to see that when he deliberately widened and hardened the generation gap, making youth the deadly enemy of age, the ironic consequence was that he made himself his own enemy. For barring untimely disaster, one thing is certain: every young revolutionary grows older.

Psychiatrist Dr. Seymour Halleck insists that every society must find a means of providing a respected place for its older members. "So long as aging means being less respected, less powerful, and less relevant to this society," he writes, "there can never be any joyous anticipation of the future." So the tragedy of the recent enmity between youth and age is seldom noted. It is, as the psychiatrist notes, that

> even as [the young] attack the adult world they become trapped in destroying themselves; if they make their parents irrelevant, they will surely make themselves irrelevant. . . . We are told that our youth are our future. Yet, unless we can create a world which offers the possibility of aging with grace, honor, and meaningfulness, no one—young or old—can look forward to the future.[14]

This gives point to something else written by Ambassador Kennan:

. . . one would like to warn these young people that in distancing themselves so recklessly not only from the wisdom but from the feelings of parents, they are hacking at their own underpinnings—and even those of people as yet unborn. There could be no greater illusion than the belief that one can treat one's own parents unfeelingly and with contempt and yet expect that one's own children will some day treat one otherwise; for such people break the golden chain of affection that binds the generations and gives continuity and meaning to life.[15]

There is no way to step outside the historical continuum which gives identity to the self—no way, that is, to defy with impunity "the golden chain of affection that binds the generations"— without tearing at the vital tissue which makes us what we are. It is simply romantic nonsense to believe that the present moment exists in isolation and immunity either from what we have already been or from what we shall yet be. Our past is never finished and done; it intrudes ineluctably into the present. Nor is our future simply uncreated; rather it reaches, and indeed sometimes rushes, forward to qualify the "now" before we know it. There is very little difference between one who, in age, despises and retroactively repudiates his earlier years, and the one who, in youth, despises and by anticipation repudiates his later years. Both break "the golden chain of affection that binds the generations" even within a single self. Both are thus forms of self-hatred from which nothing humanly useful can be expected.

Youth have sometimes been warned to be careful what they dream, since dreams have a way of coming true. So have nightmares. The tragedy of a marked generational separation is that the confident misapprehensions of youth may, in self-fulfilling prophecy, become the realities of age.

ESCAPE INTO THE EROTIC AND IRRATIONAL

At the beginning of this chapter, I said that *two* forms of the romantic escape from fate are active among us, one calling for radicalization and the other for eroticization. I have chosen to give almost all of my attention to the first, since it appears to be the more dangerous of the two. It may, in the irony of history, turn out that the second—quieter, less evangelistic, or at least differently evangelistic, and more broadly appealing to men and women from all kinds of circumstance from hippie to hard hat—may have the more lasting influence. In concluding this present chapter, I want to give at least brief attention to this second form.

Some time ago an article, appropriately in *Playboy* magazine, announced the advent of a new movement in America which is "anti-intellectual, anti-ideological and toward the eroticization of practically everything."[16] The most enthusiastic proponents of this movement are not the earthy and ignorant masses but precisely the intellectuals. The article asserted:

> For several years people from some sectors of society—*especially the intellectuals*—have devalued commitments to the life of the mind and placed a new importance on feeling. In their work, calculation, control and conformity to the rules assure "success." They get places, even as far as the moon, by following certain norms, being rational and careful. But somehow that isn't enough. The sensualists need a little freedom as well, and many are turning to what is spontaneous, personal, natural and real.[17]

So "sensitivity sessions," "encounter groups," "micro-labs," "therapy groups," and a host of other techniques intended to free the impulse life of the inhibited have been introduced into business and industrial management, professional associations, church gatherings, and college and university classrooms and dormitories. Esalen, a California prototype much imitated in "retreat" centers around the country, operates on the assumption, as one staff member put it, that "the golden era of physical pleasure is the first fifteen months of life." "The seekers at Esalen," comments the *Playboy* author, "will try anything that might help restore that early innocence."[18]

At Esalen, and one deduces in the sensualist movement at large, no epithet is more dreaded or devastating than for a "seeker" to be told, "You're up in your head!"

Esalen and its imitators, as well as the group interaction techniques which have sprung up across the land like mushrooms after a spring rain, extend an admirable, surely unexceptionable, invitation to life in "the total self," rather than perpetuating that separation of intellect from emotion, of the mental from the sensual, which seems to be expected of solid citizens in the world at large. Of course no one ought to be satisfied with less than total selfhood. No one ought to acquiesce in that internal alienation of one aspect of the self from others which social conventions sometimes seek to foist upon us.

But there is grave, ironic danger in the movement. How can one live "in the total self" while "therapeutically" letting go of the mind as if it were dispensable from total selfhood? A movement which begins by ridiculing the mind, presumably in order to free men and women from the tyranny of an intellection which imperiously excludes other faculties, is likely to end by repudiating the mind, thus delivering men and women into the tyranny of a sensualism unmodified by thought.

The substitution of impulse for intellect, and the elevation of feeling to a place of epistemological primacy, form one of the major themes in Charles Reich's controversial best-seller, *The Greening of America*. Reich, a professor of law at Yale, also demonstrates how anti-intellectualism can find its way even into the most prestigious of America's supposedly intellectual centers. Reich describes what he takes to be a new consciousness particularly among the young—Consciousness III, he calls it—which is marked by a capacity for joyousness and exuberance, loss of middle-class inhibitions imposed by rationality and institutional expectations, indifference to rank or station, and a life-style marked by wholeness and love. Clearly these are admirable traits in young and old alike, and to that extent Consciousness III ought to be befriended wherever it appears. But in an astonishing passage, Reich ascribes a peculiar wisdom to the youth of Consciousness III: "He does not 'know' the facts, but he still 'knows' the truth that seems hidden from others."[19] This new clarity arises, in Reich's view, from the ability of Consciousness III to transcend categorical ways of thinking, to get beyond artificial distinctions, for example, between prose and poetry, or to refuse to recognize the concept of "private property" as if it had a status fixed by natural law. And once one gets beyond such categorical barriers, new possibilities and relationships appear. Reich asserts:

> But the "new knowledge" is more than this; it is as if everything, from political affairs to aesthetics, were seen with new eyes; the young people of Consciousness III see effortlessly what is phony or dishonest in politics, or what is ugly and meretricious in architecture and city planning, whereas an older person had to go through years of education to make himself equally aware.[20]

So a Consciousness III drug user "knows" that the law is an instrument of oppression, whereas it would take men of Consciousness II (establishment types, that is) years of reading radical literature to arrive at a similar awareness.

Reich is certainly right in insisting that categorical thinking, uncriticized and treated with the immunity of an ontological first principle, inhibits the mind and distorts what passes for knowledge. But to propose as a serious alternative a kind of generational intuition which assumes that young people can "know" quite without being bothered by the facts is merely to substitute one form of arbitrariness for another, with results scarcely more promising. It should not be necessary to remind a professor of law that, when intuition replaces the rules of evidence, some form of tyranny will sit on the bench. And it is, to say the least, a crashing irony that, having presumably banished categorical thinking as unworthy of the new consciousness, Reich nevertheless proposes to categorize all of mankind as belonging to Consciousness I, II, or III, thus placing formidable categorical barriers of his own in the way of the new intergenerational relationships our society so desperately needs.

I see no alternative to insisting that responsible knowing— responsible intellectual work—requires as its *sine qua non* a capacity for disinterestedness. Disinterestedness means willingness intellectually to take the attitude of another, even when that attitude appears distasteful in advance. It means willingness to entertain another point of view at the level of its meaning, even though it may, in the end, be necessary to reject it at the level of its truth. It means acknowledging that one has a right to an opinion about the truthfulness or meaning of another's view only after a disciplined effort to enter into and to master it intellectually. It means willingness to get rid of oneself—one's prejudices and predilections—long enough to hear clearly what another is saying.

It means doing all of these things, not simply for the purpose of fulfilling some formal convention of abstract rationality, but for the purpose of fulfilling *a concrete moral obligation:* the obligation to assume a dignity and value in the world beyond the self not less than the dignity and value which are claimed for the self.

It means doing these things, as well, not simply in order to put down the anti-intellectual, frankly sensual, unpredictable energies of new social movements, but precisely for the effectiveness of these new movements. Much that our conventional culture values desperately needs challenge and the offering of new alternatives. But that challenge will simply be swept away if it is not thoughtful ·but only defiant, if it is content merely to flaunt and to outrage but not to persuade, if it is only a new form of arbitrariness. Lacking intellectual power, it will simply become lost, confused, and in the end killed by its own mindlessness. Lionel Trilling has insisted that, precisely in order to guard the potential creativity of the radical impulse, it must be confronted with a countervailing force: "with the mind that insists that things are so and not otherwise, that the object is as it really is, that the world is intractable as well as malleable." When intellectual mastery is not demanded to match the powers of its impulse life, says Trilling, radicalism falls "into inertness and the weariest of all conventionalities, the conventionality of an outworn radical mode." Then I want to make Trilling's conclusion my own:

> If, as I believe, the modern energy of radical thought is essentially good, then we . . . shall have to guard against subverting it by mere bland tolerance, or by a Philistine delight in its intent of outrageousness. It is best for us, it is best for the state of the general culture, it is best for the poet himself, that we do *not* establish William Blake as the Poet in Residence. When it comes to dealing with the subversive energy of modernity, the right way is to keep our doors hospitably open to a powerful and unpredictable guest, but not, by our household familiarity with him, rob him of his frightening strangeness.[21]

Part III
History
as Freedom

Chapter Six

The Coordinates
of Man

MAN ON THE BOUNDARY

Man in the second half of the twentieth century is not a new
being. However unprecedented may be the challenges his
manhood confronts, it is the same manhood which meets us
coming out of the mists of prehistory.

Read in one way, such a view may seem to require, as its
correlate, the notion that human nature is static, incapable of
change or variation. Not so at all. There are, to be sure, limits to
our manhood; and they are real limits, not merely imposed by some
arbitrary ideological scheme. Man errs and sins; he suffers and
sickens, emotionally as well as physically; he dies. To complain
about these limits is to complain about being human.

But within these limits—within what in the preceding chapters I
have called man's fate—the possibilities which combine to form a
concrete human being are almost infinite. Some of the most
influential views of man have stressed the ambivalence and
ambiguity of his nature, with possibilities which reach toward the
subhuman and the superhuman. The psalmist located man "a
little lower than the angels" in the hierarchy of creation, subject to
the Creator but made to have dominion over the creatures—"All
sheep and oxen, yea, and the beasts of the field; the fowl of the air,

and the fish of the sea, and whatsoever passeth through the paths of the seas" (Psalm 8:5, 7-8, KJV). Blaise Pascal saw man as creation's mean:

> A Nothing in comparison with the Infinite, an All in comparison with the Nothing, a mean between nothing and everything. Since he is infinitely removed from comprehending the extremes, the end of things and their beginning are hopelessly hidden from him in an impenetrable secret; he is equally incapable of seeing the Nothing from which he was made, and the Infinite in which he is swallowed up.[1]

Horace Bushnell found man at the juncture of nature and the supernatural. Man is a natural being, said Bushnell, in that he is subject to many of the necessities of natural law; but man is also supernatural, in the sense that he is able to act upon the chain of natural cause-and-effect relations from outside of it. In spite of the limitations nature presses upon him, man is thus superior to the mindless world about him. Man is a power, not a thing, said Bushnell, a power being that "agent or force which acts from itself, uncaused, initiating trains of effect that flow from itself."[2] Because man transcends the nexus of cause and effect, he is "able to act on the lines and vary the combinations of natural causalities,"[3] thus making nature the servant of man's supernatural purposes and creating out of nature what nature alone could never produce.

There is—as the biblical writer, Pascal, and Bushnell all seem to suggest—something in human nature which defies systematic ordering and which breaks out of every scheme which seeks to exhaust the meaning of humanness. If we are able to take man's measure at all, then, it cannot be done by means of a closely ordered, abstract system; neither can we measure man by asking— certainly not by commanding—him to stand still, for man is static only in a state of morbidity, and the resultant measure is dead weight. If man is to be located at all, it must be by means of *coordinates*, as the views noted above hint—coordinates which take a fix upon man while leaving him free to be what he will be and to become what he will become. By means of coordinates, we can take account of what commonly links the humanity of all of us, while protecting at the same time the singularity of each man's location in the network of human interactions.

Any number of coordinates might have been chosen, but "alienation" and "reconciliation" seem to me to catch up so much that is astonishing about being human—and perhaps for that very reason so much that is problematic about being human—that I choose these two coordinates as a means of recovering a sense of what it is to be a man. If they do not yield belief in a new man, they may at least help us toward a new belief in man.

SELFHOOD AND ALIENATION

Alienation is an important and complex human experience which has the power both to hurt and to heal us, but that is no guarantee that the term itself is widely or well understood. We ought to avoid an approach to the term through textbook definition, since that may only encourage us to depersonalize it, as if we were dealing with a distant problem rather than with a vital aspect of our own experience. I prefer, therefore, to approach an understanding of the meaning of alienation by means of synonyms which catch up its various forms and nuances, in the hope that these words will help us to identify it by identifying *with* it; in the hope that some of these words may call forth experiences of our own in which we have known alienation, not as an impersonal clinical observer, but as a personal participant. The list of synonyms is suggestive rather than exhaustive.

These are some, at least, of the forms alienation takes in us: an experience of strangeness, dislocation, doubt, negation, separation, over againstness, hostility, lovelessness, distance, otherness, outsideness, disruption, conflict, cut-offness, solitariness, disinterest, and indifference.

One of the first things to notice about this list is that every word on it describes an experience which, at certain times and under certain conditions, is a thoroughly desirable, wholly admirable experience. To feel a sense of strangeness, for example, on first visiting a country and culture strikingly different from one's own is not necessarily cause for alarm or even regret. It can be, rather, the sharp discovery—both exciting and threatening—of the remarkable inventiveness of the human spirit which has created, in times and places different from one's own, a kind of life we never guessed at. And that sense of strangeness we experience may be absolutely essential in shocking us out of our provincialism and self-satisfaction so that we are attentive to what is new and therefore free to consider what it may add to our own humanity.

Take doubt as another example. Doubt is an indispensable human response. If Meursault, the "stranger" in Albert Camus's novel, is sick, as I believe him to be, a part of his sickness is his inability to be skeptical.[4] Until the very end, as Germaine Brée comments, Meursault "is the man who answers but never asks a question."[5] Surely that very absence of a capacity to question was one of the things which made him a "stranger." Nobody ever really becomes an insider in any human enterprise, whether it be marriage or politics or art, who does not take it seriously enough to have doubts about it. No man has faith—not in himself, not in another man, certainly not in God—who has no capacity to doubt. Without doubt there is no faith but only a certain resignation.

Take hostility as yet another example. Who can deny that this world would be a vastly better place if more men were to follow the lead of Thomas Jefferson and swear "eternal hostility" to all forms of tyranny over human life?

I cannot prolong the examples, but I invite you to test for yourself whether it is true that every synonym for alienation which I have listed is, at certain times and under certain conditions, a vital and valuable experience.

I have made a particular point of this in order to correct what seems to me to be a popular but seriously defective understanding of alienation. As the term is commonly used in this age of pop-psychologism and excessive amateur analysis, and as the term is frequently served up in popular literature—each dramatist and novelist must be his own Freud, it seems—alienation is always portrayed as pathological, always the sign of near-mortal disease, always the experience from which men must be saved, whether by psychoanalysis or religion, by physical coupling or by joining themselves to some cause—almost any coupling or cause will presumably serve a useful therapy, as long as it gives the alienated one something to do!

Alienation may indeed be pathological; and I shall have more to say about that later in this piece. But to understand it *only* in pathological terms may, in fact, be a sickness—it is certainly, at best, a distortion—all its own. Alienation, as the term is used here, is intended to be value-free, descriptive rather than normative. Alienation means incongruence, lacking a relation of identity, being out of phase.

If alienation is sometimes a source of human misery, that must not prevent us from seeing that it is also the sign of man's greatness. Alienation is a mark of man's uniqueness among all of the forms of created existence that we know anything about. To be human is to be alienated; without alienation there simply is no humanness. This is not a complete definition of what it is to be human, to be sure, but it is nevertheless an indispensable term in that definition. Alienation is one of the coordinates which helps us to locate man. Let me try to say how this is so.

To be a self is to know myself to be a self. To be a self is to be aware of myself being a self. It is inappropriate to speak of a tree or a dog having a self, for what a tree and a dog both lack is self-awareness. A tree is not aware of its treeness nor a dog of its dogness, because neither tree nor dog, nor indeed any other creature we know except man, is able to view its own existence, as it were, *from the outside.* To have a self, it is necessary to be aware of oneself having a self, and even to be aware of one's awareness of having a self! Human selfhood thus means self-distance, self-detachment, self-separation, self-in-conflict-with-self, self-negating-self. In a word, selfhood means alienation from self.

More than that, to be a self is to be aware of the not-self. Other forms of life may live an undifferentiated existence, unable to distinguish the part from the whole, ignorant of otherness. But to be a man is to know the difference between I and Thou and It. In short, human selfhood means alienation—distance, distinctness—from the not-self. As Dr. Austin Des Lauriers puts it in his study of childhood schizophrenia, "Only when the outside is experienced as alien, as withdrawn from the ego feeling . . . does it assume a reality value in the experience of the individual. . . . the process of detaching the world from himself becomes, for the individual, a process of becoming more real to himself." [6]

Self-awareness means self-transcendence, and self-transcendence is just another name for that freedom which is peculiar to human selfhood. Man is aware of his own condition, but that very awareness keeps him from being victimized by his condition. Pascal said of man that "if the universe were to crush him, man would still be more noble than that which killed him, because he knows that he dies and the advantage which the universe has over him; the universe knows nothing of this." [7] Memory and imagination are two of the forms our peculiar human freedom—the freedom which is conferred by the capacity for alienation—takes, for they permit us to detach ourselves from the immediacy of the moment by retreat into a lost past or by projection into an uncreated future. So Augustine wrote:

> When I enter [the court of my memory] I require what I will to be brought forth and something instantly comes; others must be longer sought after, which are fetched as it were out of some inner receptacle. . . . Nor yet do the things themselves enter in; only the images of the things perceived are there in readiness, for thought to recall. . . . For even while I dwell in darkness and silence, in my memory I can produce colours if I will . . . yea I discern the breath of lilies from violets, though smelling nothing. . . . These things I do in the vast court of my memory. . . . There also I meet with myself, and recall myself and when and where and what I have done and under what feelings. . . . Out of the same store do I myself with the past continually combine fresh likenesses of things, which I have experienced, have believed, and thence again infer future actions, events and hopes, and all these again I reflect on, as present. I will do this or that, say I to myself, in the great receptacle of my mind, stored with images of things so many and so great, and this or that might be.[8]

Human individuation begins in an act of physical alienation. Birth is the experience of being expelled from the womb, literally cut off from an umbilical form of dependence on another organism, forced to live a separate physiological existence. Psychoanalyst Erich Fromm uses the metaphor of birth to describe the vital process of psychological individuation, the process by which a human organism becomes a mature self. The problem, says Fromm, is that psychological birth is far more difficult than physical birth. Man struggles with emotional birth in every moment of his existence, for he is tempted to flee from the discomfort of self-awareness and from the sometime terror of freedom; he is tempted in each conscious moment to flee from the difficulty and daring of birth-alienation and, as Fromm puts it, "to go back to prehuman, preconscious existence, to do away with reason, to become an animal, and thus to become one with nature again."[9] But the real "aim of life," says Fromm, "is to be fully born."[10] Life is tragedy for those who "cannot cut the umbilical cord completely, as it were; they remain symbiotically attached to mother, father, family, race, state, status, money, gods, etc.; they never emerge fully as themselves and thus they never become fully born."[11]

In his novel *Winesburg, Ohio,* Sherwood Anderson describes

one of those moments when a man faces a choice between birth and death, between a maturing selfhood, on the one hand, and a dulling, deadening refusal to accept the alienation which goes with selfhood, on the other:

> There is a time in the life of every boy when he for the first time takes the backward view of life. Perhaps that is the moment when he crosses the line into manhood. The boy is walking through the street of his town. He is thinking of the future and of the figure he will cut in the world. Ambitions and regrets awake within him. Suddenly something happens; he stops under a tree and waits as for a voice calling his name. Ghosts of old things creep into his consciousness; the voices outside himself whisper a message concerning the limitations of life. From being quite sure of himself and his future he becomes not at all sure. If he be an imaginative boy a door is torn open and for the first time he looks out upon the world, seeing, as though they marched in procession before him, the countless figures of men who before his time have come out of nothingness into the world, lived their lives and again disappeared into nothingness. The sadness of sophistication has come to the boy. With a little gasp he sees himself as merely a leaf blown by the wind through the streets of his village. He knows that in spite of all the stout talk of his fellows he must live and die in uncertainty, a thing blown by the winds, a thing destined like corn to wilt in the sun. He shivers and looks eagerly about. The eighteen years he has lived seem but a moment, a breathing space in the long march of humanity. Already he hears death calling.[12]

No one who has not experienced the precariousness of life, and in it his own vulnerability and mortality, can have any understanding of how precious life is; which is to say that to find his life, a man must first feel what it would be like to lose his life.

SELFHOOD AND RECONCILIATION

Earlier in this chapter I said that alienation is an indispensable coordinate for locating man, for defining the nature of the human, though it does not complete that definition. We have now reached the point in the discussion where it is important to supply the second coordinate, an essential but thus far missing term in the definition. Since I want to make this concrete, and as little like a formal textbook definition as possible, let us return to the quotation from *Winesburg, Ohio*, only this time we shall carry it just a bit further. The "sadness of sophistication" comes to a boy, said Sherwood Anderson, when for the first time he hears death— which man fears as the ultimate alienator—calling.

> He shivers and looks eagerly about. The eighteen years he has lived seem but a moment, a breathing space in the long march of humanity. Already he hears death calling. With all his heart he wants to come close to some other human,

touch someone with his hands, be touched by the hand of another. If he prefers that the other be a woman, that is because he believes that a woman will be gentle, that she will understand. He wants, most of all, understanding.

When the moment of sophistication came to George Willard his mind turned to Helen White, the Winesburg banker's daughter.[13]

The missing coordinate is "reconciliation," as this passage from the novel makes movingly clear. It is essential to understand that alienation and reconciliation are not opposites. It is not the case that when one is present the other will be absent. Rather they are complementary terms; they complete each other. For full human selfhood, alienation requires reconciliation, and reconciliation requires alienation.

But we need something more by way of a definition of reconciliation. Again, we must avoid depersonalizing the term. Like alienation, it is a vital aspect of our own experience and should be defined in such a way as to evoke personal recognition in us. So I propose to define reconciliation synonymically, as I did alienation; and you will not be surprised to note that each term on the list of synonyms for reconciliation is the complement of a term on that earlier list of synonyms for alienation. So:

Alienation	*Reconciliation*
strangeness	familiarity
dislocation	location
doubt	faith
negation	affirmation
separation	reunion
over againstness	withness
hostility	affinity
lovelessness	affection
distance	intimacy
otherness	oneness
outsideness	belonging
disruption	continuity
conflict	harmony
cut-offness	attachment
solitariness	community
disinterest	involvement
indifference	passion

One of the first things to be noticed about this list of synonyms for reconciliation is that every word on it describes an experience which, at certain times and under certain conditions, is a thoroughly undesirable, wholly deplorable experience. Take faith as an example. There is a kind of faith which is demonic. Whenever a man surrenders his life, wholly and uncritically, to the will of another man, or to the discipline of an institution—when, that is, he surrenders his own self-possession and instead becomes possessed—the result is that demonic destruction of the self which always comes about when a man places absolute trust in what is not absolute.

Take attachment as another example. Several years ago a man, who had been married only a few weeks, came to tell me that his wife had peremptorily left him. Her parents had appeared at the couple's apartment the night before and had said to her, "Come with us!" and without a question she went. What I discovered from further exploration of the problem was that this young woman, legally quite of age, was emotionally unable to detach herself from her childish dependence upon her parents, and the parents, children in their own right, were unable to detach themselves from her. So daughter and parents perpetuated each other's immaturity with tragic consequence.

Take involvement as yet another example. No effective medical doctor who cares about the health of his patients dares to permit himself to become deeply involved emotionally in the lives of those patients. To do so is to risk damage to his medical judgment by an anxiety about their condition which may lead him either to excessive medical caution or medical recklessness.

Again, there is no need to prolong the examples, since each of us can test for himself the validity of my contention that every synonym for reconciliation listed is, at certain times and under certain conditions, dangerous and destructive.

Let me try to make it as clear as I can that I am using the term "reconciliation" in a sense which may not be immediately grasped without explanation, but which, I am persuaded, is fully justified by the word itself and which seems to me to be more fruitful than its common connotation. I do not intend to limit the meaning of reconciliation to "the restoration of a once existing amicable relationship following a period of enmity," nor indeed to limit it to any variation on that "restoration of lost beatitude" theme. As I am using the word, it may indeed mean "restoration of lost beatitude" but only because primarily it means something simpler and more basic: it means congruence, a relationship of identity, being in phase. Once it is pointed out, the meaning is not unfamiliar. We talk of "reconciling" a bank statement, which means bringing the bank's record and our own into congruence. We talk about reconciling ideas, which means bringing them into intellectual agreement, congruence.

I have taken the trouble to try to change a familiar primary meaning, with all the peril of misunderstanding which that entails, as a means of calling attention to a problem. Since I doubt that we shall get rid of so durable a word, this is the only way I know to signal a false value transition. Everybody assumes that "the restoration of a once existing amicable relationship following a period of enmity" is a good thing, as it most probably is. Since, then, this is the common understanding of the word, reconciliation almost always goes out laden with strong positive value. But the fact is that the term does not always connote "restored beatitude," as any comprehensive dictionary or careful auditing of conversation will show. Some of its other meanings, as I have tried to show in my examples a few paragraphs above, are on occasion "good things," but they are by no means unambiguously and always so, as the examples should have demonstrated. Nevertheless, because the primary connotation of the word carries positive value, that same value is uncritically transmitted to other uses of the word which, as I have also tried to show in the examples, gets us into all kinds of trouble.

Congruence I take to be relatively value free, which is what I am striving for here. It is descriptive rather than normative; it tells us how things are or are not, not how they ought to be. Whether or not a particular kind of congruence—perhaps it is safe now to return to the use of reconciliation—is a good thing is a matter not for *a priori* assumption but for investigation.

COORDINATES AND COMPLEMENTS

Then let me return to my earlier contention, that alienation and reconciliation are complementary terms, and let me see whether I can now demonstrate that assertion of complementarity. There is a sense in which human life can be said to be a quest for models. I am not the first man to appear on the earth, and therefore I am not required to set the first precedent or to make the first test of the limitations and possibilities of my humanity. Of course, I am I, a unique, unrepeatable human event; but I am a *human* event, which is to say that, in addition to my uniqueness and unrepeatability, I belong to a general class. If I am genuinely different from other men, the continuity of my experience with the experiences of other men is at least as real a fact about me. It is precisely because my humanity is not radically different, not wholly discontinuous, that it is possible for another man to become a model for me.

So somebody has been there before me. And that, as it turns out, is crucially important, for I discover that in order to be confident of my own manhood, that manhood must be confirmed by the experiences others have of their own manhood. Internal assurance requires external reassurance, and the confirming reassurance we seek takes varied forms; a word, a look, a touch, a gesture, in each of which the other says to me, in effect, "Yes, I see that you are there, and I value your being." Without such regular reassurances, a man comes to doubt the reality of his own existence.

Thus it is possible to affirm that *awareness of my self is the awareness of others at work in me.*

When one human being seeks reassurance and confirmation, reaches out to touch and to be touched by another human being, as George Willard reached out in the "sadness of sophistication" to touch Helen White and to have his importance reconfirmed by her answering touch, it can only be because George was so aware of his own selfhood that he could identify, and identify with, that in Helen's selfhood which was like him-self and which therefore could perform the function of confirmation. Whenever one person turns to another for understanding, or offers his own understanding to the other, that can only be because he is aware of his own condition but is able to break out of it by imaginative projection into the condition of the other.

Thus it is possible to affirm that *awareness of others is awareness of my own selfhood at work in me.*

The emotional well-being of the self depends upon both alienation and reconciliation and thus provides further evidence of their complementarity. Erich Fromm says that personal well-being "means to be freely related to man and nature affectively, to overcome separateness and alienation, to arrive at the experience of oneness with all that exists—and yet to experience *myself* at the same time as the separate entity that *I* am, as the in-dividual." [14] If Fromm is right then, as regards our coordinates, human well-being requires us to affirm the necessity of each while denying the sufficiency of either.

This should rid us of the popular notion that alienation and reconciliation are the opposite ends of a spectrum, or continuum, and that maturity means the steady and deliberate movement away from the one and toward the other. It is accurate to say that maturity—emotional health—comes to us only as we dare to stand the tension between alienation and reconciliation, only as we are prepared to feel the pull and power of each, only as we are prepared each moment to face the decision as to which shall momentarily have the greater weight. An emotionally healthy life moves back and forth between the poles, now one predominating and now the other, the one insinuating doubts about the other and the other about the one. We only begin to get into emotional trouble when the tension weakens, when one comes to predominate too long or becomes permanently dominant. Then we have emotional lop-sidedness, and the more lopsided the more serious the emotional condition. When the tension between alienation and reconciliation snaps, breaks completely, there is no way to reestablish the dialectic under one's own power, and the result is a pathological personality.

When the tension weakens toward alienation, the self experiences itself as increasingly cut off, often invaded by meaninglessness, drifting toward the void. There is only the self alone with its mocking, relentless, agonizing fear of emptiness within and without. At the extreme, the senses no longer delight, relationships are vacuous, and no object in the world bears the least significance either of friendliness or hostility. So Adriana, the prostitute in Alberto Moravia's novel *Woman of Rome*, says of her own experience:

> I said to myself, "Here I am and I might be elsewhere. I might exist a thousand years ago or in a thousand years' time. I might be a Negress or an old woman, fair or short." I thought how I had come out of endless night and would soon go into

another endless darkness, and that my brief passing was marked only by absurd and trivial actions. I then understood that my distress was caused, not by what I was doing, but more profoundly by the bare fact of being alive, which was neither good nor evil but only painful and without meaning.

My dismay used to make my flesh creep with fear; I used to shudder uncontrollably, feeling my hair stand on end, and suddenly the walls of my flat, the city and even the world seemed to vanish, leaving me suspended in dark, empty, endless space—suspended, what's more, in the same clothes, with the same memories, name and profession. . . . I found no consolation in the thought that other people also acted and moved in just as futile and inadequate a way as I did when faced with this nothingness, within this nothingness, surrounded by this nothingness. . . . [15]

Thus can alienation without reconciliation terrify.

When the tension weakens toward reconciliation, the self is increasingly unable to distance itself from the realities in which it now seems quite immersed. Rather than nothing bearing any significance, as in the case of extreme alienation, everything may now seem to impinge upon the self, for good or ill. Everything matters passionately, one way or another, and the world thus becomes a welter of confusing, conflicting, even threatening significance.

Dr. Austin Des Lauriers has written that the healthy ego has a distinct sense of its own bodily boundaries, is aware of the ways in which its own bodily reality is separate and distinct from reality which is other than itself, and relates to that otherness by experiencing it as "transgressing" its own bodily boundaries. By contrast, says Dr. Des Lauriers, "In schizophrenia, these conditions are absent. The schizophrenic individual cannot relate to reality, because he does not experience himself as real, that is, bounded, separated, and differentiated from what is not himself." [16] Thus does reconciliation without alienation sicken.

TRANSCENDENCE AND LIMITATION

Alienation and reconciliation are by no means the only coordinates which help us to locate man within the continuing flux of his life. Reinhold Niebuhr's fruitful and influential description of *The Nature and Destiny of Man* utilized two related but distinctive coordinates: man's transcendent powers, and his creaturely limitations. Man, in Niebuhr's view, bears the "image of God," and this "image" is the source of the transcendence which marks man's spiritual nature. Transcendence means the power to escape the limitations of natural and historical processes; to turn physical disability to human asset, for example, or in a moment of loneliness to call to remembrance a past full of intimacy and to anticipate a future reunion with those loved. Most remarkable is this power as *self*-transcendence: the capacity to stand even outside the self; for example, to confer self-approbation or self-reprobation, and at the same time to be detached enough to judge those judgments. Considering this power, Augustine concluded that "the power of transcendence places [man] so much outside of everything else that he can find a home only in God."[17]

But even in the presence of this transcendence, man is limited and he knows it. He is often a creature of fear; he suffers disappointment and defeat; he sickens, and he knows his own final mortality; and he experiences his life under the constant threat of nonbeing.

Anxiety arises from the experienced fact of limitation; but it also arises from man's awareness that he possesses possibilities and powers whose limits he does not know. Says Niebuhr, "There are, of course, limits but it is difficult to gauge them from any immediate perspective. There is therefore no limit of achievement in any sphere of activity in which human history can rest with equanimity."[18] So anxiety has a double source: awareness of concrete limitation, but awareness at the same time that the possibilities of any given historical event are never exhausted.

Just as, in my own analysis, emotional lopsidedness—a disordered self—results from a failure to endure the tension between alienation and reconciliation, so for Niebuhr sin results from man's failure to endure the anxiety which results from the tension between transcendent powers and creaturely limitations. It is important to understand that, for Niebuhr, anxiety is not itself sin; it is, indeed, the source of our human creativity. Refusal to live the anxious life is sin, and in Niebuhr's view escape is sought by seizing either transcendence or limitation and treating it as if it were the whole truth about man. When the tension is broken in the direction of transcendence, the result is the sin of pride and of excessive self-love, the denial of man's finite and dependent character "by raising precisely what is contingent to absolute and unlimited dimensions."[19] This most commonly takes the forms of pride of power, of knowledge, and of virtue, Niebuhr observes.

When the tension is broken in the direction of finitude, the result is the sin of sensuality. "Sensuality represents an effort to escape from the freedom and the infinite possibilities of spirit by becoming lost in the detailed processes, activities and interests of existence, an effort which results inevitably in unlimited devotion to limited values."[20] There is a sense, then, as Niebuhr notes, in which both forms of sin come to the same thing in the end.

It is useful at this historical moment to rehearse this point of view because a failure to take seriously the coordinate possibilities which Niebuhr describes has unbalanced some relatively recent attempts at theological innovation. William Hamilton, one of the radical "death of God" theologians, asserted in a 1966 essay, that Niebuhr's "pessimism" was no longer persuasive as it had been in the late 1930s when the Gifford lectures were first delivered. There is, said Hamilton, a "new optimism" abroad in the land which calls Niebuhr's formulation seriously into question. That "new optimism" is to be seen, in Hamilton's view, in the fact that, in spite of Vietnam, America is not afraid and has confidence in its national future; that there is a new attitude of hope in technological achievement; that there is fresh emphasis in the arts on purposeless play; and finally, that there is in the civil rights movement "a gaiety, an absence of alienation, a vigorous and contagious hope at the center...."[21] One of the reasons, in my own view, that Hamilton's "new optimism" no longer persuades, as it may have done in 1966, is precisely that crucial evidences for it have dissolved in historical events which were upon us almost before the ink on his essay was dry. Hamilton's persuasive power lasted scarcely more than a year, just up to the civil disturbances of July, 1967; Niebuhr's persuasiveness has lasted for decades. As my own words are written, even the American military withdrawal from Vietnam has not created a new sense of national optimism or of confidence in our national future. Technology is widely recognized as the cause, even if it must also be the cure, of ecological disaster. Constructivism has captured some of the younger and most interesting among the artists. And the civil rights movement seems confused and relatively leaderless, with little contagion of hope about it.

I suggest that Hamilton's view would not have failed so soon had he taken more seriously the power of sin which is at work in historical process. In my own view, Niebuhr's coordinates are indispensable at this moment—indispensable if we are to locate man amid the confusions of our times, and indispensable in order to prevent either naive and enervating pessimism or a naive and equally paralyzing optimism, so shocked by the realities history has pressed upon us that it is unable to cope.

RESPONSIBLE SELFHOOD

Finally, consider coordinates which seek to locate man in the midst of his dynamic moral experience. Again it is a Niebuhr—this time H. Richard Niebuhr—who has provided in his book *The Responsible Self*[22] one of our generation's most suggestive and persuasive statements of the human situation. In attempting to understand himself as a moral agent, man has made use historically of several major symbols or images. One is what H. R. Niebuhr calls the image of "man-the-maker." In this image, man makes himself, directing his self-creative efforts toward a chosen end. In a similar way he acts upon events, forming them according to his own purposive intent. A second historical image is that of "man-the-citizen," which holds not that man makes himself but that he is made by the rules, spoken and unspoken, of the social units to which he belongs, most prominently the family and the community. In this image, neither ends nor means are controlled by the individual but are given to him by virtue of his presence in social units which both transcend and shape his individuality. A third image, not yet widely appropriated but superior, in Niebuhr's view, to either of the others, is that of "man-the-answerer," man engaged in dialogue, man acting in response to action upon him.

This third image is what Niebuhr calls "the responsible self," with responsibility a compound of three elements. The first element is response: "All action . . . including what we rather indeterminately call moral action, is response to action upon us."[23] But it is not, in fact, moral action unless a second element is present, namely, interpretation: "We respond to . . . events in accordance with our interpretation," which is not simply conscious and rational but includes memories, feelings, and intuitions not fully under immediate conscious control.[24] A knee jerk, as Niebuhr notes, is a reaction but it is not a "self-action," not a moral action, unless it is "accompanied and infused, as it were, with interpretation." [25] The third element is accountability: "Our actions are responsible not only insofar as they are reactions to interpreted actions upon us but also insofar as they are made in anticipation of answers to our answers." [26]

On the face of it, Richard Niebuhr does not appear to offer us coordinate means of locating man. While identifying the images of "man-the-maker" and "man-the-citizen," he rejects them in favor of a superior view of "man-the-answerer." The first two are unacceptable because they mistake the real source of human selfhood, while "man-the-answerer" points precisely to the social matrix out of which, as Niebuhr believes, the human is formed.

> To be a self in the presence of other selves is not a derivative experience but primordial. To be able to say that I am I is not an inference from the statement that I think thoughts [cf. "man-the-maker"] nor from the statement that I have a law-acknowledging conscience [cf. "man-the-citizen"]. It is, rather, the acknowledgment of my existence as the counterpart of another self. [27]

In my own reading and teaching of Niebuhr's analysis, I have been puzzled about why I found all of this at once so persuasive and so unhelpful. "Man-the-maker" and "man-the-citizen" translate quite readily into moral action, but "man-the-answerer" seems to defy direct translation into moral response. If it is relatively easy, in the presence of a concrete moral issue, to say how constructionist-man or citizen-man would respond, it is almost impossible to say what answering-man ought to do. Now I think I know why. What Niebuhr points to in the quotation immediately above is so "primordial" that it seems to me quite unsatisfactory to treat it merely as a third alternative, albeit preferred, model of moral action. Neither of the two rejected images is wholly untrue in its reflection of man; their defect is that they fail, by themselves, to tell the whole truth, so that neither is capable of standing alone. Then it may be more fruitful to think of "man-the-maker" and "man-the-citizen" on the analogy of my earlier analyses in this chapter: as the permanent poles which create that tension in the presence of which man's moral life must be lived.* If that is so, then "man-the-

*The difference between the social character of selfhood which underlies "man-the-answerer" and the social legislation which forms "man-the-citizen" is this: the former gives primary place to selves in their relations, while the latter gives primary place to laws, with selves secondary. What limits and attracts "man-the-citizen," says Niebuhr, "is a commandment, a demand, a requirement." Other selves may be viewed by legislated man as "representatives of the law, enforcers of the law, or in their obedience to it may command respect; but his first relation is to the law and not to other persons."[28]

answerer" is not an alternative to or inference from the other two at all, but precisely the ontological base line which makes it clear that each of the others is quite necessary and that neither of the others is, in itself, sufficient. Answering-man—social man—is not merely another image; it is, rather, the ground which gives rise to all human images. It is not an alternative shape for man, but the reality which conditions all shapes. It is not an alternative moral style, but the elemental human situation which judges all human styles.

THE INTERACTION OF COORDINATE POSSIBILITIES

To value a man is to know him as a unique, unrepeatable human event. To have a durable belief in man is to understand his capacity to be magnificent without ever underestimating his talent for meanness and malignity. The purpose of this chapter has been to demonstrate the dynamic process out of which our human singularity arises, and to illustrate how what is both admirable and deplorable in man takes shape in the interaction of coordinate possibilities: in the interplay of alienation and reconciliation, of finitude and transcendence, of pride and sensuality, of "man-the-maker" and "man-the-citizen," and infinitely many more.

This is the character of our human freedom, and it is awesome to contemplate. The processive character of human history cannot be repealed; manhood cannot be permanently arrested. But if this created dialectic is awesome, its very unpredictableness makes some men profoundly uncomfortable with it. For man and his institutions always to be unfinished has seemed to some in almost every historical period precisely too much freedom. Our own time is no exception. There are among us now men and women who are quite prepared to affirm history as fate, but who are unable to bear history as freedom. In their view, man is too frail to be trusted with such openness. So they choose out of the historical past some set of ideas and institutions for which they want to claim permanent validity, perhaps even divine authorship. Moreover, they seek—by giving to those parochial ideas and institutions the strongest patriotic, religious, and legal sanctions—to require of their fellow citizens a similar renunciation of freedom.

Chapter Seven

Political Fundamentalists and Other Reactionaries: The Escape from Freedom

UNTANGLING A CONFUSION

The garden beds I wandered by
  One bright and cheerful morn,
When I found a new-fledged butterfly
  A-sitting on a thorn,
A black and crimson butterfly
  All doleful and forlorn.

I thought that life could have no sting
  To infant butterflies
So I gazed on this unhappy thing
  With wonder and surprise,
While sadly with his waving wing
  He wiped his weeping eyes.

Said I, "What can the matter be?
  Why weepest thou so sore?
With garden fair and sunlight free
  And flowers in goodly store"
But he only turned away from me
  And burst into a roar.

Cried he, "My legs are thin and few
  Where once I had a swarm!
Soft fuzzy fur—a joy to view—
  Once kept my body warm
Before these flapping wing-things grew
  To hamper and deform!"

103

> At that outrageous bug I shot
>   The fury of mine eye;
> Said I, in scorn all burning hot,
>   In rage and anger high,
> "You ignominious idiot,
>   Those wings were made to fly!"
>
> "I do not want to fly," said he,
>   "I only want to squirm!"
> And he dropped his wings dejectedly,
>   But still his voice was firm:
> "I do not want to be a fly!
>   I want to be a worm!"
>
> O yesterday of unknown lack!
>   Today of unknown bliss!
> I left my fool in red and black,
>   The last I saw was this—
> The creature climbing madly back
>   Into his chrysalis.[1]

And that, if you believe its author, is a description of "A Conservative," the title Charlotte P. S. Gilman gave to her poem. I should say, rather, that is a more apt description of the fundamentalist. At this juncture of American history, it is sometimes difficult to tell conservatives from fundamentalists, partly because they appear to have the same preoccupations. Conservative and fundamentalist alike decry big government, are likely to equate regulation with regimentation, call for local control and individual initiative, and express alarm at what they view as a drift from principle to expediency (or, to put this last point differently, they are distressed at what they consider to be the abandonment of tested values for untested ones).

Though conservative and fundamentalist do, indeed, share a somewhat similar agenda and are ordinarily located at the same general end of the spectrum, they are by no means identical, witness the fact that conservatives often take great pains to dissociate themselves from fundamentalists. The conservative is likely to see the fundamentalist as reckless and irresponsible; the fundamentalist is likely to reply that the conservative is spineless and lacks the courage to follow where his professed convictions ought to lead.

This is to say, then, that the chief distinction between conservative and fundamentalist is not primarily doctrinal but behavioral. Many articles of the creed they can recite in unison, but their rituals represent rather different orders of things, different styles of life. There is, however, an intimate relationship between ritual and creed: the way in which one acts out his creed reacts back upon the creed. In other words, action has the power to work subtle changes on the ideas action is presumed to serve. In more familiar terms, if means are not carefully chosen for their appropriateness to the ends we seek, they will lead us to ends we never envisioned. And this, I think, is a clue to the uneasiness the conservative has with the fundamentalist: in spite of the fact that on occasions both sound the same, the conservative is suspicious that in the end the fundamentalist ritual will require a rewritten creed, a suspicion which is well founded.

It is a mistake, then, to think of fundamentalism as primarily an effort to conserve cherished values out of the past. Fundamentalism is, rather, a failure of nerve, an effort not simply to value yesterday but to cancel tomorrow, not for lack of interest but for lack of daring. It is rampant nostalgia which clings desperately to familiar patterns of action in a world which grows daily more unfamiliar. Its quest for simple verities is response to an increasing and accelerating complexity of life which threatens to disorient and to overwhelm. It is the expression of frustration and outrage that history does not move at the fundamentalist's command in his own desired direction. It is an insistence that all important precedents have already been set, only because there is insufficient courage to set new precedents. *Fundamentalism, in short, is fright of freedom and flight from freedom.* And since it does not trust itself to live in an open world, it conspires to prevent anyone else from doing so.

All of this means that conservatism and fundamentalism bear no *necessary* relation to each other. Sometimes, to be sure, fundamentalism is merely conservatism fermented, gone sour; but a man could become a fundamentalist without ever having passed through conservatism. The conservative is doctrinally oriented, is concerned with a particular system of coherent ideas and their translation into institutional structure and life-style. Fundamentalism is a refuge, not for the disenchanted (as in the case of romanticism) but for the frightened. Its distinctive ideas are not so much principled as weaponed, and its distinctive behavior patterns are improvised responses to what is experienced as the hostility of the emerging world.

Fundamentalism has neither formal system nor informal coherence but offers instead a program for action. This has two practical consequences. In periods when fundamentalism is aggressive, it draws a strange conglomeration of followers who, though chanting the pseudoconservative slogans, represent rather differing and sometimes inconsistent points of view. So in these recent years of fundamentalism rampant, the movement has included both those who would scrap the welfare system built over the last thirty years and those who, though ready to scrap parts of the system, would retain and extend other parts. For example, though prepared to revoke aid to dependent children, presumably because it rewards sexual promiscuity, they might like to see an enlargement of old age and survivors' benefits. There are those who support the abolition of the graduated income tax, those who support the abolition of every tax on income, and those who would retain the income tax while modifying its exemptions. And all join in lusty cheers for individual initiative, property rights, and local government. There is, then, no ideological unity in fundamentalism but only a pseudounity which comes from the fact that the movement is a coalition drawn together by a common form of political behavior—a common ritual—for aggressive attack on a common enemy.

In periods when fundamentalism is not aggressive, however—when it is leaderless, or when it has suffered severe defeat, or when the enemy is indistinct, or in certain localized situations where it has won at least temporary dominance—the lack of ideological coherence results in schism. Fundamentalism's unity lies only in its common enemy and its defensive, underdog posture, and when these are not present, its coalition disintegrates and the movement literally falls apart. It is common to decry the fact that there are, in the United States, more than 250 organized religious sects and denominations. I agree that the statistic is somewhat appalling, but it is also almost wholly misleading. More than three-fourths of American Protestantism can be located within some seven or eight major cooperating families of denominations. The remaining less than one-fourth of the church membership is scattered through an incredible number of splinter groups, most of which are fundamentalist in character. Because it lacks intellectual coherence and is largely a strategic amalgam, fundamentalism is inherently schismatic.

FUNDAMENTALISM IN RECENT POLITICS

Readers will scarcely have failed to note that, although this chapter purports in its title to deal with politics, the language thus far used is usually associated with religious behavior. This is because I find in the history and sociology of the American religious experience a type and a typology which help me to understand what has been happening in recent years in the American political experience. In American Protestantism, the fundamentalist movement began to become visible and vocal shortly after the turn into the present century, at a time when the familiar patterns of the nineteenth century were breaking up and the world was becoming a far more complex place. Fundamentalist agitation was directed against a liberal movement which had become increasingly dominant in the last quarter of the nineteenth century. Although the rank-and-file membership in the major Protestant denominations has probably never been liberal in character, liberals succeeded in capturing many of the major denominational offices and gradually possessed the theological seminaries, thus wielding an influence all out of proportion to their numbers. Since the liberals in this period were inclined to embrace enthusiastically—and, as it turned out, rather uncritically—the new movements in science and in social reform which were threatening to undo comfortably established virtues, fundamentalism was a strategy of desperation aimed at stopping the liberal rush toward the future.

Political fundamentalism has had a similar history. It became particularly visible and vocal shortly after the close of World War II and was a delayed but agitated response to the liberal politics and economics of the Roosevelt era which had enjoyed a period of relative immunity from effective attack, first by the desperate needs of depression days and then by national preoccupation with waging global warfare. But this period of immunity served to entrench the liberal drift and thus, perhaps, to make the fundamentalist fermentation all the more agitated once it began to work. Although the rank and file of the two major political parties was probably never liberal in character, liberals succeeded in capturing major political posts and gradually possessed the academic centers of the land upon which politicians have come more and more to depend, with the result that the liberals wielded a political influence all out of proportion to their numbers. Political fundamentalism was the strategy of desperation aimed at stopping the liberal movement toward a transformed American society.

What follows is an attempt at a delineation of political fundamentalism in profile. Many of the illustrations are drawn from the period of the presidential campaigns of Barry Goldwater and George Wallace, the most successful practitioners of political fundamentalism to appear on the recent American scene. And the Wallace incidents are primarily from his 1968 campaign, since in the primaries of 1972 Wallace was driven more toward the political center in an eager effort to attract voters who were not, in fact, fundamentalists themselves but who had become at least momentarily disenchanted with the candidates of both of the major parties. In consequence of this shift, in 1972 Wallace abandoned many of the fundamentalist tactics which had made him notorious in 1968 and took on, instead, a more moderate tone and style. His ability to provide vigorous national leadership in 1976 for a political fundmentalism which is, for the moment, relatively leaderless is unclear in view of the paralysis which resulted from the tragic but abortive attempt on his life late in the 1972 primary campaign.

But the analysis which follows is not dependent upon a specific cast of characters or dated by a particular set of years. It has to do, rather, with a political type which appeared vividly in the campaigns of 1964, 1968, and 1972 and which will appear again. I would not be surprised to see new leadership center in some presently unknown charismatic figure who may arise out of the group of returned Vietnam war prisoners. I sense in some of them precisely the kind of "God and country" intensity, fused in a politically exploitable ordeal in the enemy prison camps of Indochina, which could become fundamentalist dynamite.

In any case, political fundamentalism has taken deep root in localities and states, often in a form more virulent than appears in national campaigns, and this base gives it a relative permanence among us. It has made successful inroads into the hard-hat mentality and formed alliance with blue-collar backlash in many parts of the country. The trigger issues of busing to achieve racial balance and sex education in public schools gave the movement a more effective local strategy than did its earlier attacks upon fluoridation of the water supply; and these more recent issues won a sympathetic hearing and support from insecure segments of white-collar society. All of this suggests the importance, especially to those who believe that fundamentalism diminishes man, of recognizing its profile and its operational style, the more effectively to oppose it in whatever campaign or candidate.

THE STRATEGY OF SIMPLISM

Its appeal depends on a radical simplism. Protestant fundamentalism holds that the source of our human ills is to be located in man's sin, where sin is understood simply as pride and laziness, lust and self-indulgence. All human ills—whether physical or spiritual, individual or corporate, economic or political—can be overcome if only men's hearts can be put right. And lest there be any uncertainty about how that can be accomplished, fundamentalism has always been ready to reduce the entire matter to "seven steps to salvation" or some other simple formula. Neither sin itself nor the ills to which it gives rise require subtlety of analysis; the remedy takes no sophistication of the understanding. On the contrary, the fundamentalist fears that subtlety of analysis and sophistication of understanding are just other forms of the sin of pride intended by the devil to confuse men's minds and to distract them from a saving simplicity. It should not be necessary to observe that elsewhere in the Protestant movement sin and salvation, though taken with radical seriousness, are treated in a less forensic and more profound way—for example, in Martin Luther or John Calvin, in Jonathan Edwards or in Reinhold Niebuhr.

This anti-intellectualism which is characteristic of religious fundamentalism also gives character to political fundamentalism. It proudly flaunts its refusal to be detained by thought; it scorns the "pointy-headed pseudo-intellectual who can't park his bicycle straight" and thus obviously cannot be trusted with the more important matters of government; and it hints that "egghead" claims that domestic and international problems involve considerations of a complex and subtle nature are smokescreens either for inaction or for subversion. Phyllis Schlafly, whose book *A Choice Not an Echo* was one of the leading tracts of political fundamentalism in the Goldwater campaign, wrote:

> *Life* said we must beware of Goldwater because he has one-sentence solutions for national problems. According to this peculiar line of egghead reasoning, present day problems are so complex that we must have sophisticated—not simple—solutions.
>
> Contrary to this argument, civilization progresses, freedom is won, and problems are solved because we have wonderful people who think up simple solutions. It is not the complicated, round-about Rube Goldberg approach that accomplishes anything, but the direct approach that goes to the heart of the problem....
>
> Likewise, there are numerous simple solutions that confront our country today. Barry Goldwater is the man who can cut through the egghead complexities in Foggy bottom and solve these problems for us.[2]

So the simple solution to the Cuban problem, according to Mrs. Schlafly, was to invoke the Monroe Doctrine. We could have stopped the construction of the Berlin Wall, she held, by the simple expedient of closing the Soviet Embassy and the Soviet consulates in this country. And world communism would collapse if only American foreign policy would stop "helping the Communists."[3] (Parenthetically, a speaker in my town, a self-confessed Communist in the late thirties but later by his own report a member of "The Soldiers of the Cross," which he described as a Christian anti-Communist crusade, announced at a public meeting that the American CIA is financing the Soviet intelligence service!)

No one should make the mistake of passing Barry Goldwater or George Wallace off as fools, as political cartoons encouraged us to do. But not even their most fervent supporters have ever accused them of harboring complicated solutions to important domestic or international problems. They were almost wholly unencumbered by formal platform, and one searched their speeches in vain for hint of a coherent program which they were offering to the voters. Is there a tax crisis in the United States? Wallace would have saved it by removing the tax-exempt status from the giant nonprofit foundations like Ford and Rockefeller. Is there crime in the streets? Require Supreme Court justices (whose decisions on constitutional procedures have presumably made things easier for lawbreakers) to be reconfirmed by the Senate every six years, overturn by congressional action the restraints imposed on law enforcement agencies by the Court, and if necessary place troops with fixed bayonets at five-foot intervals through the public thoroughfares of Washington, D.C. Is America torn by dissent? Said Mr. Wallace to a group of Missouri state police, "I'd like to see what would happen if the government was turned over to you fellows for two years."

Absence of program is, of course, precisely what draws voters to the political fundamentalist. In a time when life has become frightfully and frighteningly complicated, simple solutions are strongly attractive to unreflective and insecure segments of the voting population. Whether or not we can persuade the unreflective and insecure, we ought to be clear ourselves that there is nothing simple about either our problems or their solutions. What has created an atmosphere of dissent and dissatisfaction, for example, is the conviction that government lacks a capacity for responsiveness to the concerns of its citizens; not simply that government refuses to alter its policies on demand, but that it lacks the will even to entertain seriously the views of its critics. The fear is abroad, and spreading, that official power is corrupt at its base, in that it uses the force of law to harass or to silence its detractors while using that same force to protect its own privilege. Even persons who are normally unresponsive politically, inclined to attribute virtue to authority simply because it is authority, are beginning to stir in growing awareness of official manipulation of public opinion, and of policy made in cynical disregard of those the people have elected to represent them.

Wallace's simple repressive society would be a grim and living caricature of the nation's worst fears. Far from being a solution to our ills, it would have been the virtual declaration of a new civil war.

When political fundamentalists have invoked the Monroe Doctrine, insisted on protecting national sovereignty, and called for "total victory" over our opponents in the world, their invocations were dangerous because they attempted to apply to problems of an entirely new dimension formulations and solutions long since outmoded. When the political fundamentalist has complained about experiments in world community and talked, instead, of nationalism in nineteenth-century terms, it is appropriate to reply that he simply does not understand the irreversible interdependence which is a brute fact of our twentieth-century existence. In the 1970s, "Fortress America" is a figment of a retarded imagination. When the political fundamentalist has demanded "total victory" over our opponents in world politics, and when he has advocated within frightening memory the giving to military field commanders the use of even limited-yield nuclear weapons as a means of achieving that "victory," it is appropriate to reply then as now that he does not understand the nature of the power he would so recklessly have unleashed, nor does he understand the politics of that power. In November, 1968, Robert Kennedy's account of the Cuban missile crisis was published for the first time, and Mr. Kennedy recounted how General Curtis LeMay urged President John Kennedy to order a direct attack on the Cuban missile bases, assuring the president that Russia would not make retaliatory response. Later in the account Robert Kennedy wrote, "One member of the Joint Chiefs of Staff . . . argued that we could use nuclear weapons, on the basis that our adversaries would use theirs against us in an attack."[4] Was that suggestion made by General LeMay? Kennedy's account doesn't specify, but it is surely not irrelevant that the general was on record as favoring the strategic battlefield use of nuclear weapons, and that he once suggested that Vietnam ought to be bombed right back to the Stone Age, if that were necessary to an American victory there. (Perhaps it is unnecessary to remind readers that General LeMay was George Wallace's vice-presidential running mate in 1968.) Robert Kennedy reflected, "I thought, as I listened, of the many times that I had heard the military take positions which, if wrong, had the advantage that no one would be around at the end to know."[5]

Not even a so-called "preventive" or "preemptive" nuclear war would result in "total victory." Beyond the indiscriminate devastation of the nuclear weapons themselves, the panic and disorder which would inevitably accompany their use—in the country of origin, not simply in the target nation—would force us to apply to our own people the controls of a police state beyond anything we have experienced in the earlier wars of this century, thus adopting for ourselves what we profess to hate in the enemy. For whom would that be "total victory"? When, to the appeal for patient negotiation and peaceful but competitive coexistence with our international detractors, the political fundamentalist cries

"Appeasement!" and "Treachery!", he simply confirms his own incompetence for the complicated tasks of modern government.

HISTORY REFRACTED

It distorts history in the service of its present interests. Religious fundamentalists appeal to the Bible for support of their peculiar views, but their use of the Bible often results in a distortion of the biblical record. In proof, for example, that the pope is the Antichrist and therefore the archenemy of God, appeal has often been made to the book of Revelation, whose symbolism is read to support such a view. There is, indeed, the figure of a beast in that book which is represented as God's enemy, and religious fundamentalists have identified that figure for centuries with whatever at the moment they happened to think of as demonic, from Napoleon to Franklin Roosevelt. Each fundamentalist has confidently assumed that Revelation is aimed directly and unerringly at his own period of history; to none of them has it seemed to occur that the biblical writer may have intended to say something about the beastly in his own years, probably a period of Roman persecution of the Christians at the end of the first century A.D.

Similarly, what political fundamentalists appeal to for precedent out of the past is often a distortion of the past. For example, one of the leaders of Young Americans for Freedom appealed to the example of Thomas Jefferson in support of the view that the American republic was originally founded on "scriptural principles." The fact is, of course, that Jefferson was no evangelical Christian at all but rather a rationalist and a deist who, if he were alive today, would be denounced by that same fundamentalist as a liberal modernist. Jefferson's view of the Scripture was so selective that it permitted him to emasculate it by choosing some portions and rejecting others, finally creating a distinctive "Jefferson Bible."

A more dangerous instance of distorted appeal to history was seen in those who, at the time of the Cuban missile crisis and since, have called for the invocation of the Monroe Doctrine as if nothing had happened in the world in the last 145 years. But as a matter of fact, when President James Monroe sent his historic message to the Congress on December 2, 1823, it contained *two* statements of policy: one was a warning to European powers not to attempt to propagate their political influence in the Western hemisphere; but the other was the announcement that the United States intended to follow the advice of President Washington by avoiding foreign entanglements and would not interfere in the political affairs of Europe. How much sense does it make, historically, to appeal to the Monroe Doctrine as an adequate response to a current hemispheric crisis, when American troops occupy Germany and American generals command the North Atlantic Treaty Organization, to say nothing of our direct and indirect entanglements in Southeast Asia and the Middle East?

THE POLITICS OF ABSOLUTISM

Its pronouncements are couched in an absolutism appropriate to deity. In the case of the religious fundamentalist, the Bible is viewed as the infallible basis of knowledge of God's will for the world, and this is the source of the confidence with which he makes his pronouncements. Fundamentalists have never quite succeeded in explaining, however, how one moves from infallible record to infallible interpretation. That is, even if the record were without error, that record does not interpret itself and must be interpreted by men who are, indeed, prone to error. Having rejected the notion of papal infallibility, the fundamentalist is in a poor position to claim it for himself or his church. And it is embarrassing to him to recognize the extent to which fundamentalists themselves have differed on what the infallible Bible teaches, for example, about the millennial age at the end of history.

Political fundamentalism extracts its authority partly from the biblical tradition and partly from appeal to natural law which, it is presumed, every honest man ought to recognize. But whatever the source, the message of the political fundamentalist claims the status of absolute truth. The "Sharon Statement," credo of the right-wing Young Americans for Freedom, opens with the words, "In this time of moral and political crisis, it is the responsibility of the youth of America to affirm certain eternal truths." One of the "intellectual" spokesmen for political fundamentalism has written that what our American society needs is "To turn from the quicksands and to find the granite. What is granite? It is truth, it is reality, it is things as they are in the mind of God. . . . In philosophy, in ethics, in aesthetics, we must return to absolutes. And in politics we must return to absolutes."[6]

There is a sense in which no one can quarrel with that. Who would dare to be against eternal truth? Indeed, the political liberal himself believes in some truths which he thinks are pretty permanent in his understanding of man and society. One of these is that all men ought to have equal rights before the law. For the liberal, I take it that is simply not negotiable; it is a fixed point in his view.

But if we would not dare to be against eternal truth, we always face a problem when we try to sort out what is eternal from what is transient. Our human preferences are conditioned both by our passions and by our past. If we are rational beings, capable often of selfless and objective thought, our rationality is also often perverted into cleverness and made to serve our own special interest. Ever since Eden, men have been taking their own private truths and demanding that other men bow down before them as if they were universal and eternal. The political fundamentalist I quoted a moment ago apparently thinks that he knows "things as they are in the mind of God." As a theologian, I can only reply that he knows more than I do. He appears to have an unmitigated confidence in human reason, a confidence more akin to the eighteenth century than to our own, and it is this which leads him to think that he can read God's thoughts after him—or perhaps even before him! It is this which permits him to announce eternal truth with untroubled confidence.

There is a second problem here as well, and I think it is much the more serious problem. For the political fundamentalist moves quite uncritically from the announcement of certain *principles,* which he thinks are eternal, to the advocacy of certain *arrangements and institutions* whose eternal validity he wants to claim. It is one thing to insist that all men ought to order their relationships by the principle of justice; it is quite another to insist that any particular social order or arrangement is so sacred that *it alone* can serve the ends of justice. Yet this is precisely the kind of misplaced absolutism in which the Young Americans for Freedom engage in their Sharon Statement. What are the "eternal truths" they want us to affirm? Not only justice and freedom and integrity. Rather, one of their "eternal truths" is "That the market economy, allocating resources by the free play of supply and demand, is the single economic system compatible with the requirements of personal freedom and constitutional government." Again, "That we will be free only so long as the national sovereignity of the United States is secure. . . ." And again, "That the United States should stress victory over, rather than co-existence with, [Communism]." But libertarian economics and particular ideas of national sovereignty are not eternal truths; they are, rather, the historically conditioned, and therefore quite fallible, programs and institutions within which men have sought to create distributive and political justice.

It is this same misplaced absolutism in which the "intellectual" spokesman above indulges. In politics we must return to absolutes he tells us. And what are these absolutes?

> We are not a democracy, we are a Republic; we are not a welfare state, we are a government that should uphold free enterprise; we don't want the state to be our orderly policeman from the cradle to the grave, we want freedom, and individual initiative, and what Emerson called "the infinitude of the private man." And in religion we must return to the granite of reality. We need to say, and to act on, the foundation of our Republic: God.[7]

This is, I think, a very revealing quotation. It is not too much to insist that the political fundamentalist will have to choose between "the infinitude of man" and God; for to speak of man's infinitude is precisely to make man his own god. Indeed, that is just the problem: the political fundamentalist's claim to absolute truth is the attempt to fob off our historically conditioned human arrangements on God and to claim him as their author.

This fundamentalist preoccupation with the so-called absolutes has a dangerous practical consequence, in that it prevents him from appreciating the subtlety which is present in our ordinary human relations and particularly in political issues. He is not able to distinguish shades and differences and is therefore given to heavy-handed judgments. A flagrant instance of this was contained in a letter I once received from a prominent midwestern news commentator during the McCarthy era. I had written to him to protest what I thought were his reckless charges made in radio comment on the political scene. This is what he wrote in reply:

> While I believe I have over the months (and even years) considered all the points you have brought up, I would point out one thing the significance of which, I believe, you have lost: that one may be pro-Communist and NOT be a card-

carrying member of the Communist Party. Accordingly, an adherent of the so-called New Deal and Fair Deal is considered at least on the road to pro-Communism, inasmuch as the Deals are steps along the road to Socialism and Socialism is Communism before it has completely shackled a people in an all-out police state.[8]

And then he added with an accusing twist, "By the way, Mr. Averill, why are you so concerned about these things? People with a clear conscience find no fault with the words I use."[9] Apart from this insufferable sense of absolute truth, he preached a dangerous doctrine. To damn the Roosevelt and Truman administrations, along with England's Labor government and the Scandinavian countries, as enemies of freedom helped no one except the enemies of freedom.

Former President John C. Bennett of Union Theological Seminary quite properly noted that, at precisely the moment when world communism was becoming more varied and complicated, both popular and official attitudes in the United States insisted on characterizing it as univocal. Bennett called for an awareness of the ways in which peculiar national traditions and interests were diluting the "universal" ideology, and he insisted that it was in the interest of the United States to recognize that the new variations would weaken communism's force and effect. "The moment you get the dramatic presentation of two different ways," he wrote, "then both become more relative and neither one can be as convincing or absolute any longer."[10] In this sense, willingness to recognize the subtle shadings of political difference would in the long run have a far more profound anti-Communist influence than would the fundamentalist's refusal to make such distinctions in the interests of his own absolutism.

One would think that, especially after the events of Czechoslovakia in 1968, it would be unnecessary to argue about differences within the Communist camp. It was precisely Communists—and in the case of party secretary Alexander Dubcek, a Communist who had been carefully trained in Moscow—who determined upon a more humane course for communism in Czechoslovakia. That the political fundamentalist was unwilling to permit mere facts to change his dogma, however, was seen in the statement by the "Soldier of the Cross" who announced, in a speech in my town at the time, that Dubcek was not a Communist at all but only pretended to be. Were that the case, of course, Dubcek would have died the day the Russian troops invaded his country. The Russians looked desperately for evidence of anti-Communist influence on the Czech liberalization policies as an excuse for their intervention; that Dubcek remained alive was evidence that they found none. Dubcek was a Communist, but he was also a Czechoslovak nationalist, and that made all the difference between him and his enemies in the Kremlin.

IS FREEDOM THE ABSENCE OF RESTRICTION?

Its view of man and society is highly individualistic. Religious fundamentalism holds that good men make good institutions and the bad men make bad institutions; good men make good laws, and bad men make bad laws. Thus its emphasis is on salvation through a changed heart. It ignores or denies the extent to which man is shaped by his culture, and therefore refuses to become directly involved in shaping a human society which will, in turn, help men to become more human.

Similarly, the view of man implied in political fundamentalism is atomistic. Left free of restriction, men will do what their good requires; and in this, the fundamentalist sounds very much like the revolutionary. So, that government governs best which governs least, and which leaves the business of governing primarily to the states and localities. Thus the atomistic view of man has its counterpart in an atomistic view of the governing process, with a consequent reduction in the power of the federal establishment.

To sharpen the issue by means of a contrast, the view of man implied in political liberalism is contained in Reinhold Niebuhr's dictum, that "Man's capacity for justice makes democracy possible; but man's inclination to injustice makes democracy necessary." [11] Thus when the liberal talks about freedom, he means that balancing of interests which maximizes the possibility of justice. Niebuhr expressed this view pointedly when he wrote that "liberalism connotes a desire to use all the instruments and authority of the political state for the advancement of justice." [12]

The liberal holds that economic freedom will result from political freedom, whereas the fundamentalist believes that political freedom will result from economic freedom. That is, the political order has priority for the liberal and is to be served by the economic order, while for the fundamentalist the economic order has priority and is to be served by the political order. The political fundamentalist's position on this matter involves a contradiction not often enough noted. While he typically holds that government ought to be subject to checks and balances of a statutory kind to prevent it from becoming tyrannical, he does not see that the economic order requires these same kinds of statutory checks and balances to prevent it from becoming greedy and irresponsible.

Moreover, in our American society business has become a kind of "secret government," whose edicts profoundly affect the general welfare. Why this "secret government" should be less in need of regulation than the agencies of public administration is hidden in the mystery of fundamentalist logic. But the reason the liberal chooses to allow the political order to control the economic order seems reasonably clear: such an arrangement guarantees to every citizen a responsible and reasonably equitable share in the decision making which affects the general welfare. That kind of equity is not available to us by virtue of our places in the economic order, for we have not such equity there. It is available only by virtue of our individual places within the political order. Furthermore, political decisions are protected from undue influence and pressure by the secret ballot, while economic decisions have no such protection. This kind of equity is precisely what the liberal means by freedom.

Is it legitimate for government to ask for legislation whose purpose it is to end practices which are discriminatory to minority groups? The standard fundamentalist response is that "you can't legislate goodwill." Of course goodwill cannot be legislated, and perhaps government would have no business legislating it if it could. But it is the business of government to see that ill will is not given legal sanction and to minimize as much as possible the economic and political advantages which may accrue to ill will. Even if I hate my neighbor, I am prevented by such legislation from putting my hatred to his economic and political disadvantage.

The other standard response of the fundamentalist is that such legislation takes away certain freedoms from the majority. But the argument over the legitimacy of civil rights legislation cannot be reduced to a simple choice between freedom and its opposite. The real question raised by such laws is not "freedom or not freedom," but "freedom for whom to do what?" A democratic society represents competing claims for freedom, and government must adjudicate those claims. When Congress passes antitrust laws and prohibits combinations in restraint of trade and price-fixing, it asserts that the freedom of the consumer to exercise choice in a competitive market is to be protected against the freedom of the manufacturer to manipulate the market without regard for consumer welfare. When a state enacts fair employment legislation, it asserts that the freedom of all citizens to gain employment on the basis of actual job qualifications is to be protected against the freedom of employers to discriminate on the basis of race, color, religion, or national origin. Recently a doctor wrote in a letter to a newspaper editor that no governmental authority should be allowed to tell us "when, where, and what to buy," referring to open-housing legislation. Perhaps that doctor has forgotten that every time he writes a prescription, he gives consent to laws which tell us just that, since drugs can be prescribed and dispensed only by individuals properly licensed by the state. I presume he would argue, as I would, that the health and safety of the public must be protected against freedom for quacks, drug exploiters, and well-meaning but ignorant persons to make unrestricted use of drugs.

FUNDAMENTALISTS VS. THE CONSTITUTION

It seeks basic alteration of the tradition under the guise of protecting that tradition. This is, I am persuaded, what happens in the religious fundamentalist's relation to the Bible. He declares its unchanging witness to be his most precious possession, while at the same time his use of the Bible as a source book for proving the authority of his own confident view of things is precisely what robs the Bible of both its authority and integrity.

The political fundamentalist sees himself as the only authentic guardian and interpreter of the American tradition of constitutional government, and as the only true advocate of freedom. There is good reason to suspect, however, that in fact he is deeply hostile to the separation of powers which the Constitution guarantees, that he really wants a basic alteration in that constitutional provision, and that fear of his own political impotence leads him to prefer political survival over constitutional principles.

Attacks on the United States Supreme Court and attempts to subordinate the Court to the Congress in violation of the doctrine of the separation of powers have been led by political fundamentalists, who thus demonstrate their hostility to the means chosen by the Founding Fathers to protect our American freedoms. In a magazine article during the 1968 presidential campaign, William F. Buckley, Jr., insisted that American conservatives were even more appalled by George Wallace than were the liberals. Conservatives were concerned, said Buckley, lest the fact that Wallace sounds, in certain respects, like a conservative would lead the public to identify him with the conservative movement in American politics.[13] If, indeed, the public made that identification, Buckley had only himself to blame. For in 1963 he wrote that he was quite out of patience with the notion that the Bill of Rights applies to everyone without moral or political distinction. He wrote:

> It is an empirical question, not to be answered by liberal dogmatic invocations, whether a Western nation can pursue a truly effective pro-Western policy while adhering to conventional libertarian attitudes toward the rights and privileges of dissent. . . . It is nothing short of preposterous to tolerate an active conspiracy in our midst; and if the Constitution is not, as presently understood, resilient enough to cope with the contemporary requirements of survival, then the Constitution should be modified.[14]

That, in my view, represents a proposal for a constitutional breach as serious as anything suggested by the fundamentalists.

In George Wallace we have had a much more open and unabashed instance of a man who sought basically to alter the constitutional tradition under the guise of protecting it. While he criticized those among the younger generation who insist on choosing which laws they shall respect and which they shall not, on the ground that no man is above the law in a democracy, George Wallace stood in the schoolhouse door at the University of Alabama in public defiance of an order of the federal court. While declaring his love for constitutional government, he found his own political fortunes in Alabama frustrated by the fact that the state constitution would not permit him to succeed himself in the office of governor. Failing to win the necessary constitutional amendment which would have permitted the perpetuation of his own rule, he cynically managed the election of his wife and continued to run the state government behind this modest subterfuge, in public and unblushing violation of the clear spirit and intent of the state constitution. A similar cynical contradiction is found in such a political fundamentalist as Senator Strom Thurmond of South Carolina. Thurmond impugned the personal and legal integrity of almost every member of the Supreme Court because that wins more public applause than do attacks directly on the Bill of Rights. Yet it was at the Bill of Rights that Thurmond really aimed in his criticism of the Court, whose justices had sought in cases of civil rights, free speech, and the constitutional rights of prisoners to protect the freedoms the bill guaranteed to all citizens. Thurmond charged the justices with being "soft" on pornography because of free-speech decisions which refused to suppress the circulation of certain motion picture films. Thurmond had no scruple against the use of these same films for his own political profit, however, and during the hearings on the confirmation of Associate Justice Fortas to be Chief Justice, he arranged to show the films in the rooms of the United States Senate because Fortas voted with the Court majority in refusing to suppress them.

Finally, the political fundamentalist would like to change the traditionally nonpolitical role of the military in American public life. In those parts of the world where the military holds the balance of power, politicians must pander to military support. Under such circumstances, the orderly procedures of government by ballot and legislation are constantly menaced by arbitrary military whim. It is precisely this which portends in the desire of political fundamentalists to create a coalition with military leadership.

EXORCISING THE DEMONS

It depends for its emotional power on the invocation of a popular demonology. Fundamentalism, whether in its religious or political form, is a movement of frustration and of desperation. Outraged by liberal programs and the disproportionate power liberals have had in influencing public policy, and frustrated in its attempts to win a share of that influence for itself, fundamentalism has accumulated a considerable reservoir of hate. It therefore needs a set of demons against whom it can vent this emotional energy, on whom it can heap its outrage, and from whom it can presumably salvage its own wounded ego by invidious comparison. Religious fundamentalism has always had Lucifer himself as a considerable resource, and it has fulminated fulsomely against that fallen angel. But it has found it necessary to give the Devil face and form and so has created a demonology. The demons change from time to time, since what is identified as demonic is not wholly stable. For Protestant fundamentalists, Roman Catholics in general and the pope in particular have been identified as the Devil's progeny, along with infidels, heretics, and all manner of dissolute persons. For political fundamentalists the list is led, of course, by Communists and followed by fellow-travelers, but the list is in fact almost endless. It has included those "pointy-headed intellectuals who can't park their bicycles straight"; guideline writers in the Department of Health, Education, and Welfare who can tell you how and when your local public school ought to integrate; hippies and homosexuals; anarchists, draft-card burners, and draft evaders. These demons are so important to fundamentalism that it would fall apart if they were to disappear. George Wallace was shrewd enough to know that, and he told the truth when he said that the youthful anti-Wallace demonstrators who attended his rallies won him votes.

As a result of this ritual of demon invocation and demon exorcism, there is in both religious and political fundamentalism a latent violence. Protestant fundamentalism has found a socially acceptable language of violence in its descriptions of hell and the fate of the sinner. Observers of the Wallace campaign in 1968 noted the air of violence in his rallies, not in the activities of the young dissenters who were usually present, but in the Wallace regulars who could hardly contain their enthusiasm and excitement when Wallace described what would happen if a protester ever lay down in front of *his* car! "Run over him!" the advocates of law and order shouted. And if, late in that campaign, Wallace gave up the promise to run over the anarchist in the roadway, his followers were sure, by that time, that they knew what he intended to do, and they identified themselves with him in the act of crushing evil. This note of latent violence was less in evidence during Wallace's primary campaign in 1972, partly because by this time all Americans had had their fill of it domestically and in Southeast Asia, and partly because Wallace himself fell victim to it in the midst of that campaign when he was wounded in an assassination attempt.

The present prominence and influence of the political fundamentalist is, as I insisted at the outset, evidence of a widespread failure of political nerve among us. It is a sign that an alarming number of American citizens have lost confidence in the desirability of an open society. If the fundamentalists should win an increasing measure of real power, it will threaten a subversion of the American political tradition, and an attendant diminishment of man, more serious and more effective than any foreign conspiracy could dream. That power grab can only be thwarted by the mobilization of all Americans who dare to believe that human freedom is worth all it risks.

Part IV
History
as Relation

Chapter Eight

The Matrix
of Man

THERE IS A GRACE IN LIFE

Peer Gynt, the drama by Hendrik Ibsen, is a powerful and perceptive delineation of man's problematic quest for self-identity. Young Peer was a wastrel—brawler, braggart, liar, drunkard—known for his flagrant disregard of almost everyone and everything. Even his mother, to whom he was touchingly attached, called him "a hopeless ne'er-do-well" and went grieving to her grave. The lovely Solveig, the only other person for whom Peer seemed to have any regard, was repeatedly hurt by his excesses.

There is something too extreme about Peer: his antics are too bizarre, too calculated to shock, his apparent gaiety and wit a bit too desperate. These are not the acts of one who simply has an excess of youthful exuberance; they are, rather, the actions of a deeply troubled spirit seeking to disguise its trouble. Early in the drama it becomes clear that Peer is engaged in a frantic and fruitless search for self-significance. In spite of the appearance that he commands life, he admits inwardly that his own existence is "empty, ugly, dreary," a dreadful burden. It is a burden he seems unable to share, perhaps because he has a talent for building walls rather than bridges, perhaps because he assumes that self-significance, if it is achieved at all, must be sought as a lonely prize.

127

So, standing in the night outside a hut in which Solveig waits for him, Peer speaks his desperation with a double meaning Solveig does not quite grasp:

> Solveig. What do you say?
> Peer Gynt. Dear, you must wait. It's dark, and I've a heavy load.
> Solveig. I'll come and help you bear the load.
> Peer Gynt. No, do not come! Stay where you are! I'll bear the whole of it.
> Solveig. But, dear, don't be too long.
> Peer Gynt. Be patient, child; whether the time is long or short, you must wait.
> Solveig (nodding to him). Yes, I will wait.[1]

So Peer leaves her to chase his phantom self halfway around the world, through revolution and shipwreck. One day he sits peeling an onion, removing first one layer and then the next, always expecting to find substance at the core; but when the last layer is removed, there is nothing. So it is with his own lonely quest for substance: layer after layer of Peer comes away, but when all are gone, there is nothing. Then it is an aged and sobered Peer Gynt who returns, after years of wandering, to Solveig. And there, in the predawn darkness, he experiences in their meeting a grace he could not have expected and speaks a confession he would not otherwise have dared:

> Solveig. 'Tis he! 'Tis he! Thanks be to God. (Gropes for him.)
> Peer Gynt. Tell me how sinfully I have offended! . . . Cry out, cry out my sins aloud!
> Solveig (sitting down beside him). You have made my life a beautiful song. Bless you for having come back to me! And blest be this morn of Pentecost!
> Peer Gynt. Then I am lost! . . . Unless you can solve a riddle!
> Solveig. What is it?
> Peer Gynt. What is it? You shall hear. Can you tell me where Peer Gynt has been since last we met?
> Solveig. Where he has been?
> Peer Gynt. With the mark of destiny on his brow—the man that he was when a thought of God's created him! Can you tell me that? If not, I must go to my last home in the land of shadows.
> Solveig (smiling). That riddle's easy.
> Peer Gynt. Tell me, then—where was my real self, complete and true—the Peer who bore the stamp of God upon his brow?
> Solveig. In my faith, in my hope and in my love.
> Peer Gynt. . . . Oh, hide me, hide me in your love![2]

Nothing I know, in life or in literature, speaks more powerfully than these words of Ibsen to the meaning of that wisdom about our human selfhood cited from Richard Niebuhr in chapter six and which I want to elaborate more fully now: that *to affirm one's own selfhood is to acknowledge one's existence "as the counterpart of another self."* [3]

"All real living is meeting," wrote Martin Buber [4] in confirmation of Ibsen's insight; and in the meeting of an I and a Thou is to be found that quintessential grace without which life could never have reached the level of the human. This is the primordial mystery of my manhood: that I am able to internalize the experience of the other and to have my own experience internalized by that other; that the other may become the intimate without evaporating his otherness for me or my otherness for him. And the fact that we are able to describe *how* this happens—as I shall attempt to do in this chapter—in no way reduces our wonder *that* it has happened at all, the awesome fact that creation has come to this.

Man's problematic character springs in significant measure from the fact that he is a peculiar being whose history is a *social* history, woven out of the interactions of a community of such beings: beings visible and invisible, known and unknown, past, present, and—strangely—still to come, and yet mysteriously a community all the same. To be a man is thus to be a self-in-relation. To be a man is to "have" a history which the self both creates and receives as a gift.

SELFHOOD AND HUMAN INTERACTION

Some years ago, the *New York Times* reported that Pennsylvania officials had found a female child of five or six years of age "tied to an old chair in a storage room on the second floor of a farm home." When found, the article said, the little girl was

> wedged into the chair, which was tilted backwards to rest on a coal bucket, her spindly arms tied above her head. She was unable to talk or move. . . . "The child was dressed in a dirty shirt and napkin," the officer said. "Her hands, arms, and legs were just bones, with skin drawn over them, so frail she couldn't use them. She never had enough nourishment. She never grew normally, and the chair on which she lay, half reclining and half sitting, was so small the child had to double her legs partly under her." [5]

As the story was later pieced together by investigators, the little girl was the second illegitimate child of a mother then in her late twenties. The mother lived with her father and other relatives in the farm home where the child was found. The father's anger over his daughter's behavior was so intense and so permanent that he did not want to see this second child; so she had been kept in the upstairs room since birth. The mother had only fed the child over the years, largely on great quantities of milk; she had not bathed, trained, supervised, or caressed the girl. She denied having tied the child, but it appeared that in earlier years the child had been confined in a crib and was later tied to a chair in order to prevent her from falling down the stairs. An older brother, also illegitimate, ignored the girl except for occasional ill-treatment. A sociologist who investigated reported that "Anna's social contacts with others were then at a minimum. What few she did have were of a perfunctory or openly antagonistic kind, allowing no opportunity for *Gemeinschaft* to develop."*

When first found, Anna was described as "completely apathetic, . . . limp, supine . . . immobile, expressionless, indifferent to everything." She was taken to a county institution for care. It was not clear at first whether she could see or hear. Within a few days, however, she responded to the ticking of a clock, though not to speech or to hands clapped near her head. Her eyes began to wander, though it was impossible to tell whether she was looking at anything in particular. Her physical reflexes were found to be entirely normal. She neither smiled nor cried, and the only sound she made was an occasional sucking with the intake of her breath. After ten days in the county home, however, she was more alert, able to fix her attention, had more expression, and handled herself better physically. She had located her tongue and was beginning to discriminate tastes and to show visual discrimination. But she had not yet learned how to seek attention or to indicate her wants; she could not chew or control her elimination. Hand play was entirely asocial, though she did like to rub foreheads with her nurse. Her attention could be concentrated only momentarily.

Six weeks later, nearly two months after she was found, there was little change, and it was not until seven months after being found

*Ferdinand Tonnies, who gave the term sociological currency, defined *Gemeinschaft* as "community," meaning "all intimate, private, and exclusive living together." "In *Gemeinschaft* (community) with one's family, one lives from birth on, bound to it in weal or woe." It is important to note that "the expression bad *Gemeinschaft* (community) violates the meaning of the word."[6]

that she could laugh and make a sound like "da." When tested in the eighth month by a standard developmental scale, she was below one year of mental age, though her chronological age by this time was nearly seven. After a little more than a year she showed marked physical improvement, laughed heartily, and once or twice made a sound with her lips that seemed verbal. Her interest in others was more obvious, her responses more definite and discriminating, and she could take some steps when held.

Because the county home where she was being kept was rather isolated, populated only by adults who were often preoccupied, so that she was in a room alone often with the door closed, it was decided to move her into a foster home. A month later she had shown remarkable improvement. The foster mother, said the sociological investigator, gave "unremitting attention, repetitive correction, and countless small rewards and punishments, mixed always with sympathetic interest and hovering physical presence. These Anna was getting for the first time in her life." Now approaching seven years of age, she was more like a normal one-year-old for the first time. By her seventh birthday she was able to walk a few steps alone, to respond to verbal commands, to recognize familiar faces, to express by bodily movements her desire to go for a ride in the car, to seek and to enjoy attention. Anna died at the age of ten of a physical disorder and had not progressed far beyond this point, except for greater physical control.

When compared with other isolated children, according to the investigating sociologist, these similarities occur: almost universal failure to learn to talk, hence failure to master their cultural heritage; and nearly universal sensory abnormality. A feral child named Kamala, who had been found at the age of eight, could speak only forty words after six years of tutoring. Said the investigator: "They developed responses suitable to their surroundings. Hence their subsequent inability to learn is attributable to the difficulty of uprooting fundamental, basically intrenched habits formed by earlier experience." In Ohio, Isabelle, an illegitimate child of six and one-half years of age, was found kept in seclusion in a dark room by a deaf-mute mother.[7] Communication had only been by gesture. The child's behavior toward strangers, especially men, was frightened and hostile, like an animal. After a year and a half, this child was bright and energetic, spoke well, walked, and ran without difficulty. She reached mental normality within two years and by age fourteen had passed the sixth grade. This child had learned to speak very early after being found and as a result proceeded to develop rapidly; by contrast, Anna never received prolonged and expert attention, had not learned to speak, and thus was prevented from growth toward mental normality. The sociological investigator concluded that "isolation up to the age of six, with failure to acquire any form of speech and hence failure to grasp nearly the whole world of cultural meaning, does not preclude the subsequent acquisition of these." If one were to ask how old an isolated child could be without permanent retardation, the answer is probably not as high as fifteen but may be as low as ten.[8]

Experience with severely isolated children confirms the view that

> ... human nature is determined by the child's communicative social contacts as much as by his organic equipment and that the system of communicative symbols is a highly complex business acquired early in life as a result of long and intimate training. It is not enough that other persons be merely present; these others must have an intimate, primary-group relationship with the child.[9]

Psychoanalytic theory, about the formation of human nature out of certain wishes which are inherent in the organism and which are responsible for the series of developmental states through which the human individual moves, is in this view simply mistaken.

THE NEED FOR INTIMACY

These observations about human organisms which have begun life under conditions of extreme isolation provide an appropriate setting for the theme of this chapter, namely, that *the self is formed in social interaction;* and they provide as well some useful illustrations of what it means to talk about the self in these terms.

First, we need to understand what it is that marks man off from other forms of animal life. That difference is to be found in man's peculiar freedom, his capacity not simply to be driven unthinkingly by his urges but to decide what he will do with his urges. Psychosomatic studies suggest that there is no such thing as a purely biological drive or instinct in man, that there is no form of behavior which man's body commands which he cannot modify by conscious or unconscious, but still not instinctual, intent. The body demands that its hunger be satisfied. Man, however, may gorge himself with so much food that he makes himself sick, perhaps because he desires to win the blueberry pie-eating contest or in order to compensate for a sense of loneliness and unfulfilled dependence; or he may deny his body's demand for food, perhaps because that is cheaper than buying an entire new wardrobe to fit his more than ample proportion, or because by engaging in a hunger strike he can draw the attention of the world to a cause in which he passionately believes. Again, the body demands that its sexual energy find an outlet. Man, however, may become a Don Juan who exhausts himself in sexual debauchery in order to prove his virility, or he may become a celibate who removes himself wholly from sexual contact in order to devote himself single-mindedly to other activities or because he is afraid to become intimate with another person. So, says anthropologist Loren Eiseley, in man, "unlike the case in the world of animals," instinct "is . . . reduced to a minimum."[10] And in a similar vein, psychoanalyst Erich Fromm remarks, "In contrast to the animal, which in its instincts has a 'built-in' mechanism of adaptation to its environment, living completely within nature, man lacks this instinctive mechanism. *He has to live* his life, he *is not lived by it.* . . ."[11]

And what is it in man which gives him this peculiar freedom? It is his mind—that is, his capacity for reflection and imagination—his ability to see how things are related to each other and to bring together combinations of things in relations which have never existed before, his ability to be aware of his own existence and to be aware of other centers of existence—that is, of other men—his capacity to remember and to anticipate, his teachability.

Man is born with a brain, but brain alone is not mind. The brain, as Dr. Eiseley puts it, is "peculiarly plastic . . . intended to receive impressions from the social world around it." Man enters upon life with a brain, but the mind is largely unformed and must be grown. "His childhood is lengthy," says the anthropologist, "because his developing brain must receive a large store of information and ways of behavior from the social group into which it is born."[12]

Man's mind, then, is formed in social interaction out of the impressions which he receives, the behavior he learns, the mental and motor skills which he practices, all because of the affectionate pressure of relationships in the intimate community *(Gemeinschaft)* in which he is nurtured. So, says Dr. Eiseley:

> The demands of learning thus placed upon the human offspring are greater than in any other animal. They have made necessary the existence of a continued family, rather than the casual sex life of many of the lower animals. Although the family differs in many of its minor features in distinct societies, it is always and everywhere marked by its tender and continuing care of the human offspring through the lengthened period of childhood.
>
> ... To the student of human evolution this remarkable and unique adjustment of our peculiar infancy to a lengthened family relationship between adults is one of the more mysterious episodes in the history of life. It is so strange, in fact, that only in one group of creatures—that giving rise to man—has it been successfully developed in the three billion years or so that life has existed on the planet. Family life is a fact that underlies everything else about man—his capacity for absorbing culture, his ability to learn—everything, in short, that enables us to call him human. He is born of love and he exists by reason of a love more continuous than in any other form of life.[13]

Humanness is marked, then, by man's capacity for mind, and mind is the result, for one thing, of man's location in an intimate and affectionate community in which his brain can grow the social experience it needs to become mind. Under these circumstances, it is not surprising that Anna, when she was first found, was described as "completely apathetic ... expressionless, indifferent." There is no evidence that she lacked brain capacity; her organs were intact, and her reflexes were normal. If what it takes to be human were built into the organism, if it were simply a matter of instinctive development from the inside, then there would be no reason why children such as Anna and Isabelle should not have been within the bounds of normality when found. Instead, Anna, though only one month short of her seventh birthday, had a mental age of less than one year. And note that she suffered from more than mental retardation. Her eyes and ears did not begin to function normally until she was placed in the county home and provided with something approaching normal human contacts. And the sociologist who investigated her situation remarked, as I noted earlier, that it is common for children who have experienced extreme isolation that though they may not be diseased or deficient in the physical condition of their sense organs, they nevertheless are abnormal in their ability to use these organs. So not only is the mind retarded, but so also are the organs of sense, by the absence of an intimate and affectionate community in which our humanness can be nurtured during the very critical first years of our lives.

LEARNING TO SPEAK

There is a second condition for the growth of a mind. In addition to the intimate and affectionate community, the *Gemeinschaft,* there must also be language. I have just been noting that mind is formed out of the impressions which we receive, the behavior we learn, the mental and motor skills we practice because of the affectionate pressure of relationships in the intimate community into which we are born. But to receive impressions from another, to learn behavior from another, to experience the affectionate pressure of another, means to be able to take the attitude of the other into myself and to be able to modify my own behavior and experience by means of that communication. I do not directly experience the pleasure or pain of another person. The pain or pleasure of the other is expressed in sounds or gestures. I can learn from the experience another person has of pleasure and pain only if I know what those sounds and gestures mean. When a mother repeatedly says "Good" to her child and accompanies that verbal symbol with a caress which the child experiences as pleasurable or with a reward of food, the child eventually learns what the verbal symbol means and learns to internalize its meaning, even without the physical reward. When a mother repeatedly says "Bad" to her child and accompanies that rather different verbal symbol with a slap or the withholding of food, the child eventually learns what that verbal symbol means and learns to internalize its meaning, even without the physical punishment. Language, then, is the system of gestures and sounds by which one is able to identify the experience of the other and to take that experience into himself as the basis for the modification of his own experience and behavior. The ability to learn from others' experience saves each of us from a frightful amount of bother—it prevents pain, delay, and the useless repetition of acts already tested. More than that, it makes us relatively at home with experiences and aspects of the world even before we come upon them firsthand ourselves, and thus eliminates unnecessary and unfruitful strangeness and anxiety. It opens to us vicariously worlds of experience which we shall never see but without which we should be humanly the poorer.

But notice something important which takes place in this

process. By internalizing the experience of another person, I do not simply learn something about his experience; I also learn something about my own. When I am permitted to participate in the feelings of another person, the result is that I begin to identify, to clarify, and to sort out my own feelings, including my feelings about myself. This is why a J. D. Salinger or an Albert Camus, a Bob Dylan or a Woodie Guthrie can be so important to a whole generation of people. "He says what I have been feeling but could not put into words" is the way we often describe what such people do for us. Did Salinger or Dylan create the feeling in me? Not necessarily at all; but he did help me to recognize it, to clarify it, and thus to free it to form my own response to the world. And when we say about another, "He says what I have been feeling but could not put into words," we also pay unconscious tribute to the importance language has for us. For the fact is that we are uneasy with our feelings, often even threatened by them, until we can put them into words, that is, until we can get them out, look at them, and name them, which is what language helps us to do. Simply being able to name a feeling reduces its threatening character, just as being able to name a physical illness often makes it seem less dire.

All of this, then, is to say that I become a self only to the degree that I am able to participate in and to internalize the experiences of others. I begin to be an individual to the degree that I am enabled to break out of my monadic insularity by the gift of language. George Herbert Mead, a social psychologist who was one of the most important interpreters of man in this century, put the matter in these words:

> To the extent that the animal can take the attitude of the other and utilize that attitude for the control of his own conduct, we have what is termed mind; and that is the only apparatus involved in the appearance of the mind.
>
> I know of no way in which intelligence or mind could arise or could have arisen, other than through the internalization by the individual of social processes of experience and behavior, that is, through this internalization of the conversation of significant gestures, as made possible by the individual's taking the attitudes of other individuals toward himself and toward what is being thought about. And if mind or thought has arisen in this way, then there neither can be nor could have been any mind or thought without language; and the early stages of the development of language must have been prior to the development of mind or thought.[14]

If there is no human being, no self, without mind, and if serious limitations in language impose serious limitations on mind, this helps us to see why, in the illustrations with which I began this chapter, Isabelle was able to reach her mental maturity in two years after she was found in isolation at age six and one-half, and why Anna, on the other hand, had scarcely progressed beyond a mental age of one year when she died at the age of ten, more than four years after she had been found. Anna never learned to speak, perhaps because, even in the county home where she was first placed after being found, she was not given continuous expert care but was often left alone because of the preoccupations of the staff of the home. The foster mother, to whom she eventually went, was persistent and well-meaning, to be sure, but not sufficiently expert to help Anna overcome the withdrawal by means of which she had become adapted to six years of dark isolation. Isabelle's situation was significantly different. She had learned a crude communication from her deaf-mute mother by means of gestures. Upon being found by the authorities, she was the object of continuous expert care, with the result that she learned very rapidly to speak, and with her language skill came her development toward both mental and physical normality. In both cases, language made the crucial difference.

No one who has seen the story of Helen Keller as portrayed in *The Miracle Worker* can be in any doubt about the astonishing consequences which result from the intimate and affectionate pressure of another human being, from the persistent and patient effort to teach a language of gesture, which together transformed a helpless and apparently hopeless organism into a rich and rewarding human life.

SELFHOOD AS CONTINUING SOCIAL PROCESS

It should not be necessary to remind us, though it sometimes seems to be, that the importance of affectionate intimacy and of language does not end with the end of our childhood. Intimacy and communication continue to be important to us, because *selfhood is a continuing social process* and not a fixed skill which we receive permanently at the conclusion of our childhood apprenticeship. This can be demonstrated, for example, by asking, What is man's ultimate weapon against man? The answer, I think, is loneliness.

This is the real, if not always explicit, reason that punishment in our culture takes its peculiar form. When a child misbehaves, he is banished from association with the rest of the family and sent off to his room. A young man who is having a difficult time in bringing a young woman around to his way of thinking and of behaving decides that a few lonely nights and weekends may change her mind; so he stays away for a while. Society expects to persuade an offender not to repeat his offense by isolating him for a period of weeks or years; and when all other forms of punishment fail to break the will of a defiant prisoner, he is placed in solitary confinement. Indeed, for one who has experienced it, the threat of solitary confinement may be terrifying enough to make him change his ways. For political crimes, the ultimate weapon of the nation is exile, separation from the people the politician loved and sought to lead.

Or, in order to see the importance of affectionate intimacy in a different way, ask: What form of human suffering is more acute than any other? I think one will not answer that question by an attempt to scale the various intensities of physical pain from least to most. It is not physical pain alone which creates suffering. There is no anguish conceivably more intense than *to be in pain alone.* The Christian tradition insists that God demonstrated his love for man by giving up his immunity as God and by experiencing for himself human life at its extremity. It is no accident, then, that the symbol of that divine love is the cross, on which the pain of physical death was joined with the dereliction which came with being utterly deserted by all those for whom Jesus cared.

Jean-Paul Sartre makes a character in "No Exit" say that "hell is other people." I think he is precisely wrong. Hell is, rather, the absence of the intimate other. In the Old Testament, for example, one finds the psalmist fervently praying to God to be spared from Sheol, not because that abode of the dead was a place of fire and physical torment, but rather because, as one commentator has defined Sheol, it was "a land of silence and forgetting."[15] I am persuaded that we have mistaken the New Testament idea of hell when we see it as a place of eternal physical discomfort to which God may banish us. As I read the Epistles particularly, it means that if we insist on being what we are, having done what we have done, refusing to accept the forgiveness of God, then God will finally accept that verdict. It does not mean that he will cease to care for us. It does mean that he will leave us to ourselves, if that is what we want. There is, I think, no more accurate way of stating the meaning of hell than this: hell means being left to ourselves.

When, for example, physical intimacy is present but the self is withheld and the selfhood of the other is made a matter of careless or callous disregard, the result is not humanizing but demonic. So in Albert Camus's novel *The Fall,* Jean-Baptiste Clamence boasts of his successes with women: "I used to achieve my ends just about whenever I wanted." He admits that he loved none of them, but he comforts himself with the reflection that "true love is exceptional—two or three times a century, more or less. The rest of the time there is vanity or boredom." Not, he hastens to add, that he is incapable of love; except that his regard is always directed toward himself. Well then, "It is not true, after all, that I never loved. I conceived at least one great love in my life, of which I was always the object." Finding chastity gone and love continually elusive, Clamence at last gives himself up to debauchery, which for a time he finds "liberating because it creates no obligations. In it you possess only yourself; hence it remains the favorite pastime of the great lovers of their own person. It is a jungle without past or future, without any promise above all, nor any immediate penalty. . . . On entering, one leaves behind fear and hope."[16]

Does Camus intend it solely as coincidence that the inscription over "The Inferno" was "Abandon hope, all ye who enter here"? I think not. Hell is proximity without involvement, closeness without communication.

See, too, how language continues to be a critical need for us long after we have first learned to use it, and how we depend for our continued mental and emotional well-being on communication. It is a frightful thing, for example, to be "sent to Coventry," which means to be given the silent treatment. No one is exactly sure why that English city came to be a synonym for silence. But when, for instance, a factory worker refuses to abide by the work quota his fellow workers have set and insists upon working at his own pace, word is passed that he is to be "sent to Coventry." From that time on, no one in the factory speaks to him. His shop is the same busy, buzzing place as before, crowded with workers; but no one speaks to him, and no one replies by so much as a look or a gesture when he speaks. It is a cruel but effective device, and it frequently leaves the man utterly broken, thoroughly demoralized, and finally unable to function at all.

We cannot live well, with our morale wholly intact, it would appear, without the confirmation words provide. Feelings and actions, however vivid they may be, simply are not enough. So a man or a woman wants to be told, "I love you!" regardless of all the intimacies of touch and all the little considerations of romantic courtesy. Words seal reality.

Perhaps I ought to repeat the point which these illustrations and observations are intended to make. It is that the importance of affectionate intimacy and of language does not end with the end of our childhood, because selfhood is a continuing social process. My self is not a static entity once given and then effortlessly retained; rather, my self is in a continual process of becoming. Or to put it in a slightly different but equally important way, my selfhood is a gift which I may continue to receive only under the conditions of intimacy and communication with other selves.

If only we understood this better, it would save us from many tragic mistakes, detours, and delays. What anxiously preoccupies many men and women is the quest for self-fulfillment—feeling real, complete, whole, finding a sense of significance which will make it possible to live with enthusiasm and joy. We expect to find those things by searching out the self, by exposing all the dark recesses of the psyche on the assumption that somewhere within the self there must be a source of energy which will free us to be and to do all those wonderful things, if only we can find it. So we engage in endless hours of self-reflection and self-analysis. We examine and reexamine our own entrails, as it were, expecting to find in our own substance the clue to the life that eludes us. Or, what in the end amounts to the same thing, we engage in endless hours of talk, usually about ourselves; and even when it is talk ostensibly about others, it often turns out to be only an inverted and indirect form of discourse about ourselves. So we live in a cocoon, always hoping one day to emerge a butterfly. This is, in fact, the problem with what passes for "falling in love," why we so often become disillusioned with the experience and find it ultimately empty. What we call "falling in love" is sometimes only infatuation, the momentarily fascinating experience of gazing intently into the eyes of a man or a woman and finding there what most fascinates us about ourselves. Infatuation is only a form of self-love, indirect and inverted like so much of our conversation. In the end it disillusions us because it is only the reflection of ourselves that we see in another person and because, for that very reason, it is powerless to contribute anything, to add anything, to my self which is not already there. So infatuation becomes emptiness, all the more unhappy if undiscovered until after marriage. That remarkable French author-philosopher-airman St. Exupery somewhere wrote that love is not two people looking intently at each other; love is, rather, the experience of looking together at the world.

Self-fulfillment is a will-o'-the-wisp, a myth, a mirage, a false ideal. There is no feeling of reality, of completeness, of wholeness, no sense of significance leading to enthusiasm and joy, which does not come as a gift from beyond myself. Psychotherapist Dr. Viktor Frankl puts the matter this way:

> The extent to which subjectivism misses the point of true human cognition becomes obvious as soon as one recalls the fundamental truth that only insofar as a person is capable of ignoring and forgetting himself is he able to recognize anything in and of the world. Only as he moves to the periphery of his attention can he become properly aware of objects beyond himself. This can be illustrated in the case of the eye which sees itself, or something in itself . . . only where there is a visual defect. The more the eye sees itself, the less the world and its objects are visible to it. The ability of the eye to see is dependent upon its inability to see itself . . . the more cognition actually becomes mere self-expression and a projection of the knowing subject's own structure, the more it becomes involved in error. In other words, cognition is true cognition only to the extent that it is the contrary of mere self-expression, only to the extent to which it involves self-transcendence.[17]

Jesus put the matter much more directly when he said that if a man would find himself, he must first be willing to lose himself. So it is that only when I aim at the good of another man can I begin to find my own self fulfilled. It is in giving another new reason for hope that I may find my own hope returning. In helping another out of his confusion, I begin to find growing clarity. In filling the loneliness of another, I may find my own emptiness disappearing. In giving another man's life back to him, I may find myself in possession of my own life for the first time.

CULTURAL MEANINGS AND SELF-IDENTITY

At the beginning of this chapter, I said that if the intimate other is absent and interpersonal communication impaired, the result is failure to master the cultural heritage, inability to grasp the whole world of cultural meaning. If the failure is only partial, the result will be varying degrees of human impoverishment; if the failure is complete, there is no human selfhood at all. I want now to describe some of the means by which culture shapes self.

Most basically of all, anthropological evidence suggests that our world view—the way we perceive the real and our location in it—is socially formed. In a recent study, Jerome Bruner and Patricia Greenfield point out that in Western society individuation is considered to be a product of increasing age, with childhood the period of collective consciousness and with maturity the time of personal independence. In the Wolof culture of Senegal, however, the reverse is true. There distinctive desire and intentionality are imputed to children, while adults are expected to subordinate desire and intentionality to group will. The older the Wolof grows, therefore, the more his individuality merges into the collective.[18] This reversal of Western expectations goes well beyond the Wolof, as the authors note, for in a broader way the value placed on individualism in European cultures contrasts sharply with the predominating socialism of the African cultures.[19]

These differences between European and African outlooks are to be accounted for, say Bruner and Greenfield, by differences in language; and we have already seen how language is both social product and social carrier. Wolof children, when asked to group like physical objects together, are able to solve the problem, for example, by selecting all objects which are yellow. But when they are asked *why* the selected objects are alike, the question itself is not understood. Before the Wolof child is exposed to European education, he does not distinguish between *thought* and *thing*. "Thought and the object of thought seem to be one. Consequently, the idea of explaining a *statement* is meaningless; one can only explain the external event."[20] The Wolof language contains words for specific colors, for example, but no abstract word for "color," just as it supplies no abstract word for "shape." Because the Wolof child has available only words for which concrete objective referents exist, he assumes that his concrete words (e.g., yellow, banana) are of the same order of reality as the object they designate. **Thus thought is not distinguished from the object of thought.**

When, however, the Wolof child goes to school and learns French, he is introduced to a language which differs from his native tongue at two vital points: it provides him with abstractions—with concepts as well as labels; and it is written, thus permitting him to employ his abstract symbols in an abstract process. As a result of learning French, the Wolof now begins to distinguish between his own thought and the things about which he thinks. Thought and object are no longer one. When word and thing thus become separated, "verbal realism" is destroyed because, in a written language, words are "there" without the referents which they designate.[21] The word "banana" exists on paper as an independent object even in the absence of the fruit itself. And this change makes way for a striking change in the way the Wolof views the world and his own relation to it, as Bruner and Greenfield explain:

> When names . . . no longer inhere in their referents, they must go somewhere; and the logical place is the psyche of the language user. Thus, separation of word and thing demands a notion that words are in a person's head, not in his referents. Meaning varies with the particular speaker, and the notion of psychological relativity is born.[22]

With it is born an individuality which is aware of its own peculiar grasp of objects and events, of its own distinctive outlook upon the world, in contrast perhaps to other individuals or to the collective.

This shift in perception comes about, not only because of the availability of abstract terms but also because the child is now able to participate in an abstract activity: writing. To write is to *use* terms apart from their objects, since the writer can neither merely point to objects nor attach simple labels to them. "Writing, then, is training in the use of linguistic contexts that are independent of immediate referents."[23]

These changes which occur when the child learns a new language only begin to point to more sweeping changes which will follow, as Bruner and Greenfield make clear. For the separation of *thought* from *thing*—the loss of a "verbal realism"— breaks up the solidarity of the Wolof's world. "Once thought has been dissociated from its objects, the stage is set for symbolic processes to run ahead of concrete fact, for thought to be in terms of possibility rather than actuality."[24] The capacity for increasing abstraction simply intensifies the shift away from collective perceptions toward idiosyncratic views.

Thus the cultural tool of language shapes all of our perceptions, including—and this is the most important conclusion for our present concern—*self*-perception.

The meanings of manhood and womanhood are defined by the culture, and the ability to identify oneself depends directly upon the accessibility of that cultural heritage and experience. In the West, adolescence typically is that period in the development of a maturing self when he is capable of sufficient distance from, and independence of, the primary group to permit him to begin to work at his own identity rather than being content to live out an identity prescribed by the primary group. But note that neither the timing nor the content of the search for self-identity is the result simply of an inner chronology, as should be clear from the fact that many men and women scarcely reach that stage, while many others scarcely ever get beyond it, regardless of chronological age. Adolescence is the period in which the maturing individual has been readied by the nurturing community to take on his own identity; and it is no accident that adolescence is also the period in life when "hero-worship" is at its height. The onset and duration of adolescence may vary from place to place and from time to time; what does not seem to vary is the fact that adolescence is the search for models. The sources of those models will change with times and fashions: they may be drawn from star athletes, motion picture or television personalities, pop artists, or political or military figures. Closer at hand, they may be drawn from teachers, the parents of friends, or professional men and women in the community. If for some reason adult models are not accessible or sufficiently compelling, then models will be drawn from the peer culture. The primary fact, however, is that cultural imitation is essential to growing clarity of self-identity; and frequently there will be a series of imitations, sometimes of conflicting styles, as various identities are "tried on," as it were. Negatively too, models are important, for they teach us what, in our own manhood and womanhood, we intend to avoid. So in any event, it appears to be the case that one can eventually become himself only if he is permitted temporarily to take on the identity of someone else.

Or again, the attitude one takes toward life is socially formed.

Take love, for example, for many the fundamental clue to the attitude one ought to take, both toward the life that is and the life that ought to be. The word "love" is not like the word "table." When I say *table*, I mean neither more nor less than some particular object to which I can point. I ask for a table, and when one is brought, I am satisfied that it is exactly what I wanted; or if I am dissatisfied, it is only because I know that the precise object which I desire exists, if only the arrangements committee for my meeting had not been so stupid or lazy as to overlook it. *Love* is a different kind of word. Its meaning is always larger than any given act; it is always more than any settled accomplishment. The word "love" has grown out of the collective experiences and aspirations of men; centuries of agony and ecstasy have given to that word subtleties and overtones of meaning. And that is, indeed, why *love* is such a powerful word: it can reach deep into my own experience and lay a claim upon me precisely because it comes out of the depth of experience. It rises up out of a cultural heritage which reaches beyond our own time and catches up a funded wisdom of incredible range and persistence. More human sensitivity has been poured into that word than we can even guess at. I can invent a new piece of furniture, but I cannot simply invent a word like *love*. Such a word must be learned, in all its richness of meaning, from those who have already lived it, and who in their own turn have been given that word out of a heritage which reaches far beyond themselves.

More than that, I can sustain my faith in love as a desirable attitude toward life only as I participate in the human community of those who believe in it. Love, whenever it appears under the conditions of history, is never complete; it is always partial, always eluding us in its fullness. There are experiences, furthermore, which make us wonder whether, in the end, love is an adequate response to life in this sometimes brutalizing world. So love is unstable and problematic. There is no simple demonstration by which its truth can be certified. By myself, I may doubt more than I believe, not simply doubt the adequacy of love but doubt any attitude toward life, any faith in life. There is, therefore, no substitute for belonging to a congenial community of people of whom one can ask certain crucial questions: Do you see what I see? Do you feel what I feel? Do you mean what I mean? Sociologist

Peter Berger holds that every world view, every faith, is a "conspiracy": that is, it can be maintained only through membership in a social situation whose members (the "conspirators") take that world view for granted. "Only the madman or the rare case of genius can inhabit a world of meaning all by himself," Berger writes. "Most of us acquire our meanings from other men and require their constant support so that these meanings may continue to be believable." [25]

Yet again, we cannot perform satisfactorily in a social role—as a husband or wife, father or child, doctor, lawyer, or Indian chief—unless that role has social confirmation; unless, that is, the role is supported by the attitudes and expectations of society. Anyone who has ever played cowboys and Indians knows that you can't play the role of a fast-shooting, sharp-eyed cowpoke if the kid who is supposed to be the Indian won't stay dead. There is nothing more disconcerting to the would-be hero than to have his supposed victim wandering about the yard in patent disconfirmation of his heroism. So we also become threatened, frustrated, insecure, and eventually unable to function at all if our roles do not have social recognition and endorsement. A doctor would finally lose his professional and personal self-confidence if no one ever came to consult him, if no one permitted him to do what doctors do, if, that is, there were no social acceptance of his role as a doctor. Parents are frustrated by children who do not acknowledge parental authority, who refuse, that is, to confirm the authenticity of the parental role. And a child may be demoralized by parents whose permissiveness, attempts at "understanding," and insistence on treating him as if he were already an adult deny him confirmation of his authenticity as a child. Perhaps we can understand why police authorities were so intensely angered, even provoked to violence, when college-age demonstrators called them "pigs" and refused to behave in the respectful and circumspect way people are supposed to behave in the presence of civil authority. When a large body of people refuses to confirm the authority role of the policeman, his frustration erupts into violence precisely because his social role—and with it his identity and value as a man, which are quite inseparable from his role-perception—is endangered. Conversely, even though a person may lack full technical competence to function in a particular role, the fact that it has broad social acceptance and confirmation—the fact that people *do* act as they are expected to in relation to one who occupies this role—can free that person to fill the role with amazing success, as certain notorious impersonators have demonstrated.

Finally, consider that, by means of tradition and expectation, society contributes substantially to anxiety-reduction for each individual. When someone I care about dies, I am relieved of the anxiety which would go with being the first person in the world ever to experience bereavement. There are certain traditional ways of handling the experience of death which are given in the cultural heritage—certain procedures, gestures, and rituals, forms of socially supported emotional release, ideas about death with which to manage the experience conceptually—all intended to permit the bereaved to face the fact of death with a minimum of disorientation.

When social practice and social usage define appropriate conduct in a variety of concrete situations which might otherwise be strange or unsettling, they are designed to reduce the anxiety of the actors in these little scenarios. So it is expected that a man who has just won an election will go through the ritual of open-handed magnanimity toward the man he has just defeated and make it clear that he considers him a worthy opponent in spite of all the nasty things that were said during the campaign. An actor who has just won an award is expected to thank all those responsible for his achievement, from the studio janitor to his mother. Men whose wives have just had babies are permitted the proud symbol of passing out cigars as an accepted social demonstration of their virility. In each case, the awkwardness of finding oneself the object of some public attention and being expected to "say a few words" is overcome by the availability of familiar conventions which satisfy practically everyone and offend almost no one.

So it is that sexual identities, world views, social roles, and responses to anxiety-producing situations are given, confirmed, and made effective in social interaction.

SELFHOOD AND SINGULARITY

At the conclusion of the preceding chapter, I said that to value man is to know him in his unpredictable singularity and complexity. Yet read in one way, much that I have written in this chapter might seem to cast quite a contradictory image. Rather than singularity, the kind of social interaction I have been describing might seem to require a stultifying conformism. Rather than guarding man's power to initiate, social interaction might seem to locate the sources of effective power almost wholly outside the individual. Two considerations persuade me that this is far from being the case.

For one thing, every impression which the self receives from its social surroundings receives a problematic reception. Each self, though socially formed, has a distinctive outlook upon the world which is possessed by no other self who has ever lived. There is a law of physics which says that two bodies cannot occupy the same space at the same time. Translated into our present discussion, this means that, though I may indeed *participate* in the experience of another person, I do not *occupy* his life space. He alone occupies it, just as I alone occupy my own. He and I literally see from different angles, and the *meaning* of what we see thus differs in its angularity. Furthermore, although each self is touched by natural and social events which have a shaping influence upon its developing selfhood, no two selves occupy precisely the same intersection of these events, which means that no two selves are touched by precisely the same events. Therefore the complex of meanings which emerges out of events impinging upon developing selves may be for each self as unique as the events in combination are unique. So the angle of vision and the uniqueness of the intersection which selects and collects impressions combine to free a man for criticism and for questioning, for creative openness and for conflict. Social interaction, thus, is not a process of mechanical reduplication, nor does it make man simply a hapless victim with no power to modify or resist the actions of society upon him.

If man's singularity is thus guarded, what of the power of initiative which our human dignity requires? That concern is answered, I think, by recalling that we are dealing with social *inter*-action. Not only are there significant others whose influences shape my growing self, but in turn I am the significant other for selves whose existence I touch. The social self is not formed only in being acted upon but also in acting. The self whose definition emerges out of social process is itself active in influencing the definitions of other selves, and thus, reflexively, shapes its own selfhood. If it is true that I *receive* selfhood as a gift, it is also true that I *give* selfhood as a gift. Says the Italian dramatist Ugo Betti, "That's what's needed, don't you see? *That!* Nothing else matters half so much. To reassure one another. To answer each other. Perhaps only *you* can listen to me and not laugh." [26] When I care, and indeed when I dare, enough to do that, the miracle of social *inter*-action occurs.

So in this process there need be no diminution of my singularity or my power to influence events.

It is precisely in the dialectic—the dialogue—between the self and its others that the most delicate, not to say desperate, of our human problems arise. There can be no adequate selfhood apart from adequate social relations; which means that, at those moments in individual history or those periods of corporate history when "meeting" is most difficult, selfhood is most precarious. Such moments are, of course, built into the rhythms of change through which all human beings pass: from childhood to adolescence, perhaps, or from the life of activity to the life of retirement. Such periods also emerge, less rhythmically and predictably, from the peaks to the troughs through which our common history passes. And precisely because we are *social* beings, the inner modifies the outer, and the outer works its change upon the inner.

We are at a time now when *the loss of the other* is a commonly confessed experience, with selfhood more than ordinarily in jeopardy—more than ordinarily problematic—as a consequence. There are many sources of our situation, but Philip Slater has remarked upon one of its most notable ironies. "One of the major goals of technology in America," he writes,

is to "free" us from the necessity of relating to, submitting to, depending upon, or controlling other people. Unfortunately, the more we have succeeded in doing this the more we have felt disconnected, bored, lonely, unprotected, unnecessary, and unsafe.[27]

Perhaps nowhere is the loss of the other, and the consequent loss of the self, more pointedly and poignantly in evidence than in the crisis in sexuality which seems almost to have reached epidemic proportion in our culture. It is this crisis of intimacy which I want now to examine.

Chapter Nine

Crisis in
Sexuality:
The Loss of the Other

THE SERIOUSNESS OF SEXUALITY

There is sexual crisis in us and among us these days. Not that there is anything very new in that. Ours is by no means the only generation to find itself bewildered by that mysterious human potency we call sex. The Victorian era had its element of sexual crisis no less than did the flaming era which followed the death of Victorianism.

Indeed, where in history is such a crisis *not* to be found? The truth—too often obscured by our tendency to look for the causes of critical conditions only in external events, whose unwitting victims we can then claim to be—seems to be that human sexuality is itself the crisis, which external events do not create but to which they contribute a certain tone and texture. "Critical," says *The Random House Dictionary of the English Language,* means "involving grave uncertainty, risk, peril. . . . "[1] If that is not a complete description of our sexuality—and it assuredly is not—it is nevertheless an essential element in the description, one which gives the lie to popular notions that sex can be treated casually or indifferently. On the contrary, wherever there is intercourse, there is a human transaction. There is no such thing as indifferent orgasm.

What is there in sexual intimacy which touches us ineluctably at the core? There is, for one thing, our human nakedness. We seldom fully realize how powerful a force body image is upon our sense of well-being—how essential a favorable body image is to our own self-esteem—until the body suffers mutilation or change. See it at its most extreme: when a woman experiences the removal of a breast, or a man experiences genital amputation, the psychic consequences are often severe. Depression arising out of self-revulsion may be intense and may continue so unless plastic surgery succeeds in restoring an acceptable image of the body upon which our dignity seems so to depend. Painful, but usually less pathological, are the agonies women endure who think their breasts are too large or too small; and painful, too, are the self-reproaches men suffer with genital organs which seem oversized or undersized. Many of us have experienced the self-disgust which may come with only slightly excessive weight or only moderately misshapen limbs. Fashion happily provides us with clever ways of masking many of our supposed physical defects, of creating the illusion of a more ideal body image than we actually possess— masking the situation not only from others but, much of the time, even from ourselves.

Lest anyone conclude from these remarks that our body image matters only where it appears to be defective, let me hasten to add that even a favorable image apparently cannot be taken for granted—is not a matter of indifference to the one who holds it. All of us know exhibitionists of various kinds who engage in flagrant display of whatever they consider their best physical features; indeed, we all have some element of exhibitionism in our own makeup. We are complicated combinations of the recluse and the exhibitionist. Even our perceived self-perfections and self-satisfactions require the confirmation of others, it seems.

And that, I think, is the significance of our attempts both to hide ourselves and to exhibit ourselves. Selfhood is no private affair; it requires social confirmation, as I tried to show at some length in chapter eight. If there is no confirmation of our identities as men and women from those whom we perceive to be men and women, then we cannot function effectively as men and women ourselves. And it is not surprising that self-identity should be reduced to bodily perception. It is, after all, by our bodies that we are identified by others. But more than that, each of us is a psychosomatic unity, so that there is no awareness of the self by the self which is not also, at the same time, awareness of bodily existence. To be aware of myself as a self is to be aware of my behaviors, and what is behavior except the self given bodily expressiveness? So when we hide what we suppose are our bodily defects, is it not because we fear that not only the body but the self which is identified with and by the body will be revealed as defective and fail thereby to win the approval, the confirmation, of others without which no self is intact? When we exhibit ourselves, subtly or flagrantly, is it not in the hope that our flawlessness will be recognized and approved and our identities secured thereby?

How, then, shall we understand a period like our own in which nudity is more and more common, in films and in popular advertising, on the stage and in public? It may, on the one hand, be evidence of an age in which men and women dare such display because they are uncommonly secure in, and confident of, their identities. Would that that were true! Yet every other indicator suggests that it is not. Millions of men and women have become disillusioned at their failure to find the sense of significance they need where the public relations of our culture had led them to expect it: in the comforts of affluence and in the heroics of war. Dissatisfaction with the self has literally run riot, both among the privileged and the dispossessed. Drugs and drink, compulsive sleep and compulsive work are the heavily traveled escapist routes by which we have fled into self-forgetfulness. Adolescent behavior prolonged into what we once thought to be mature years and the high incidence of neurotic disorder alike have suggested a preference for fantasy over reality.

If, then, the new nudity is not evidence of our confidence, perhaps it is evidence of the contrary. Discovering that riots, drugs, drink, sleep, work, prolonged adolescence, and neurosis cannot confer upon us that fugitive sense of significance, perhaps we are witnessing a work of desperation, for only something like desperation could generate the energy necessary for so radical a change: from withdrawal to exposure. So now we are baring our bodies, and thus, with both symbolic and literal power, exposing our selves in a desperate effort to be noticed. For only if we are noticed, warts and all, is there any hope of being confirmed.

Or if this explanation will not quite do, then perhaps a slight variant will: when we strip away what covers the body, it may be with the expectation that a substantial self will also be uncovered where neither we nor the world have quite found it before.

When I listen to the ways in which the new nudity is justified by those who practice it, I am convinced that this is at least the right neighborhood of explanation. Nudity, a practitioner will almost always insist, "permits me really to be myself." It means giving up the "artificiality" of clothing for the "realness" of the naked self; it means renouncing the "hypocrisy" of the social conventions represented by clothing in favor of a new human "authenticity"; and it means refusing the binding "restraints" of dress and embracing a new "freedom" in nakedness. Recently a top fashion model said, in explaining why she had agreed to be photographed with her nubility showing, "You become more important and more real in the nude. You're not encumbered with someone else's fantasy of fashion." I am further encouraged to link nudity to the quest for selfhood by the fact that nude psychotherapy appears to be growing in popularity.

What we are witnessing in our generation is, I would insist, not a new thing, though, as I suggested earlier, its tone and texture—its urgency, for instance—are historically distinctive. Nakedness cannot be a casual matter for reasons that run deeper than recent historical events. Self is prematurely reduced to the body (when, in civilized history, has it not been?) so that exposure of the body means also exposure of the self; and with every exposure comes the critical risk of confirmation or rejection. This is what makes sexual encounter so critical, for there is no sexual contact without exposure, usually to the sight of another but always to the touch of another. What makes it even more intensely critical than mere nudity is that in sexual encounter attention is focused upon those parts of the body which are most powerfully and elementally symbolic of maleness and of femaleness, whose physical form and "effective" function are expected to carry the heaviest burden in testing manhood and womanhood. If this sounds like erotic mystique, let us admit at once that it is, so common as to be all but universal in our culture; but we need to understand that a mystique is a confession of the power the mysticized phenomenon holds over us which prevents us from touching it casually.

SEXUAL ENCOUNTER AND THE LOSS OF CONTROL

There is another reason why full sexual encounter must be seen as noncasual and as critical; for in addition to the nakedness of our bodies, there is also a certain emotional nakedness and vulnerability in the experience. Let me suggest an imperfect but interesting musical metaphor. We may be very good at orchestrating many of the moment-to-moment aspects of our existence—controlling our own tone and tempo, keeping our relationships in harmonious balance, permitting now this voice quality and now another to be heard. We may even attempt to orchestrate certain aspects of our sexual experience, or find an orchestration already written out for us in sex handbooks, planning seduction and foreplay in advance, perhaps with considerable success. But we cannot compose the cadenza, which is both musically and sexually the climax of the movement. Indeed, when we labor self-consciously to reach it, it becomes all the harder to arrive at. We do not create the power of that climactic moment; rather, we are carried along by that power. It is not the artist but the art which takes control, drawing out from us responses which may be surprising or shocking, ecstatic or frightened. In that sexual cadenza, emotions otherwise kept carefully in check may come pouring forth; capacities for warmth or withdrawal, for tenderness or for brutality, nowhere else expressed, appear; selfishness or selflessness are unmasked; joys and fears are confirmed; needs and sufficiencies cry out which are not otherwise guessed at; language is used which, in any other context, would seem inappropriate. Even when the total effect is fulfilling, the experience is nevertheless unsettling, precisely because it defies our conscious control and has the power to reveal, whether we will it or not, the dimensions of a self nowhere else exposed in quite this way. So Paul Tillich has warned:

> The ecstasy of love can absorb one's own self in its union with the other self, and separation seems to be overcome. But after these moments, the isolation of self from self is felt even more deeply than before, sometimes even to the point of mutual repulsion. We have given too much of ourselves, and now we long to take back what was given.[2]

There is at least one other reason for asserting the critical nature of sexual encounter. It is that the learned "dos" and "don'ts" of our culture have perhaps more to do, directly and indirectly, with our bodies generally, with the erotic parts of our bodies particularly, and with sexual taboos most specifically, than with any other form of human activity. These carry the sharpest overtones of approval and disapproval and therefore bear the largest burden of our moral self-consciousness, so that we do not exercise them, even in their "normal" functions, with complete impunity. It is this moral burden which creates the likelihood that sexual experimentation under socially unacceptable circumstances will result in trauma or failure. Not even the supposedly "liberated" younger generation is very successful in escaping its own moral history, as psychiatrists in health centers for university students regularly testify. One of the reasons that married couples, whether or not they engage in full intimacy prior to marriage, often find it difficult to achieve a sense of freedom and satisfaction in their sexual relationship is that they simply cannot internalize the social fact that what was so long disapproved is now, by instant transformation of social degree, approved. Often this inability to shift the moral burden persists well into marriage and may, in some instances, be indelible.

It would be easy to place the entire responsibility for this situation upon a middle-class society which values rational behaviors it can regulate but is insecure in the presence of nonrational potencies which defy planning and control, which knows what to do with words but is frightened by feelings. Part of the responsibility does lie precisely there, but by no means all of it. Sex viewed as a moral matter did not first appear with the rise of the middle class in Western society. That view exists in all human groupings; and if the approved and disapproved behaviors vary somewhat from culture to culture, and indeed change with the times even within a single culture, the fact that a moral dimension is universally recognized in some form represents an acknowledgment that in our human sexuality there is radical power both to hurt and to heal. That is what makes it a moral matter; and as long as that power exists in it, sex will continue to be a moral matter whether we will it so or not. It is because human sexuality is moral in the most elemental sense that it is, always and everywhere, a critical form of human behavior.

SEX AND THE HUMAN PROBLEMATIC

Sexual behavior is one of man's most problematic forms of

activity. For all of the reasons adduced above, it is critical behavior, "involving grave uncertainty, risk, peril." It should not be necessary to add that its profound ability thus to hurt is intimately tied in with its profound ability to heal. The paradox is only apparent: if it could not hurt us, it would not so heal us; if it could not heal us, it would not so hurt us.

Those who assert rather simplemindedly that "sex is fun!" will probably be scandalized by this view of the seriousness of our sexuality. If "fun" means "frivolity," then the scandal is fully intended. I do not believe that sex can be frivolous, and one can treat it as if it were, only if he is willing to be ignorant of its real significance for our humanness. But this certainly does not mean that one should not enjoy sexual humor, should not engage in sexual light heartedness and teasing, or should not take frank delight in sensual delicacy and intensity. These we ought to have a perfectly good conscience about; which leads me also to make it quite clear that I intend to rebuke as well the unhappy ignorance of those who assert simplemindedly that "sex is sin!" It is a matter of embarrassment to me as a Christian man that this view usually claims religious sanction, as if the ideal Christian were an asexual being who indulged in coition solely out of reluctant reproductive necessity, if at all. The truth is quite otherwise. There is no incompatibility between the physical and emotional joys of sex and the requirements of a godly life. Indeed, godliness is expressed and experienced precisely in and through our sexuality. Dietrich Bonhoeffer expressed what I am bound to believe is the proper combination of ecstasy and seriousness when he wrote:

> . . . speaking frankly, to long for the transcendent when you are in your wife's arms is, to put it mildly, a lack of taste, and it is certainly not what God expects of us. We ought to find God and love him in the blessings he sends us. If he pleases to grant us some overwhelming earthly bliss, we ought not to try and be more religious than God himself. For then we should spoil that bliss by our presumption and arrogance; we should be letting our religious fantasies run riot and refusing to be satisfied with what he gives.[3]

Indeed, I doubt that one can really "make fun of" anything that he does not take with real seriousness. Lacking seriousness, "fun" readily becomes parody, and parody becomes cynicism or dismissal. Without seriousness, "fun" is simply a form of unbelief, whether the subject be sex or God. I doubt, at the same time, that one can really be serious about anything without the freedom to "make fun of" it. I am free to "make fun of" my wife's love only if I am really secure in it, only if I really believe in it. If I cannot "make fun of" it, it must be because I am too uncertain of it, because its reality is too fragile, and because I must constantly reassure myself of its truth by determined repetition. I can "make fun of" God or sex only if I have a proper respect for their significance in human life, only if I really believe in them. If I cannot "make fun of" them, it must be because of my fear that anything less than a fully serious statement might shatter them, that their importance depends upon my assertion of it. Seriousness without the ability to "make fun of" our commitments is also a form of unbelief.

At the moment, those who assert that "sex is fun" seem most intent upon converting our society to the gospel of sexual "liberation," so that assertion deserves a further test. Nowhere has the natural, fun-loving view of sex been more persistently and powerfully stated than in the contemporary novel and drama. Yet the mood which the current generation of novelists and playwrights has served up in books and plays is commonly marked by a kind of doggedness and determination which suggest that sex is more a work of desperation than of delight. What is called natural turns out rather to be compulsive, and what is called fun seems often touched with terror.

This point has been made persuasively for me by the New York drama critic Walter Kerr. While he wrote the article, from which I take the following excerpts, before some of the more recent forms of sexual explicitness in books, films, and plays, I doubt that these more recent events would cause him to modify his judgment markedly. Kerr notes that, far from viewing sex these days as an embarrassment, we affirm it "as an act that is beautiful in itself and beautiful in all its implications. . . . Meaning to honor our natures as our natures are, and to honor them in clear good conscience, we approach the subject of sex in a candid, generous, accepting, and even admiring manner."[4] It is understandable, then, that we have wanted to free our art forms from their Victorian constraints in order that they may be able to reflect this new affirmative sexuality.

> We have freed them. But the reflection is most strange. What do our novels and our plays show back to us? Almost without exception, an image of sex that is violent, frustrated, shabby, furtive, degrading, treacherous and—more and

more—aberrant. . . . For the most part, as we spy upon sex [through the eyes of novelist and playwright] we seem to be spying on failure.[5]

So his ironic conclusion is this: "What we proclaim as noble we present as nasty. If no Victorian ever said so much about sex, no Victorian ever said anything so unpleasant about sex."[6]

Kerr's interest in the matter is not primarily that of a moralist; he is interested rather in what appears to be a blatant cultural disjunction: the fact that "we give formal assent, in our pronouncements, to an act regarded as beautiful while giving formal assent, in our [artistic] images, to the same act regarded as ugly." He is driven to wonder which of these things represents the real truth about our condition.

> Forced to vote, I am afraid I should have to come down in favor of the mirror as being the truer record of our minds: it is much easier to spot a lie in a play or a story than it is in a conversation. Unless I have overlooked a sizable body of contemporary literature in which sex is seen to be precisely as healthy an activity as we proclaim it to be, I am compelled to conclude that no matter what our voices say when we are talking for effect, when the eye of the mind begins to do its work it photographs sex as a dubious pleasure. With the click of the shutter, there is a sound of doubt.[7]

If Walter Kerr is right, my earlier contention is confirmed. Absence of seriousness about sex—insistence on treating it as an act with no profound consequences, a natural vitality made unnatural by any restraint, a touch with power to thrill but not to threaten— seems curiously to prevent its enjoyment and turns it instead to parody, cynicism, and finally to boredom. If lack of seriousness is, in fact, a form of unbelief, it is self-fulfilling prophecy, for it results in a kind of sexual experience in which no one could possibly believe.

CRISIS AND INCOMPETENCE

If external events do not create the critical nature of our human sexuality but rather contribute a certain tone and texture, as I suggested at the beginning of this chapter, that does not mean that we can ignore events in our effort to turn our sexuality to humanly creative purpose. It is, therefore, of more than passing importance to note that there is something peculiarly ironic about the sexual situation our own generation faces. We are, by all odds, the best-educated victims of sexual crisis in history. There has probably never been such open, unabashed discussion of sexual matters as there is today—not merely a flagrant, defiant openness which delights to flaunt the problem, but a serious, dogged openness which seeks answers to the problem in education and discussion.

So the mass media bombard us with sex, served up in unprecedented explicitness, sometimes merely for titillation and display, but often for purposes of education. Parents are intent as never before upon giving their children adequate information about the sexual side of life, either because they value sex or because they are frightened by it and seek to arm their children against it. And churches, schools, and youth clubs are more aware than ever of their roles in the sex education of the young.

Education and openness have assuredly had their effect. When it comes to our bodies, we know how to call things by their right names. When it comes to the origins of life, children are no longer kept in the dark by vague and sometimes ingenious metaphors but are told frankly where babies come from. When it comes to dating, the adolescent has a pretty good idea of how his own physiology functions. And when it comes to marriage, the manuals on sexual technique have been faithfully consulted. The irony is to be found in the fact that this generation has nevertheless produced a record of sexual incompetence of staggering proportion, which all our openness and education have failed to prevent and have been helpless to dispel.*

Writing from his German prison cell in the midst of World War

*Let me make it unmistakably clear that I have no sympathy whatsoever with hysterical attacks from right-wing extremists of the John Birch variety who, having failed to forge a formidable political weapon with the fluoridation issue, have seized upon sexual instruction in the public schools as eminently exploitable. Most of their charges represent an outrageous distortion of such programs as those prepared by the Sex Information and Education Council of the United States (SIECUS) and make use of propaganda so sensational and lurid in its own right as to constitute a form of pornography all its own. To be sure, not every program of public-school sex education has been wisely conceived. Some of them are too explicitly physiological; some provide information before there is readiness in the child to understand and handle it. That our schools are properly engaged in sex education is, I think, axiomatic in a sex-saturated culture in which youngsters need all the guidance they can get. That schools, as well as parents, need to treat human sexuality in terms larger than the biological is the burden of what follows in this chapter.

II, Dietrich Bonhoeffer made a comment which at first reading may seem irrelevant to our problem but which on deeper reflection may illuminate that irony. Shortly after a severe air raid he wrote,

> People are talking quite openly about how terrified they were. I don't quite know what to make of it. Surely terror is something we ought to be ashamed of, something we ought not to talk about except in confession, otherwise it is bound to involve a certain amount of exhibitionism. On the other hand naïve frankness can be utterly disarming. Yet there is also a cynical, I might almost say ungodly, kind of frankness, the kind generally associated with drunkenness and whoredom, which is a sign of chaos.[8]

I would suggest that much of the frankness about sex in this generation is a sign of our chaos, of a world in which our human connections are in a state of serious disorganization, a world in which little that is really human is left. We have talked openly about sex with the best of intentions, hoping to bring order out of the chaos, to recover our humanity. But we have frequently engaged in a misplaced frankness, and the result is a deepened crisis and incompetence. Our frankness is misplaced because it assumes that the problem will be solved when we lose our fear of four-letter words and dare to call things by their right names.

SEX AS RELATION

In all our talk about sex we have commonly forgotten one thing, namely, that sex is a relationship, that it depends upon the quality and character of our responses both to ourselves and to other men and women. Our sexuality is assuredly physiological, but it is also personal which is to say that it entails our whole being. It is a biological function, but it is equally a function of our own self-estimate and our estimate of others. Indeed, it is quite possible for a person of apparent physical health, with all his genital powers organically intact, to be sexually powerless, and it is equally possible for one who suffers from physical defect to find genuine sexual fulfillment. A purely genital definition of what it is to be a man is seriously defective. Whether or not a man can function effectively as a man in relation to other men depends not simply upon his having the right physical equipment to confirm that identity; it depends most basically upon the models of manhood that are available to him and his ability to establish his own identity as a man in relation to those models. Whether a man can function effectively as a man in relation to a woman depends not simply on ample genital endowment but, first, on the character of his own self-identity as a man in all the aspects of his being, then on the quality of the communication that exists between himself and the woman, and then on the character of their personal responses to each other.

In this crisis of sexual incompetence, it is not our information alone which is defective but our relationships. Researchers into juvenile behavior have concluded that the boy of twelve to sixteen is frequently unable to locate himself in the human pattern our contemporary culture provides. He simply does not belong, and there are few relationships adequate to provide the desperately needed sense of belonging, so that he is, as it were, "an orphan in an alien universe." He lives largely in a female world, with the dominant figures—his mother and his teachers in the schools—overwhelmingly women. Too often he has no significant role to play in the family, nothing upon which the proper functioning of the family really depends that can be authentically identified as boy's work—unlike his sisters, who are still able to be significantly integrated into the day-to-day operations of the family. He may find little satisfaction in study, but he is too young to quit school, too young to go to work, and too young to get married. Yet he is too old to be treated as a child. The questions he is learning to ask and the burgeoning excitements he is beginning to feel are not the questions and excitements of childhood, but they do not readily find the satisfactions and fulfillments which are open to adults.

This problem is intensified by the distance of the father from the family in typical middle-class homes. Since the father is away from home most of the boy's waking hours, they spend little if any time together. When the father is at home, he may be too preoccupied to give the boy any real attention. When they come into conflict, as they inevitably will, the father is likely to complain that he can't get through to the boy and doesn't understand him. Since the boy seldom if ever sees his father at work, he may have only the vaguest notion of what his father does, of what it is to do a man's work in the world. Consequently, because he has no significant and compelling model of manhood available, the boy comes to know little of what it means to be a man.

As a result of his failure to find a role to play in the world of home and school, which are regulated by relatively inaccessible adults, the adolescent male is forced as a matter of self-survival to create his own society among his peers. In this society there is a role to be played. Loyalties among its members are intense and the discipline sometimes exacting. There is an accepted hierarchy of values which gives meaning and purpose to the relationships. In the absence of the father, the peer group takes on the function of forming the boy's image of manhood.

The total effect of this process is that the adolescent attempts to establish his own identity as a man by imitating imitation men. If this results in behavior which claims maturity but actually caricatures adulthood, no one should be surprised.

It is not difficult to trace the source of at least a part of the crisis of sexual incompetence to just this situation. It is painful to be uncertain of one's own manhood, and in his uncertainty the adolescent may either withdraw and become sexually nondescript or may put his sexuality to the test to assure himself that he really is a man. But the tests available to him are almost exclusively physical, for that is the way our society customarily defines maleness. He must establish his maleness by physical prowess or by sexual prowess or by both. It is perhaps no mere coincidence, then, that fraternity initiations frequently involve two kinds of activity: language which is freighted with sexual reference, to demonstrate the candidate's ability to handle that aspect of experience with the requisite aplomb; and activities to test his physical endurance.

Sexual experimentation among males of high school and college age may thus frequently be traced to an inadequate sense of male identity; and the more intense the sense of inadequacy, the more likely it is that experimentation will become compulsive promiscuity. Although the sources of homosexual pathology are not certainly known, it is difficult to believe that what I have just described has not contributed measurably to the high incidence of homosexual experience among American males.

This is not, however, the only consequence of the phenomenon noted by the researchers who study juvenile behavior. If the problem of successful integration into the life pattern is less intense for girls than for boys, this does not mean that girls escape suffering certain consequences of the father's distance from the family or the absence of other significant adult males in their school experience. Sexuality is established and identified in part by the models of our own sex that are available to us, but it is also established and identified by models of the opposite sex. Healthy sexuality depends in part on the adequacy of our relationships to mature members of both sexes. And since in the absence of the father the girl who is growing into womanhood is as much deprived of an adequate model of manhood as is her brother, the result may be to render her own sexual identity inadequate.

Perhaps this, too, is responsible for at least a part of our incompetence. The young woman who has been deprived of an adequate image of maleness may simply withdraw from male society, in which case she may become incapable of sexual response; or she may develop unusually strong attachments to men. It is significant in this regard that the largest proportion of marriages of girls eighteen years of age or younger are between them and older men. According to one study, only 10 percent of the girls who marry in high school choose high-school-age boys.

Other relational voids make their own contributions to our sexual incompetence. Unhappiness in marriage is a serious national problem. If one marriage in four ends in divorce these days, the proportion of marital failure is even higher among those who have been divorced and remarried. But this tells only part of the problem. As one researcher has noted, some studies show that as many as one-third of all marriages may be unhappy though still legally intact. Certainly the unhappiness in marriage which afflicts many parents has consequences for the children of those marriages; and if the children are not emotionally crippled, they are lucky to escape emotional disadvantage. One national group which considered this particular problem concluded that something should be done to break up what it called "the circle of circumstances which keeps producing sexually mixed-up people with sexually mixed-up kids who become the parents of more sexually inadequate people."

MISPLACED EXPECTATIONS

So sexual incompetence can be traced to the loss of the other, to human relationships in disarray. And there is a twist to the problem which compounds both its difficulty and its seriousness. It is the popular expectation that, if indeed our relationships are disarrayed, the solution is to be found by rushing as quickly—and as frequently—as possible into sexual embrace. Articles, advertisements, books, and films have led us—sometimes subtly, often explicitly—to assume that the key to a sense of interpersonal well-being can be found if only we can learn to be "good in bed." There is no doubt that, in addition to simple prurience, this expectation accounted for the sales records of books like *The Sensuous Woman* and *The Sensuous Man*. They were searched expectantly for tips on just the right touch to trigger meaningful closeness.

Indeed, we have learned to expect sex to deliver us from whatever most desperately besets us. Into the sexual act we carry all of our yearnings for satisfaction and significance in the hope of instant orgasmic transformation. Is it any wonder, then, that we fail sexually, that we come away from our liaisons profoundly disappointed, and that, instead of leaving us filled, they simply deepen the void? Sexual embrace is delicate and fragile and cannot bear the whole weight of our desperation.

Moreover, there is more to intimacy than being close. Sexual embrace can confirm, deepen, and communicate intimacy; but two bodies rubbing frantically up against each other are powerless, by means of that friction alone, to create intimacy *ex nihilo*. When in marriage two people find that something is lacking in their relationship, they are likely to turn to the sex manuals to find out what went wrong with their technique. But all the technique in the world cannot bridge the loneliness which grows between two people who no longer have anything important to say to each other. When true mutuality is missing, there is no marriage, whatever the law may say, and sex is futile. That does not mean that we must despair of reconstructing the relationship, for reasons I shall try to make clear in the next section; but it does mean that that reconstruction is unlikely to be successful if it is built upon the attempt to achieve a new sexual virtuosity.

If we were assuredly right to lift the long silence which had made sex furtive and disreputable, we were surely wrong to expect that candor would make us competent. So we have been betrayed by a misplaced openness: we are inexperienced and ineffective. *Sexual inadequacy can be traced, not to a lack of information but to the loss of the other.* Adequacy will require a quite different kind of openness—the kind that goes by the name of love.

To love another is to acknowledge that other as a unique, unrepeatable human event. Love is the recognition of dignity, the discernment of worth in another, not merely because he is useful or fair to look upon, but because he participates in the miracle and mystery of being human. Love is communication, the willingness to enter deeply and significantly into another's experience and to allow that other access to my own depth. Love is the self-forgetfulness which makes it possible to participate in another's good, the ability to live in a relation of intimacy while still permitting the other to be the other. Love is the destiny for which men are made.

LOVE IS HARD WORK

Love, these days, is an "in" thing. That fact is announced in the most unlikely of places, from sweat shirts to bumper stickers. And it is sometimes announced in the most unexpected of ways. An undergraduate of my acquaintance recently picked at random a name from the local telephone directory, dialed the number, and said without preliminary to the startled subscriber on the other end of the line, "I love you!" Had it not happened, by the happiest of accidents, that the subscriber in question was a lonely widow, seventy-two years of age, the response the student received to his unabashed profession might have been less poignant than, in fact, it turned out to be—or at least, poignant in a very different way!

In spite of the varied signs that love is "in," however—or perhaps because of the very saturation of these signs—I am apprehensive that love may be so far "in" that it is, in reality, already on its way out. "In-ness" often has just that consequence. *Sic transit gloria mundi,* someone may be tempted to observe. After a time, even the sublimest of experience begins to bore. Why should we expect it to be otherwise in our current love affair with love?

Why indeed? Surely there is something that we ought more than ordinarily to regret if our current preoccupation with love does turn out to be merely another fad which goes as quickly as it came. At the beginning of this book, I cited Archibald MacLeish's 1969 warning that we are living in a time of the "diminishment of man." If only we knew, now, how to keep love alive and growing, this could become the generation known in history for its refusal to yield to man's diminishment and its determination to see him restored, instead, to something of the image in and for which he was made.

For man is made by Love for love. That, at least, is the Christian view of the matter. Man unloving and unloved is man diminished, undistinguished from the meanest object in creation. Man loving and loved is man completed, the crown of the creative possibilities which God has placed within our reach. So when God loves us in Christ—so the Christian faith confesses—he gives us the one thing we need for our full manhood. If each of us is not to consent to the diminishment of his own manhood or to contribute to the diminishment of another man, we must learn to live the love which God has given us and for which he has made us.

Oddly enough, the real nemesis of love at this particular moment of history is probably not anything so dramatic as the organized power of some new hate. Simple disillusionment will be enough to bring an end to this new openness to the possibilities of love which has so recently come among us. I fear that many who have been attracted by love's bright promise may have rushed into it without really understanding it and may thus give it up prematurely, may think themselves ready for love's physical nakedness when it is moral nakedness love requires, and may find that it is not so easy of access as they had thought at first.

If, rather than give consent to a fading fad, we are to keep it alive and growing, we shall have to reconsider love; we shall have to relearn what love is about; and we shall have to find the wit and the will to overcome the misconceptions about love which are so pervasively and powerfully at work among us.

And what will it mean to reconsider love? For one thing, it will mean giving up the popular misconception that love is a natural talent, a spontaneous welling up and reaching out, over which no conscious control can be exercised. Either I am a loving person, or I am not, in the popular view; either I am drawn to that man or woman, or I am not. In any case, there is very little I can do about it. If the spontaneous impulse to love is absent, then I must accept that as the verdict of the fates, or wait in the hope that one day I shall be taken captive by the feeling for which, in the meantime, I can only yearn. So the misconception runs.

I have the impression that marriages founder regularly on this fallacy. When one marriage partner discovers that his feeling for his mate has changed, he is likely to accept that fact passively, as if it *ought* to be so if it *is* so. And if asked about it, he may simply reply, "I just don't love her anymore," as if that statement had a kind of self-evident conclusiveness about which there was nothing more to be done or said. I have the impression that relationships between parents and children regularly disintegrate around the same confident misapprehension.

But it is a mistake to believe, as we so commonly do, that behavior must follow feelings, that we cannot act unless we have first felt, that I cannot—indeed, that I need not—*act* lovingly if I don't *feel* loving. The fact is that our feelings often follow where our behavior has first led.[9] Consider the case of a man who takes up a point of view in an argument, not because he has any real feeling for the view, but just for the sake of the argument. Entering enthusiastically into the game, he attempts skillfully to turn aside the objections of his opponent and to fashion persuasive support for his adopted view. Often the result is that what began as an exercise ends as a conviction! The reasoning and the evidence he managed to turn up in the course of the debate may have something to do with his change of mind, of course; but equally important, the player discovers, in the course of imitating the behavior of a man of particular conviction, that he is able to carry off that imitation competently, and, more important, that he likes the way the behavior feels. So imitation is transmuted into authenticity.

Role playing, a technique whose uses range from serious therapy to training for job interviews, rests solidly upon the expectations that feelings can be made to follow behavior. Clinical evidence and practical experience join in demonstrating that when I take upon myself a role which I would not normally accept and may not initially welcome, and when I engage in a serious game in which I play out that role with reasonable conscientiousness and imagination, modifications not just in my overt behavior but in my feelings about that role can occur.

There was a time when I found it offensive to speak of "making love." That sounded too contrived and mechanical, and I was sure that love could only be love if it were spontaneous and natural. Now I take a quite different view of the matter. Kingsley Amis was right, I think, in what he did with Ronnie and Simon, the lovers in his novel *I Want It Now*. As one reviewer describes it, Amis "has Ronnie and Simon imitate love for selfish reasons until pretense becomes the real thing."[10]

Love, as I am now sure, is a *practiced* response to life. Love always requires some degree of self-displacement to make room for the beloved, and self-displacement is never easy. It has to be worked at. To focus attention deliberately on the full sound of another's voice takes enormous discipline, given as we all are to the prepossessing notion that our own voices are the most compelling sounds in creation. Because love is a practiced response to life, love means having to say "I love you" and having to act out the meaning of those words even at moments when I don't feel very much like it. To do so is not so much hypocrisy as it is an exercise in self-fulfilling prophecy: it is the imitation which produces the reality. If I say "I love you" to my wife only on those occasions when that is for me a deeply and spontaneously felt experience, the occasions when it is, indeed, deeply and spontaneously felt are likely to become fewer and fewer. If I am persuaded intellectually that I ought to treat each man with a dignity which befits his manhood, I cannot wait to begin such treatment until an awareness of that dignity becomes for me an overwhelming experience. Rather I must begin to *practice* it first as an intellectual conclusion, as a decision to be made about a concrete person, as a step to be taken toward a real man or woman. Only then does love have any hope of becoming a felt reality.

Perhaps we would all agree that love is an art. But the trouble with all great art is that it appears deceptively easy. Whenever I hear the choir of Kings College, Cambridge, at Evensong in the magnificent college chapel, I am stunned by the utter effortlessness of the sound. The clarity of tone, the liquidity of line, the elevation of mood which soars to the fan-vaulted ceiling and beyond, all seem in that moment to be of celestial origin. Yet the truth is that such perfection of artistry is the product of untold hours of *rehearsal* and of a disciplined sublimation of each chorister to the temperament of the music. Though it is far from the popular view of the matter, there is in all great art not only the ecstasy of spontaneous discovery but the agony of hard work.

And so with love. Who does not *work at it* will not be *found by it*.

LOVE AND OUR MORAL NAKEDNESS

Work is not the only obstacle to love. There is also a kind of nakedness in it for which we may not have bargained. The physical nakedness which goes with the sexual kind of "making love" may appeal to us or not, depending upon a complex of psychological factors. But to "make love" in the more broadly human sense which I am discussing here requires a *moral nakedness* which even the most eager lover finds difficult to welcome at first.

Let me put the matter in slightly different terms. Love can only grow in us and among us where there is both the will to forgive and the willingness to be forgiven. To forgive does not mean that actions are forgotten or overlooked. To be forgiven is surely not the experience of having something to "live down"; it is, rather, the experience of finding someone to live with! Forgiveness is the determination, on the part of the one forgiving and of the one forgiven, to keep all of the human options open, rather than to foreclose some or all of them in punitive or guilt-ridden response to what is regarded as a moral fault. Forgiveness, as Werner and Lotte Pelz have written,

> is the action which lets the other find sympathy where he expected vindictiveness, concern where he expected hatred, generosity where he expected retribution, which gives much because it expects much, which recreates new opportunities for the other, because it apprehends the world as a vast bundle of opportunities.[11]

Forgiveness is the determination to keep all of the human options open: I know of no better definition of love than that.

But if I am to forgive another man, that will require me to give up something I very much value: my sense of moral superiority in the presence of another person whom I consider an offender. For me to forgive that man—on these terms, to reach out and restore him to a relation which he may have violated or even despised—requires in me a kind of moral nakedness. It is the recognition, even in the presence of his offensiveness, that when we are stripped to our human essentials, that man and I are very much like one another. Blaise Pascal expressed the daring act of moral imagination upon which forgiveness depends, when he said that I must always consider the offensive one,

> so long as he is alive, capable of being illuminated by grace, and to believe that in a short while he may be fuller of faith than I myself, while I, on the other hand, may fall into the blindness which is now his.[12]

But if it is difficult to forgive, how very much harder it is to be forgiven! Forgiveness received and accepted requires another kind of nakedness no one of us is likely to welcome. It is the recognition that what I could not do for myself, another has done for me. Once I have squandered life—not simply my own life but, inevitably, the lives of others as well, since what I am always entails the being of others—I cannot take back arbitrarily what I have as arbitrarily yielded. Since I gave away what was not mine to give in the first place, no act of my own will is sufficient to recover it. Life squandered can never be retrieved; it can only be received. It can never be taken back *by me;* it must be given back *to me.*

Life is always a gift, whether in that act in which I was first created or in those continuing acts of forgiveness by means of which my life is restored to me. Forgiveness is the cement which holds life together, since it is the refusal to accept any relationship as permanently broken; it is the determination to give back to another man the life he has willfully or witlessly given up.

But for all its restorative power, that gift may not be received gladly. Gratitude for life's gifts and graces does not come easily to any of us; indeed no gratitude comes easily, for it is an acknowledgment of my own need which another has seen and supplied. But I do not like to admit that there are some things I cannot do for myself. I prefer to think of myself as self-sufficient, omnicompetent. And forgiveness is the hardest of all gifts to receive, not only because it requires me to admit a radical need but also because it forces me to accept a radical judgment: *I am a waster of life!* It is bad enough that I know it; but forgiveness offered means that someone else knows it, too, and I am frightened by my moral nakedness before that knowledge.

Yet if it is really forgiveness which I am offered, it means that the other does, indeed, know my fault but refuses to turn that knowledge to his own advantage. So in the end, my life is in danger only if I refuse the gift, the life that is handed back to me in forgiveness. Forgiveness, as I have already said, is a refusal to accept any relationship as permanently broken. But if I refuse to accept forgiveness when it is offered, then I consent to live a broken life and thus thrust myself into a loneliness which is very unsafe indeed. For loneliness always turns us intensely, even desperately, in upon ourselves, and in such an anxious state we are not even capable of loving ourselves, cut off as we are from the love of others. We do not love ourselves with our anxious self-regard; rather we consume ourselves; we "eat out our hearts," as it were. And like the snake that swallows its own tail, the process is definitely subject to the law of diminishing returns!

But when forgiveness is given *and received,* it can work miracles. It can even restore a lost virginity! In spite of its long history, I cannot consent to the notion that virginity is simply a matter of the genitals. There is nothing inherently pure about sexual inexperience, and there is nothing inherently impure in sexual experience. Man is more than the animal, and human sexuality is more than cyclical heat. It can be, rather, an occasion for exquisite tenderness, for intense pleasure intensely shared, for the confirmation of womanhood and manhood, for a willing act of co-creation. Surely it is fulfillment, not defilement, which we may find in such "knowing" of another human being.

Virginity is a moral matter, not a physiological one. Its proper meaning is not inexperience but *wholeness,* purity only in the sense of *integrity.* Loss of virginity does not necessarily occur in the breaking of the maidenhead for a woman, or in the first vaginal penetration for a man. Indeed, we do not know whether these bare physical facts are morally significant until we examine the quality of the relationships within which they occur. *Virginity is lost only when integrity is broken because sexual relationships are dishonest.*

William Hamilton has argued, persuasively for me, that human acts are either appropriate or inappropriate depending upon whether or not they honestly symbolize the nature of the relationships within which they occur. If I am warmly embraced by a total stranger whom I meet under the most casual of circumstances, said Hamilton, that embrace is a dishonest symbol of our actual relationship. And if I casually shake my wife's hand on first being reunited with her after a long and regretted absence, that too is symbolically dishonest. So sexual intercourse, whatever else it may be, is inescapably symbolic communication. It is moral only when what it "says" about a relationship is really true, and it is immoral only when it "says" more about the relationship than can honestly be said. So, as Hamilton wrote, since sexual intercourse "involves such utter self-giving, such utter commitment and concern for the other, it can *honestly* express only a relationship which itself knows humility, trust, and selflessness."[13] Because the sexual act is so critical to our humanity—because it has such power to confirm or to disconfirm our identities as men and women, because it releases emotions and impulses which otherwise we manage to hold in check—it can be safely entered into only in a relationship which is so structured as to be able to bear that intensity, that intimate disclosure of physical and emotional nakedness, and their continuing effects upon the two people involved long after the orgasmic shudders have ceased. The sexual act is therefore an honest symbol only of that relationship in which two people are both willing and able to sustain and endure, to take delight in and growth from, the most continuous, varied, intimate, and all-embracing living together. In any context less serious and whole, it is dishonest.

I cannot fail to follow this line of argument to its clear implication, however much it may depart from received and entrenched meanings. There are, in the definition of virginity urged here, both sexually experienced virgins and sexually inexperienced men and women who have given up their virginity: the former because their sexual life is of a piece with their true relationships, the latter because, in spite of an actual relationship of full and continuing mutual responsibility, they refuse to participate in the sexual act which is its most appropriate symbol. To "say" too little is as much a lie as to "say" too much!

Virginity is the presence of wholeness, integrity. It is lost only when that wholeness has been broken by acts of sexual dishonesty. But virginity can be recovered, and love regained, in the giving and the accepting of the gift of forgiveness, whose power it is to heal what has been broken and to make life whole again.

INTIMACY NEEDS AN INTERMEDIARY

There is at least one more obstacle to be removed if we are to avoid disillusionment with love, if we are to reconsider love in order to keep it alive and growing. It is the notion that immediacy is the same as intimacy, that love is both created and sustained only in the most direct encounter of one person with another.

There is, indeed, more to intimacy than being close, as I insisted at the end of the section entitled "Misplaced Expectations"; and just so, there is more to love than the immediacy of relationship. But the further—and perhaps the harder—truth is that love, whether it be conjugal love or that neighbor-love to which the New Testament calls us, *can never be achieved by direct person-to-person efforts.*

It is simply a human fact, against which we must continually struggle, that what begins as love, or what touts itself proudly as love, often turns demonic. Love is readily and regularly confused with the absorption of one life by another; humility and selflessness can become the most subtle and dangerous forms of aggression against another human being; and what begins as service to another is often transformed by imperceptible and therefore irresistible degrees into manipulation and domination. Such are the similarities between each of these sets of terms— between love and absorption, for example—and such is our talent for self-deception, that we easily persuade ourselves that we are engaged in the former while wreaking the human havoc of the latter.

Love, whatever else it may mean, can be nothing less than the ability to live in intimacy while permitting the other to be the other. So, if we are to find a capacity for loving intimacy, we shall have to maintain a certain distance from the beloved—not the kind of distance which occurs when I withhold something of myself from the relation, but rather the kind of distance in which my self-giving is lifted up in an act of transcendent mediation. It is not my habit to look regularly to Kahlil Gibran for guidance, but here at least he is close to the mark when, in *The Prophet*, he writes of marriage:

. . . let there be spaces in your togetherness. . . .
Love one another, but make not a bond of love:
Let it rather be a moving sea between the shores of your souls. . . .
Sing and dance together and be joyous, but let each of you be alone,
Even as the strings of a lute are alone though they quiver with the same music.
Give your hearts, but not into each other's keeping.
For only the hand of Life can contain your hearts.[14]

Love recognizing the full otherness of the other: nothing short of that will do. But *how* to overcome our human propensity to get too close is the problem. It is just here, I think, and primarily here, that the Christian faith speaks its distinctive word on love. Christians have often tried to say that what makes Christianity distinctive among the world's faiths is that Christ gives mankind a new *definition* of love. The *agape* of the New Testament—love even for the unlovely—is a higher form of love which has little in common with our natural loves, we have insisted.[15] Even if that comparison were true—it is far from proved either historically or philologically and may, in fact, represent an attempt to take theological gain from etymological obscurity—there is something else in Christian truth which is far more profound in its impact upon our human loves than any definition could be. Dietrich Bonhoeffer saw it when he insisted that Jesus Christ is the mediator who "saves" my love for another from becoming absorption, or aggression, or manipulation. It is *only when Christ stands between us* that the other can continue to be the other in his relation to me. Paradoxically, *real intimacy requires an intermediary, through whom the other is loved for what he is and not merely for what I wish him to be.*

  Gibran pointed out the need for mediation; Bonhoeffer named the mediator. So Bonhoeffer wrote:

> As only Christ can speak to me in such a way that I may be saved, so others, too, can be saved only by Christ himself. This means that I must release the other person from every attempt of mine to regulate, coerce, and dominate him with my love. The other person needs to retain his independence of me; to be loved for what he is, as one for whom Christ became man. . . . Because Christ has long since acted decisively for my brother, before I could begin to act, I must leave him his freedom to be Christ's; I must meet him only as the person that he already is in Christ's eyes. . . . Human love constructs its own image of the other person, of what he is and what he should become. It takes the life of the other person into its own hands. [Mediated love] recognizes the true image of the other person which he has received from Jesus Christ; the image that Jesus Christ himself embodied and would stamp upon all men.[16]

  It is this same insight, more broadly stated, that Paul Tillich has given us in his remarkable sermon on "Loneliness and Solitude." "Only the presence of the eternal can break through the walls that isolate the temporal from the temporal," he wrote, thus asserting in his own distinctive way that the recovery of the most intimate human relatedness must be a work of transcendent mediation. To be a man is to be alone, wrote Tillich the existentialist. "We are always alone, each for himself." But our aloneness is conquered in solitude, which is life lived in the presence of the eternal. So Tillich the Christian wrote:

. . . we can never reach the innermost center of another being [by direct search or assault]. . . . But we can reach it in a movement that rises first to God and then returns from Him to the other self. In this way man's aloneness [his ability to be the other] is not removed, but taken into the community with that in which the centers of all beings rest, and so into community with all of them. Even love is reborn in solitude. For only in solitude are those who are alone able to reach those from whom they are separated. . . . One hour of solitude may bring us closer to those we love than many hours of communication. We can take them with us to the hills of eternity.[17]

That, at last, is what it means to know that we are made by Love for love!

So it leads us, in the final section of this book, into the transhistorical, to which the distinctive powers of our personhood are ultimately traced.

Part V
History
and the
Transhistorical

Chapter Ten

The Inexpugnably Personal

WHAT DOES IT TAKE TO LIVE?

Some time ago a young woman of my acquaintance wrote herself a note, which said:

> Life lasted a year then ceased altogether. That was almost sixteen months ago. After it stopped, I found myself here in Hell surrounded by other nonliving creatures. Some strange bite has occurred in my outer ear four times today like a mosquito or fly biting a deaf person—no irritating warning. This is one of the tiredest nights in my remembrance. But it doesn't matter. From now on I'm going to buy postcards and send them to people or myself.
>
> Goodnight rapidly. Goodnight vapidly. What's the use? Hope my clock alarms me tomorrow.

Not everything that young woman was feeling when she wrote those words comes clear to us as we read them now. The details of her apparently unhappy autobiography are too few for us to know precisely what it was that troubled her. What does come through with poignant clarity is her complaint against a life she found just barely livable.

That is, at odd moments, a complaint any of us may make. Someone has said that the trouble with life is that it is so daily. Perhaps experience of the sheer dailiness of life may lead us to ask the question about what makes life livable. And when we ask, we know that it is not just a question about what it would be nice to have to make life easy and pleasant. It is, rather, a question about what we *must* have if life is to be lived at all.

What does it take to live? That is the most radical question a man or a woman ever asks—radical in the original meaning of that word: it goes to the *root* of life. Just the capacity to ask such a question is evidence of both the grandeur and the misery of man. Man alone, among all the varieties of created life that we know anything about, is a problem to himself. In the problematic situation we experience not only the limitations of life, but also the freedom to envision new possibilities and the imagination to recreate the world for their accomplishment. The animal handles the question about what it takes to live by instinct: a little sharpening of the claws here, a bit of killing for food there, a brief procreative heat when the glands stir the blood. Only man takes his life in his own hands by questioning it: What is there in life that I cannot do without? What is there which, having, makes life worth living in spite of all else, and not having, makes life not worth living in spite of all else?

The older we grow, the more urgent our questioning of life becomes. In our younger years, we are protected against experiences of disequilibrium by home and community and thus seldom, if ever, are we really faced with the peril and promise of questioning life's livability. But as our childish dependence wanes, life gives us experiences which threaten to throw us off balance—experiences not only overwhelmingly bad but also overwhelmingly good: joys, successes, failures, tragedies, demands, surprises. Unless we have made anchorage in something pretty firm, pretty permanent as life runs, we are in danger of being toppled by successive shocks. So life forces upon us the question about that irreducible minimum on which we are finally prepared to wager what we have and are.

I dare say, in fact, that each of us *is* the answer he gives to the question *"What does it take to live?"* Reduce life to its essentials, strip away the cosmetics and the padding, and what is left *is* you!

PERSISTENT ANSWERS TO THE ROOT QUESTION

Throughout the long career of mankind, several competing— and apparently permanent—answers have been given to the question about what it takes to live. Some have answered, "Pleasure!" The one absolutely indispensable thing necessary to make life worthwhile, as this point of view would have it, is experience to delight the eye, to warm the body, to set our senses tingling, to bathe us in a sea of pleasurable feeling. If a man is what he answers, then to answer, "Pleasure!" means: *I am the sensations which dance on my nerve ends.* So what makes man man, what moves at the heart of man, is a will to pleasure.

Sigmund Freud gave ontic status to the pleasure principle, and his views have been seized upon as conferring legitimacy upon a popular hedonism, since it is commonly assumed that if a thing is "natural"—as Freud held the pleasure principle to be—it must also be desirable. In Freudian psychology, the pleasure principle gives energy to the id, and the id, as Calvin Hall has written in explication of Freud,

> is the foundation upon which the personality is built. The id retains its infantile character throughout life. It cannot tolerate tension. It wants immediate gratification. It is demanding, impulsive, irrational, asocial, selfish, and pleasure-loving. It is the spoiled child of the personality. It is omnipotent because it has the magical power of fulfilling its wishes by imagination, fantasy, hallucinations, and dreams. It is said to be oceanic because, like the sea, it contains everything. It recognizes nothing external to itself. The id is the world of subjective reality in which the pursuit of pleasure and the avoidance of pain are the only functions that count.[1]

Devotees of the pleasure principle constitute a considerable cult these days, with each member, by definition, his own high priest. Advertising offers overwhelming evidence that pleasure is the most salable commodity on the market today. When a product has no other virtue—when it does not improve our looks, or make us wiser; even, indeed, when scientific studies indicate that it may be positively harmful to our health—it can still sell millions of units on the single promise of providing "more pleasure." So, as drama critic Walter Kerr has noted, "the visual world about us is largely made up of handsome commercial invitations to ladies, liquor, and lazy days on the beach." But Kerr has noted something else as well:

> . . . the fleshpots, even when they are visited and not merely yearned for, seem to brew very little in the way of sustained contentment; they give rise, rather surprisingly, to a fury. The most disenchanted face one sees in the newspapers is the face of the playboy who ought, by the standards enunciated in all of those

commercial invitations, to have had the most fun. (He has had fun, too, and let's not pretend that he hasn't. Why hasn't it been enough for him?)[2]

There is a very odd thing about pleasure, and that is the way in which it very quickly and regularly displeases us. The playboy's fun has not been enough for him because the pursuit of pleasure is, in its very nature, insatiable. Once he becomes accustomed to one level of pleasurable intensity, the experience jades and he loses interest, unless intensity can be turned to a higher level. The reason the pursuit of pleasure leads to fury, as Kerr suggests, lies in the fact that the pleasure seeker is first disappointed at discovering that his pleasures do not permanently please—a discovery which he makes again and again, regardless of the level of intensity to which he may rise—until at last that disappointment turns to outrage over his betrayal by a pursuit from which he had been led to expect better things.

In Jean-Baptiste Clamence, Albert Camus intended to draw the portrait of an ironic "hero for our time," a man whose condition aggregates the vices of our generation. So the "hero" of *The Fall,* a man of considerable charitable as well as legal reputation, confesses that his life was early focused upon sensuality alone, the quest for pleasure and for conquest. He tells us that he lived simultaneously with two women, one an experienced prostitute and the other a well-born innocent whom he undertook to tutor in the ways of the world; he moved easily and acceptably in homosexual society; and he sought glory in public demonstrations of a prodigious alcoholic capacity. Yet each of these quests for sensual fulfillment came hard up against a barrier within Clamence himself. In the case of alcoholic dissipation, he says, "... it was my liver, and a fatigue so dreadful that it hasn't yet left me. One plays at being immortal and after a few weeks one doesn't even know whether or not one can hang on till the next day."[3]

Pleasure, compulsively and furiously pursued, leads to the outskirts of madness. So a pathetic, exhausted, debauched Clamence, physically and psychically sick to death at the end of the novel, essays bravado but produces only a whimper of defeat:

> ... I am happy—I am happy, I tell you, I won't let you think I'm not happy, I am happy unto death! Oh, sun, beaches, and the islands in the path of the trade winds, youth whose memory drives one to despair![4]

Thus does pleasure cease to please.

When faced with the question "What does it take to live?" some have answered, "Power." The one absolutely indispensable thing necessary to make life worthwhile, on this view, is experience of one's own increasing grip upon the world. If a man is what he answers, then to answer, "Power!" means: *I am the restless and aggressive energies by which I seek to dominate and domesticate my world.* So what makes man man, what moves at the heart of man, is a will to power.

This view has taken its greatest intellectual force from the German philosopher Friedrich Nietzsche, in whose writings the will to power was given a striking boldness of statement. "I test the *power* of a *will*," Nietzsche wrote,

> according to the amount of resistance it can offer and the amount of pain and torture it can endure and know how to turn to its own advantage; I do not point to the evil and pain of existence with the finger of reproach, but rather entertain the hope that life may one day become more evil and more full of suffering than it has ever been. . . . The object is to attain that enormous *energy of greatness* which can model the man of the future by means of discipline and also be means of the annihilation of millions of the bungled and botched, and which can yet avoid *going to ruin* at the sight of the suffering created thereby, the like of which has never been seen before.[5]

This view is what made Nietzsche so thoroughgoing an opponent of the Christian ethic:

> What is it that we combat in Christianity? That it aims at destroying the strong, at breaking their spirit, at exploiting their moments of weariness and debility, at converting their proud assurance into anxiety and conscience-trouble; that it knows how to poison the noblest instincts and to infect them with disease, until their strength, their will to power, turns inwards, against themselves—until the strong perish through their excessive self-contempt and self-immolation; that gruesome way of perishing, of which Pascal is the most famous example.[6]

German National Socialism was a match for Nietzsche in the brutality of its ideological articulation; and while the Nietzschean philosophy has boasted many practicing adherents in the American society, only with the emergence of a violent new radicalism during the past decade has an ideology of power been articulated here with anything approaching Nietzsche's bluntness. When Eldridge Cleaver boasted that the Black Panthers would one day shoot their way into the United States Senate and there cut off the head of Senator McClellan, a new political rhetoric burst ominously on the American scene.

Yet there is an odd thing about power, too: regardless of how much of it we may possess, we never lose the fear of our own powerlessness. Dictators are among the world's most insecure men. There was perhaps no more absolute dictatorship anywhere in the world than in beautiful and bedeviled Haiti, and there was surely no dictatorship in the world where the fearful, frightened insecurity of the dictator was so palpable in the land. Perhaps it never occurred to Francois Duvalier, as Bertrand Russell thinks it did not occur to Nietzsche,

> that lust for power . . . is itself an outcome of fear. Those who do not fear their neighbours see no necessity to tyrannize over them. Men who have conquered fear have not the frantic quality of Nietzsche's "artist-tyrant" Neros, who try to enjoy music and massacre while their hearts are filled with dread of the inevitable palace revolution.[7]

Behind the insecurity of power is the awareness on the part of those who possess it of their own immediate weakness and vulnerability in the very presence of that power. Power must be enlarged, lest it be lost. Power breeds insecurity in direct proportion to its own apparent absoluteness. Who could blame the tyrant who feels betrayed by such an outcome? So power unbalances the human spirit: the philosophic contemplation of such power as Nietzsche declaimed does not even leave the philosopher himself unscathed, as Nietzsche's tragically disturbed life suggests. Part unbearable vulnerability and part the result—as Nietzsche feared—of contemplating the injustices which the tyrant must perpetrate if his rule is to be perpetuated, power may lead to the outskirts of madness, in the petty principalities of home, office, church, shop, or school, as well as in corporate bureaucracies and the councils of state.

Thus does power cease to protect.

When faced with the question "What does it take to live?" still others have answered, "Success!" The one absolutely indispensable thing necessary to make life worthwhile, on this view, is the experience of my own ability increasingly to turn the world to my own gain and to occupy the summits of public attention. If a man is what he answers, then to answer, "Success!" means: *I am the sum total of the world's recognition of me.* So what makes man man, what moves at the heart of man, is a will to achievement.

Whether or not the Protestant ethic is responsible for the rise of capitalism has been warmly debated ever since Max Weber first suggested the connection at the beginning of this century.[8] What is not subject to debate is the connection between the Protestant ethic of nineteenth-century America and a gospel which asserted the godliness of wealth and business success. The American experiment was achievement-oriented from the first, made so by the necessity to tame a wilderness. But when industrial capitalism first came to America, the challenge became one of taming an unregulated economic frontier, with rewards for successful achievement of which the farmers in that earlier wilderness could scarcely have dreamed. It was Presbyterian Andrew Carnegie, the steel baron, who coined the term, "the gospel of wealth," and who was its premier practitioner; but the chief evangelists of that gospel were such men as Episcopal Bishop William Lawrence of Massachusetts and Baptist preacher Russell Henry Conwell.[9] Carnegie, Lawrence, and Conwell linked godliness with riches and morality with success; nor did they shrink from the converse implication, namely, that ungodliness is linked with poverty and immorality with failure. Religious as well as secular versions of this gospel have shaped the subsequent American experience, so that most of us bear the marks of these flawed but influential equations. Few of us are able, therefore, to avoid moral self-congratulation at our successes, and few of us are able to escape the sense of moral doom at our failures. From success we expect beatitude, and from failure we think we deserve what we get.

Yet, in spite of the formidable assurances which are virtually built into us by popular religious and secular pieties, there is an odd thing about success, too, and that is its failure to confirm the sense of self-importance we expect from it. Two passages from contemporary literature mirror the lived experiences of countless men and women. One is from Arthur Miller's play *Death of a Salesman*. Hap and Biff were the sons of Willy Loman, the salesman. Biff was a ne'er-do-well wanderer, but Hap had stayed in the hometown and worked at a business which had rewarded him well. When, after a period of separation, the boys are reunited, Biff says to Hap, "Are you content, Hap? You're a success, aren't you?" And Hap replies, "Hell, no!" Surprised, Biff asks, "Why? You're making money, aren't you?" And Hap responds:

All I can do now is wait for the merchandise manager to die. And suppose I get to be merchandise manager? He's a good friend of mine, and he just built a terrific estate on Long Island. And he lived there about two months and sold it, and now he's building another one. He can't enjoy it once it's finished. And I know that's just what I would do. I don't know what . . . I'm workin' for. Sometimes I sit in my apartment—all alone. And I think of the rent I'm paying. And it's crazy. But then, it's what I always wanted. My own apartment, a car, and plenty of women. And still, goddammit, I'm lonely.[10]

The other passage is from Eric Hodgins' novel *Blandings' Way,* in which Jim Blandings, a phenomenally successful New York advertising man, has these reflections:

He had worked for Banton & Dascomb long and loyally, and almost every year . . . his responsibilities and rewards had increased. Yet he never began a week's work without this same thrill of alarm. So far as he could analyze what his inner being was saying to him it went like this: Blandings, you are an incompetent. You know nothing, you have no gifts, you have no background of solid accomplishment whatever. But you belong in the classification of *lucky* incompetents: that is to say, whenever you have been at your incompetent worst, people have been looking the other way. . . .

. . . It is not just that I am an incompetent, or even that I am a lucky incompetent. It is that I cannot bear to think of the success of my deceits. . . . every now and then someone nods sagely when *I* say something. . . . it merely makes me feel overwhelmed with guilt, shame, and alarm. . . . I said it with a confidence I did not feel—instantly ready to modify it, take it back, reverse it, or re-explain it in such terms that nobody would know what I was originally talking about. That I should have caused agreement among a group of grown men to some proposition in which I myself felt no solid faith—this is the worst of all, the hardest to bear. . . .

God, thought Mr. Blandings, his thoughts on a long reach, in the whole roll call of business enterprise is there no one else like myself? There are the ruthless and successful, the bitter and successful, the proud and successful. Am I the only example of the *frightened* and successful?[11]

Thus do our successes fail.

MEANING AND MORALE

Why does pleasure no longer please, power cease to protect, and success fail? For one thing, pleasure, power, and success in men work like instincts in animals: they live us, we do not live them; they drive us, we do not drive them; they possess us, we do not possess them.

Moreover, each of them is subject to circumstances well beyond our control. The single-minded pursuit of pleasure simply makes us all the more incompetent in dealing with the inevitability of pain. Power is not freedom but entrapment; as the poet Edwin Markham said, wherever there is one slave, there are two. He for

whom achievement and recognition are the bemusing preoccupations must constantly pander to the capricious changes in the
tastes of the judges.

Not the least of their treacherousness lies in the fact that each of
the three tempts us to overestimate our capacities and thus ends by
making a mockery of our pursuit. Pleasure leads to the un-
pleasantness of hangover, indigestion, and physical debility.
Power beguiles us into thinking that we are immune to the
limitations of ordinary morality, and then even a trivial illness
terrifies us with its reminder that there are no immunities. And
because of the drive for success, as the Peter Principle reminds us, a
man tends to rise to the level of his incompetence![12]

Then why do men so commonly seek thus to give meaning to
their lives? Partly, I suppose, because they represent three
permanent and important aspects of our human experience.
Pleasure *is* important: life is flat when it does not bring delight,
joy, and sensual satisfaction. Power *is* important: powerlessness
makes a man a virtual nonentity, unable either to shape events or to
resist them. Success *is* important: in a world like ours, as Edgar
Friedenberg has remarked, one "who does not know what he is
good *at* will not be sure what he is good *for*."[13] So each of these
carries some meaning, even very important meaning.

And meaning for life is not an elective for any of us. Meaning,
says theologian Langdon Gilkey, means "a sense of the value of
what we do," and that sense of value frees us for effective living. But
meaninglessness, "the despair or hopelessness that nothing ,is
worthwhile, that there is no open future for us, makes it impossible
for us to use our powers."[14] Life is not simply a matter of
maintaining those powers of the body upon which continued
physical existence depends; it is, as well, a matter of maintaining
that strength of meaning upon which the *morale* of the human
spirit depends. When morale goes, the will to live weakens and
dies, and the body sickens and settles at best (or is it worst?) into a
living death. When morale is high, the human spirit often
miraculously defies the most stunning physical ravages; and if it is
not, in the end, able to defy the death of the body, it nevertheless
goes to that death with spirit untrammeled.

What gives pleasure, power, and success such desperate durability is their promise to secure our *morale*. When they fail to do that,

as regularly they do, we suffer a shocked loss of morale which Paul Tillich calls "existential disappointment"[15]: the discovery that what we had thought were means to the good life are, in fact, powerless to confer upon us an abiding sense of well-being.

Failure to find any meaning permanently worth living for results in what psychoanalyst Viktor Frankl calls an "existential vacuum." For the man in that vacuum, "No instinct tells him what he has to do, and no tradition tells him what he ought to do; soon he will not know what he wants to do."[16] This "existential vacuum" leads to a spiritually and physically enervating boredom. Frankl writes perceptively about that "Sunday neurosis" which is so common a phenomenon among us, a "depression which afflicts people who become aware of the lack of content in their lives when the rush of the busy week is over and the void within themselves becomes manifest."[17] Suicide, alcoholism, and delinquency are among the forms of behavior which Frankl thinks can often be traced to the boredom of an empty, because meaningless, existence.

So what makes man man, what moves at the heart of man, is a "will to meaning."[18] *Man means what man is, man is what man means!* The more limited the meaning, the more diminished the man. That is why pleasure, power, and achievement betray us to the point of meaninglessness when we seek to build a significant life upon them. Each is a limited good which delights to masquerade as an ultimate. Each grows increasingly imperialistic and all-preoccupying, impatient and intolerant of any other meaning, until at last man, reduced to that single dimension, loses the versatility which effective life requires. The more inclusive the meaning, the richer the man. The one absolutely indispensable thing necessary to make life worthwhile is that perspective from which it is possible to see life whole and to make affirmative sense of what we see.

Then where are we to find that ultimate—all-comprehending, omnicompetent—meaning upon which our humanhood seems so critically to depend? Not, let it be clear, in some cosmic "fortune cookie." The "fortune cookie" fallacy assumes that ultimate meaning must be discontinuous from my ordinary experience, that it rests with the inscrutable fates, and that if it appears at all, it will be suddenly "out of the blue." Breaking it open, I will find there the clue which will transform my existence. This is why, for some of us, the ringing of the telephone awakens a vague sense that perhaps something fateful is about to be announced, and why, for others, the arrival of the mail is looked upon with daily expectation bordering on spiritual excitement.

Yet surely any meaning so external and esoteric, so unfamiliar as that expected in the "fortune cookie" fallacy, would be unable to transform the very familiar round of quite unesoteric duties which comprise our daily lives. Rather than permitting us to take them up with new enthusiasm, it would only estrange us from them all the more by its alien lure. Unless I am very much mistaken, the meaning we need can transform our very ordinary existence only if it is already resident within it, only if it is intimate as well as other, only if it is not merely strange but strangely familiar. This is—not incidentally—why Christian orthodoxy has always insisted that redemption comes, not by means of a divine hero who descends among us effortlessly from above to whisper an alien clue, but by means of an obedient man who transforms the possibilities of life precisely by living them. And this is—also not incidentally—why Moses rebuked those who expected deliverance from historical crisis to come from some beyond:

> . . . this commandment which I command you this day is not too hard for you, neither is it far off. It is not in heaven, that you should say, "Who will go up for us to heaven, and bring it to us, that we may hear it and do it?" Neither is it beyond the sea, that you should say, "Who will go over the sea for us, and bring it to us, that we may hear it and do it?" But the word is very near you; it is in your mouth and in your heart, so that you can do it (Deuteronomy 30:11-14, RSV).

Nearly opposite to the "fortune cookie" fallacy is the "butterfly" fallacy, to which I referred without naming it in chapter eight. What men want is an experience of realness, of importance, and of satisfaction which will make it possible for them to live with enthusiasm and joy. Those who practice this fallacy think to find those things by searching out the self, by exposing all of the dark recesses of the psyche on the assumption that somewhere within the self's own substance there must be a source energy and insight which will free them to be and to do all those wonderful things, if only it could be found. So they engage in hours of inwardness, hoping that out of it all there will emerge a new form of life which can take wings and leave behind the husk of the old. They live, that is, in a cocoon, always hoping one day to emerge a butterfly.

This is a fallacy, however, because any meaning which emerges thus out of loneliness is likely to be a very lonely meaning. It is unlikely to put us in more creative touch with the outer world of problematic relationships; in the end, it is unable even to touch our problematic inwardness which is, in part, the mirror image of those relationships.

A third fallacy is the "do-it-yourself" meaning. It assumes, not that the mysterious clue to life's significance will one day appear "out of the blue," nor that it will emerge in primordial loneliness from within, but rather that every man can fabricate his own meaning, rough-hewn out of the random materials life hands him, forged out of his determination to have it so. As long as life does not move massively against him, a man can persuade himself that he has succeeded in shaping it to his design and can despise those who have not the will to do likewise. But good times are not the acid test; the crucial question is whether his self-made significance can withstand those times when life does not support his personal preferences and nurture his plans, when it does not hold him up but threatens to strike him down. The answer is that no significance is any stronger than its source. If what a man fabricates partakes of his strengths, it also participates in his weaknesses, is subject to his limitations, and is susceptible to his vulnerabilities. If he is not to be defeated when trouble comes, there must be resources for the maintenance of a meaning larger than himself—resources whose very largeness transcends any situation which threatens to undo him.

Finally, and nearly opposite to the misplaced activism we have just examined, there is the fallacy of the "guaranteed annual meaning," which passively expects that life will hand us a minimum level of significance just because we are alive. But we mistake the nature of the human situation if we think of it thus as a one-way process. It is, rather, dialogic as we saw in the last chapter. That means that, just as we have questions to put to life, it has questions to put to us. Dr. Viktor Frankl has given pointed expression to this latter form of questioning:

'Ultimately, man should not ask what the meaning of his life is, but rather must recognize that it is *he* who is asked. In a word, each man is questioned by life; and he can only answer to life by *answering for* his own life; to life he can only respond by being responsible.[19]

THE FINAL CONTINGENCY OF OUR EXISTENCE

So we ask again: What is the meaning we need if life is to have savor, if—in spite of persistent problems—life is not to be *ultimately problematic?* Perhaps we can approach an answer by seeing that life would, indeed, be ultimately problematic if we were simply "orphans in an alien universe." If we are the unintended products of sheer randomness, if the life process has no stake in our existence, if our being has no value for the whole of being, if the goods to which we aspire are accidental and evanescent, if life cannot be seen whole because there is no coherence in it which links each to all—if this is the way life is, then it will seem to us an indifferent business at best. But indifference, under such conditions, would not be the last word, nor indeed the worst word. "The inscrutable power by which we are is either for us or against us," wrote H. Richard Niebuhr. "If it is neutral, heedless of the affirmations or denials of the creatures by each other, it is against us, to be distrusted as profoundly as if it were actively inimical. For then it has cast us into being as aliens, as beings that do not fit."[20]

Put positively, the meaning we need if our existence is to have point and purpose is *assurance that life can be trusted.* The question of meaning or meaninglessness is, fundamentally, a question of "trust or distrust in being itself," as Richard Niebuhr insisted.[21] That is, meaning or meaninglessness is at bottom a matter of faith. "Faith is the attitude of the self in its existence toward all the existences that surround it, as beings to be relied upon or to be suspected."[22] Trust or distrust is the elemental ingredient which qualifies all of our encounters, whether with man or with nature; it is the radical constituent of selfhood.

Yet, social being though man is, as I tried to show in the preceding chapter, it is at the point of this radical life-orientation that each man is most uniquely individual. It is true, of course, as Richard Niebuhr readily admitted, that my own trust or distrust is influenced by all of the interactions of acceptance or of suspicion which make up my commerce with other selves; yet no other self or group of selves can displace me from the radical immediacy of my relation to the power by which I am. Ultimately, then, *"faith as trust and distrust is inexpugnably personal."*[23]

What theology affirms on the basis of religious experience, psychotherapy confirms on the basis of clinical experience.

Psychotherapist Dr. Andras Angyal takes a similar view of the root importance of life-trust to our developing personhood. Every human being, says Dr. Angyal, has a dual pattern of organization, with one pattern marked by realistic confidence and hope, and the other marked by diffidence and anxiety. The first, he asserts, is the pattern of health; the second the pattern of neurosis, with the emotional condition of the individual dependent upon which pattern is ascendent.[24] Emotional health, then, depends precisely upon our ability to affirm the trustworthiness of life, while neurosis is rooted in the faith that life is ultimately problematic.

When we arrive at this point in our self-understanding, we come unavoidably and frighteningly up against the fact of the *final* contingency of our existence. For however much we may succeed in fashioning certain proximate security arrangements—life insurance, job tenure, a savings account, a fallout shelter—we know that they are all subject to ultimate annihilation. However much we may succeed in grasping satisfaction from pleasure, power, and success, and thus in persuading ourselves in our daylight hours that we are the masters of our fates and the captains of our souls, there come to all of us those waking moments in the middle of the night when a nameless terror invades and reduces all our satisfactions to anguish. So we are stalked all our life long by a vulnerability which forces us to ask how the power of being itself is disposed toward our frail existence. Is it, in the end, for us or against us—not simply when we come to the end of our time, but at those regularly invading moments when we come to the end of our tether?

Whether or not that question can be answered by more than a mocking echo will depend upon whether or not there is any way through from the contingent, where we perch so precariously, to the noncontingent; from those proximate realities, which inspire both trust and distrust, to an ultimate reality in which that ambiguity is finally overcome. Not everyone will find this kind of language congenial. For the secularist it says rather too much with its implied theism; and for the religious traditionalist it says rather too little, since it fails to give theological concreteness to that implication. Then I want to insist that the secularist and the religious traditionalist possess a common deficiency: neither gives sufficient attention to that primal awareness of ultimacy which is the most fundamental and most human of our human experiences. As a result, the secularist makes vigorous intellectual denial that the term "ultimacy" has any substantive reality, all the while ordering his practical anxieties as if it had; and the religious traditionalist makes vigorous practical affirmation that "ultimacy" does have substantive reality, all the while trying to imprison it within static intellectual categories as if it were not really ultimate at all.

Both fail to understand what theologian Langdon Gilkey has recently been at some pains to point out, namely, that to speak of God at all is not, in the first instance, to speak of a being. God language does not designate surface realities, such as objects, or even neatly defined rational concepts. To speak of God is, first, to designate "a region of ultimacy and mystery that surrounds and undergirds the finite."[25] Nothing so definite as "God," in the traditional Christian meanings of that term, appears when we look into that depth. We may, in fact, experience a Void there, but it is, says Gilkey, a special kind of Void—one which is unconditioned and final, which teaches us about our creatureliness with chilling effect, since it leads us not alone toward death but—finality of finalities—toward the threat of nonbeing. It leaves us with nothing of our own, no place to stand or to turn, no way out. It is, thus, the Great Negation. If, however, an answer were to come forth from this region, it would be no less unconditional and absolute. It would be the Great Affirmation, infusing and suffusing every particle of being with its signification.

But whether utter emptiness or only hiddenness, the Void is, in either case, an unavoidable encounter with ultimacy and transcendence for the secularist as surely as it is for the religionist.[26]

INTIMATIONS OF ULTIMACY

Is there an answer hidden in the Void? Sociologist Peter Berger believes there is, and in *A Rumor of Angels*[27] he has suggested an intriguing way through to it. Sociology and psychology have customarily dealt with man's religious consciousness—his awareness of the transcendent—as a projection. That is, viewed from the angle of human behavior—which is the only view appropriate to a behavioral science—religion is a human construct; it is man's historically conditioned, socially organized response to those things which he meets at the margins of life, with death the marginal situation *par excellence*.[28] Critics of religion— Freud and Feuerbach, for example—have used the concept of projection as a means of dismissing the religious consciousness. Notions of the transcendent, in their views, are mere wishful thinking, man's wistful effort to find in the cosmos what is not, in fact, there.

Berger quite agrees that the religious awareness is a human construct. Whether its subject—the transcendent—is real or merely illusory, it is still true that man bears considerable responsibility for the peculiar shape which his response to that subject takes. To speak of a projection, therefore, is to speak only of the man-side of the religious awareness; whether or not there is an Other-side is a question into which behavioral science has no competence to enter. Furthermore, relativizers Freud and Feuerbach can be given their own relativizing treatment: their views are also projections, in the same behavioral science meaning of the term. And there is neither logical nor empirical reason to conclude that their efforts to empty the universe of any transcendent meaning are any less susceptible to mere wistfulness. The relativizing sword cannot be made to cut one way if it is not permitted to cut the other way as well.

Behavioral science, then, can only describe the man-side of the phenomena it treats; whether or not there is another side must simply be left open from the point of view of scientific inquiry. But humanly the matter cannot be left there, since man is more than scientist. There is no reason to doubt the descriptive accuracy of the frequently reiterated observation that the transcendent is excluded from the consciousness of many of our contemporaries. Albert Camus spoke for them in his remark, "We live in an unsacrosant moment in history."[29] But even after we have agreed that the "contemporary consciousness is such and such," Berger still insists that "we are left with the question of whether we will assent to it."[30] Given the fact that wherever in human history the transcendent has appeared, it has appeared as a projection, what may we do with that fact? We need *not* conclude, as did Freud and Feuerbach, that it has appeared as a *mere* projection. There is no reason, Berger insists, why *both* perspectives may not coexist: "What appears as a human projection in one [frame of reference] may appear as a reflection of divine realities in another. The logic of the first perspective does not preclude the possibility of the latter."[31] Indeed, Berger finds it instructive that in mathematics, for example, man's imaginal projections appear to correspond to an external mathematical reality. If one asks how this is possible, Berger replies that man is, after all, a participant in the same overarching system of reality, so that there is a correspondence between the structure of his own consciousness and that of the empirical world. Thus "Projection and reflection are movements within the same encompassing reality."[32]

If this is indeed the case, Berger holds that one would not be misled in expecting to find in man, the projector himself, traces of that supraempirical reality of which his projections may be, in some respects at least, the mirror image. So we need to "seek out what might be called *signals of transcendence* within the empirically given human situation" and the *"proto-typical human gestures* that may constitute such signals."[33] These latter are certain human acts which are so common that they appear to be essential aspects of man's *humanum* as such.

So, for example, man's order-making activity is such a gesture and may thus be a signal of transcendence. The effort to create order is an attempt, in the face of threatening chaos, to create a place in which things are put right, where meaningful relationship rather than maddening randomness rules. But there is in this activity a cosmic intuition that it is not merely in our little human enclaves where things are put right, but that in a deeper sense *everything* is all right. So, says Berger, our human propensity for order is an invitation to "Have trust in being."[34] Such trust is, indeed, "an experience that is absolutely essential to the process of becoming a human person. Put differently, at the very center of the process of becoming fully human, at the core of *humanitas*, we find an experience of trust in the order of reality."[35] And what is so irrational about an inductive faith which believes that what is essential to a human being is a reliable clue to the nature of that larger being to which the human belongs?

If we grasp Berger's argument thus far, we can follow him in tracing other signals of transcendence. Man is *homo ludens;* so essential is the playful that human culture could not exist without it. Following Johan Huizinga, Berger holds that "play sets up a separate universe of discourse, with its own rules, which suspends, 'for the duration,' the rules and general assumptions of the 'serious' world."[36] Play thus insinuates into the world of temporality a distinct structure and quality quite unlike that of time, namely, eternity. Berger says of little girls playing hopscotch in the park:

> They are completely intent on their game, closed to the world outside it, happy in their concentration. Time has stood still for them—or, more accurately, it has been collapsed into the movements of the game. The outside world has, for the duration of the game, ceased to exist. And, by implication (since little girls may not be very conscious of this), pain and death, which are the law of that world, have also ceased to exist. Even the adult observer of this scene, who is perhaps all too conscious of pain and death, is momentarily drawn into the beatific immunity.[37]

So man's capacity, in play, to suspend temporal "seriousness" is a clue to a deeper dimension where time, which often seems to us so brute and final, is itself but creature; and pain and death, time's seemingly ineluctable allies, are overcome.

Since self-realization is a process rather than an achievement, our *humanitas* is essentially future-oriented. "An essential dimension of this 'futurity' of man is hope."[38] It is hope which gives a man courage in the face of danger and death, hope which intuits an ultimate realization beyond these marauding powers which seek to wrest the future from us. We could not speak our defiant "No!" to death, were it not that we had caught the signal of an ultimate "Yes!" beyond all the ravages of history.

It is a historical truism to declare that moral judgments are relative to time and place. In the extreme, relativism makes morality merely a matter of taste. Yet there are deeds so monstrous that their moral condemnation admits qualification neither of time nor place. Adolf Eichmann is morally offensive, not alone in all the worlds we have experienced but in all the worlds we can imagine. How are we to account for this sense of absolute and universal moral outrage when empirical evidence seems to favor relativism? We are faced with a simple choice, Berger insists: deny that there is any moral truth, though that would require us to suppress what we experience vividly here; or look beyond the so-called "natural" for a validation of what we certainly experience. Choice of this second alternative is surely more than arbitrary preference; for condemnation of the Eichmanns of history "does not seem to exhaust its intrinsic intention in terms of this world alone. Deeds that cry out to heaven also cry out for hell."[39]

Finally, Berger finds a signal of transcendence in comic gestures—in our perceptions of "discrepancy, incongruity, incommensurability."[40] The most fundamental discrepancy of all is that between man and the universe. "It is *this* discrepancy that makes the comic an essentially human phenomenon and humor an intrinsically human trait."[41] Humor both recognizes and relativizes this discrepancy. Most of all, it delights to unmask the pretentiousness of all those finite creatures who masquerade as absolutes. The comic exposes the ultimate weakness of naked power; it robs tragedy of its apparent finality; and it makes fun of man's apparent entrapment within the dimensions of time and space. "By laughing at the imprisonment of the human spirit, humor implies that this imprisonment is not final but will be overcome, and by this implication provides yet another signal of transcendence—in this instance in the form of an intimation of redemption."[42]

Propensity for order, play, hope, moral outrage, the comic—essential qualities of our humanitas, all—may well be signals to us that hidden in the ultimate Void there is affirmation. What Berger proposes is a modest method for discerning the character of the ultimate. Its modesty does not derive from any lack of full seriousness or of significance as a method, but from the fact that it makes no claim to display an authoritative "revelation." Beginning with the most elemental of human experiences, and with the conviction that the human is ontologically continuous with the cosmic, it works through "intimations" of transcendence rather than with supernatural seizures. Its data are clues and signals, not "Thus saith the Lord!" pronouncements. It represents the same distaste for theological arrogance and overstatement—the *odium theologicum*—which was expressed by the late Carl Michalson, who once said that the Christian gospel "fell upon the ear of the world with all the force of a hint." The authority of the method proposed by Berger lies simply in its ability to touch the consciousness of other men and to invite them to look into the depths of their own intimations. This by no means settles the classical issue of revelation, but it does reject decisively the view—traceable to the younger Karl Barth—that man has no talent at all for tracing out the divine, and that there is no reliable knowledge of God apart from God's own deliberate and special self-disclosure. Berger sounds, rather, like the younger Harry Emerson Fosdick, who once wrote, "I do not believe that man ever found God when God was not seeking to be found. The under side of the process is man's discovery; the upper side is God's revelation." [43]

THE DISCLOSURE OF THE ULTIMATE

Yet, for all their usefulness, their rich suggestiveness, even their indispensability, the intimations to which Berger witnesses stop short of adequacy. What we need, I have said, is assurance that life can be trusted. But need cannot simply be hypostatized into ontological fact; and however grateful we may be for signals of transcendence, they alone cannot sustain us in the hard places. So whether or not there is a cosmic answer which corresponds to our need must still be phrased as a question.

One things seems to me surpassingly clear: the ultimate will not finally be tracked to its lair by our human craft and cleverness. If man possessed the wit to define the ultimate and then to judge whether this or that reality qualified, man would himself be ultimate by virtue of possessing in himself the standard of ultimacy. On the contrary, ultimacy can finally be known only when, in some manner which accords with its own nature, it appears and announces itself. This is what Christians have meant by revelation, but the insight to which I am pointing here is not simply the result of a special theological tradition. Viktor Frankl, writing not as theologican but as psychoanalyst, reaches a similar conclusion; for, in rejecting Sartre's notion that "man invents himself," Frankl insists rather that "the meaning of our existence is not invented by ourselves, but rather detected." [44]

When the ultimate does appear and announce itself, we may confidently expect that man's most precious notions of what the ultimate is and does may be taken by surprise and stood quite upon their heads. This is the significance of Reinhold Niebuhr's assertion, that in the experience of the biblical men, the Christ who came was not the Christ who was expected.[45] The meaning which is then and there detected may be one which, viewed in merely finite terms before the ultimate appeared, was rejected as humanly unpromising. That is surely why it has always been difficult for

Christians, to say nothing of other men, to believe that they are really made by Love for love, that Love is really sovereign in all the reach and range of being. The ultimate apart, love seems so fragile and delicate, and we find it hard to believe that final security is to be found in the vulnerabilities into which love delivers us. Thus may ultimate wisdom contravene the human.

Not, to be sure, that the ultimate could appear and announce itself without ambiguity, in all the fullness of its ultimacy. No merely finite creature could stand that kind of disclosure. So the ancient author of Exodus depicts Moses on Mount Sinai, protected by a cleft in the rock as God says to him,

> "I will make all my goodness pass before you, and will proclaim before you my name 'The Lord'; and I will be gracious to whom I will be gracious, and will show mercy on whom I will show mercy. But . . . you cannot see my face; for man shall not see me and live" (Exodus 33:19-20, RSV).

With disclosure of the ultimate there must always be a hiddenness; and in spite of the faith such disclosure may arouse in us, there is always ambiguity. But now it is an ambiguity we can stand; for it is not merely what we can grasp which sustains us, but *that by which we are grasped!*

Revelation may occur within the most intimate experience of the self. There is in each of us, as Paul Tillich has so eloquently said, an awareness of being known beyond our own knowing—indeed, of being known even more intimately than we know ourselves. The idea of a socially formed conscience, useful as far as it goes in explaining this experience, does not suffice to account for the profundity of the awareness and the depth of its hold upon us. It seems, says Tillich, that our most secret thoughts and desires are "manifest in the whole of being" and

> produce eternal repercussions. Does anybody really believe that he can escape from the responsibility for what he has done and thought in secret? Omniscience means that our mystery is manifest. Omnipresence means that our privacy is public. The centre of our whole being is involved in the centre of all being; and the centre of all being rests in the centre of our being.[46]

We are terrified by such nakedness and we seek to escape from such exposure. Yet, terrifying as it is to be so intimately known, there is something else present in that experience: namely, an awareness that, in being ultimately known, there is not only judgment but also promise of healing for the brokenness which is there revealed.

In Albert Camus's *The Fall,* Jean-Baptiste Clamence confesses that the strange, transcendent laughter, which first awakened in him the realization of his own moral enormity, was both disturbing *and hopeful:* "there was nothing mysterious about that laugh; it was a good, hearty, almost friendly laugh, which re-established the proper proportions."[47] So, if we are intimately and ultimately known, that knowledge serves the purpose, not of our destruction, as it might be expected to do, but of our redemption; that is, it restores our lost worth. "It points," Tillich wrote, "to the friendly presence of an infinitely creative wisdom. . . . There is a grace in life. Otherwise we could not live. The eyes of the Witness we cannot stand are also the eyes of One of infinite wisdom and supporting benevolence."[48]

Revelation may also occur in the encounters of public history. Christian faith affirms that the life and death and resurrection of Jesus of Nazareth is such a revelation. If there is one thing which marked his ministry, it was a determination to overcome the enmities which divide men within themselves and separate them from each other and from their ultimate ground. No man who despises himself can love a larger life; self-disgust inevitably turns outward into misanthropy and deicide. So Jesus thought to effect the reunion of men with the larger life by offering to each a forgiving acceptance. It was not an ignorant acceptance, but one which looked with compassionate candor upon human waywardness and perversity. In him, men found a new meaning for forgiveness: it was not the experience of having something to live down, but the experience of finding someone to live with! And something else was new as well. Unlike the limited acceptances we give to each other, which free us only momentarily and partially, and then usually only when we are in the actual presence of the accepting one, the acceptance they experience with Jesus seemed to defy limitations of time and boundaries of place; it seemed, oddly, even to put them into a new relationship with nature. So men began to confess that Jesus had done for them what only the ultimate could do. When they discovered, to their astonishment, that death could not hold him, the final seal seemed set upon his significance: *the universe is on the side of life like that!*

Is it? Can life be trusted so, if not on the strength of such signals and disclosures, then on the strength of some others? Each man must answer for himself, must take these ambiguities into himself and there decide whether or not they reveal the presence in life of what it takes to live. Here social imitation and interaction reach their limits. I cannot hitch a ride on another man's hazard. Faith is not transferable; it is "inexpugnably personal." That is both man's loneliness and his solitude. In that risk is both "the pain of being alone" and "the glory of being alone." [49]

Chapter Eleven

History over
Our Heads:
The Recovery of Hope

AN URGENT QUESTION

One question I find myself asking with increasing frequency and urgency in these days. It is a question which has not occurred to me to ask in quite the same way at any time in the last thirty years; yet it impresses me just now with peculiar pertinence and poignance.

The question is this: *Is there any hope for man in what is left of this century of our discontent?*

If there is a nub to the problematic character of man's contemporary ambience, I wrote in the opening chapter, it is that we do not know what kind of man will emerge out of the upheavals of our time, nor indeed whether anything recognizably human will emerge at all. There is danger in putting the matter so—the danger of falling into a pernicious and annoying form of historical pride which assumes that, whatever other generations of men have had to endure, fate has reserved for us a special election and eminence: to live at history's darkest moment. I do not intend either the assessment with which I began this volume, or the question to which I now address myself at its conclusion, to reflect that kind of pseudocomparative nonsense. It is nonsense, partly because history is a very inexact science and offers no reliable method for deciding what its darkest moment might be, and partly because as an intuitive estimate such a judgment about our own times would be too simple to be trusted.

When William Butler Yeats came to his conclusion about what he called "the growing murderousness of the world," he wrote a poem ironically entitled "The Second Coming," in which he complained:

> Things fall apart; the centre cannot hold;
> Mere anarchy is loosed upon the world,
> The blood-dimmed tide is loosed and everywhere
> The ceremony of innocence is drowned;
> The best lack all conviction while the worst
> Are full of passionate intensity.[1]

When Yeats wrote that, it was an attractive exaggeration. It was attractive because it is sometimes easier to think better of oneself if one can think the worst of the world; and it was an exaggeration because it was too unsubtle to appreciate the real complexity of things. There is more truth about the times in the words with which Charles Dickens began his classic *Tale of Two Cities:*

> It was the best of times, it was the worst of times,
> it was the age of wisdom, it was the age of foolishness,
> it was the epoch of belief, it was the epoch of incredulity,
> it was the season of Light, it was the season of Darkness,
> it was the spring of hope, it was the winter of despair,
> we had everything before us, we had nothing before us. . . .[2]

Indeed, Dickens' description of England in 1775 has an astonishingly contemporary ring about it:

> In England, there was scarcely an amount of order and protection to justify much national boasting. Daring burglaries by armed men, and highway robberies, took place in the capital itself every night; families were publicly cautioned not to go out of town without removing their furniture to upholsterers' warehouses for security. . . . prisoners in London gaols fought battles with their turnkeys, and the majesty of the law fired blunderbusses in among them, loaded with rounds of shot and ball. . . . musketeers went into St. Giles's, to search for contraband goods, and the mob fired on the musketeers, and the musketeers fired on the mob, and nobody thought any of these occurrences much out of the common way.[3]

They are not, as we should by now have good reason to know, much out of the common way. Contradiction and contrariness, violence and disorder, are the stuff out of which history seems permanently to be made; though whether or not such categories are adequate to describe the full range of our historical experience is the question which will preoccupy most of this final chapter. I do not deny that we may make legitimate and useful comparative judgments between one historical period and another. I only insist that to assert the unparalleled darkness or wickedness of one's own age is a perverse and self-pitying boast, not unlike that perversion which drives some men to boast of more depravity in their own behavior than they have either the wit or the stamina to accomplish.

> Once in a moment of passion
> I cried in desperate grief,
> "O Lord, my heart is black with guile,
> Of sinners I am chief."
> Then spake my guardian angel
> And whispered from behind,
> "That's vanity, my little man,
> You're nothing of the kind!"[4]

Human history is inherently problematic, as I have been at some pains to show. Perhaps there has never been a period in which it could not have been said, We do not know what kind of man will emerge, or indeed whether man will emerge at all. To be sure, not until now have men had access to the science of personality alteration by chemical means, or to the technology of global suicide. But long before the science and technique of human diminishment became precise and automated, other effective means were at hand. Slavery is virtually as old as man himself; and the brutalization and perversion of the human was, in some respects, even more ingenious in ancient times than in our own, for since they could not be mass-produced and mass-induced, they required even more by way of virtuosity and imagination.

Still, man's remarkable ability in the past to survive as a problematic self in a problematic world is no guarantee of his continuing survival. While I detect no serious imbalance, on an objective estimate, between the problems and the possibilities this age offers, I do detect something profoundly troublesome at a deeper level: *a growing depression of the spirit in the presence of our problems* which has not been present, to the same degree at least, at any time in this century and which, coupled with the ancient arts and the new sciences of the inhumane, creates a predisposition to disaster.

I detect now the signs of a growing hopelessness about our condition, not so much in our formal pronouncements as in our mood and our morale. So anger is abroad in almost epidemic proportion, infecting every segment of society. And if occasionally it is an anger directed at a specific grievance, more often it is unfocused, generalized, likely to boil up at small provocation or at none, almost as if life itself were the grievance.

There is increasing rejection of lawful process, and in its place resort to forms of capricious behavior. And if occasionally deliberate defiance is the only strategy conscience has in opposing some unconscionable evil which uses order for its own protection, more often these days defiance is being used to secure for ourselves conveniences to which our conscience gives us no right at all.

More and more, shouting takes the place of persuasion. And if occasionally a shout is necessary to command the attention of a distracted world, once that attention has been gained, we have lately become so fascinated with the large sounds of our own voices that we have forgotten how to engage in conversation.

I submit that unfocused anger is a sign of disappointment that life isn't what it used to be—though it probably never was. Indiscriminate defiance is the work of frustration when events refuse to move at our own private command. And shouting is the final recourse of those who, knowing that they cannot be triumphant, nevertheless insist on entering their complaint against history. These are the shapes hopelessness takes in our time. So perhaps it is not surprising, as a friend recently observed, that "hard rock" music has taken on an apocalyptic sound—has become "music to end history by"!

So I ask with some urgency: Is there any hope for man in what is left of this century of our discontent? Is there anywhere cause for hopefulness to which we can ally ourselves? Are there any grounds for believing that the world is other than, at hopeless moments, it seems to be? Is there any source of optimism for the future which is not mere wishful thinking?

My answer to all of these questions is a confident, "Yes!" I am persuaded that the angry, defiant shouters of our time are not, as they may claim, the victims of some political conspiracy, or worse, of some inscrutable determinism. Rather they have been victimized by their own historical shallowness. History discloses its own grounds for hope. The history of our era is shot through with hopefulness, if only we have the eyes to see it.

THE IMPROBABLE BECOMES POSSIBLE

There is, for one thing, the fact that *history is a source of genuine surprise.*

Who could have believed that one of the most powerful presidents in the history of the United States—a man who, by all the evidence, enjoyed his power as fully as any has done—would voluntarily relinquish that power and consent to his own early retirement? Everything about it was unlikely—his stubborn pride, the value he placed on iron will in the face of adversity, his own sense of historical destiny, his determination to see a dirty job through to what he thought a proper conclusion. It is not important that, once he had disavowed further political ambition, some could see the signs of its coming by looking back, or that others could insist that it was precisely his stubborn pride which dictated voluntary retirement rather than risk marginal victory or even defeat. All of that came *after* the surprising, unpredictable event, not before it.

Who could have believed that a modern state actually engaged in fighting a war could mount a nationwide debate about the moral justification of that warfare? It has happened twice within a decade—in France with respect to Algeria and in the United States with respect to Vietnam. Yet everything about that was unlikely. Individuals may sometimes swallow their pride and admit error, but for nations such self-effacement is simply impossible: that is the shibboleth we had learned to repeat. Patriotism is the enemy of self-criticism, and self-criticism in wartime leads to electoral disaster: those were the almost universally accepted axioms of our political "realism." So it seemed utterly clear in 1964 that the bare handful of men in the United States Senate who asked embarrassing questions about the Vietnam war would be repudiated by their electors and swept into obscurity by the growing outrage of our national pride. After the number who asked such questions had grown into the hundreds of thousands, we could look back and detect some of the moral and political and economic influences which brought about such a great change, but that is unimportant.

All of that came *after* the surprising, unpredictable event, not before it.

Who could have believed that history had anything important left for Angelo Giuseppi Roncalli to do? Everything about that was unlikely. Cardinal Roncalli, the patriarch of Venice, was nearly seventy-seven years old when his name was put forward as a compromise candidate in the papal election of 1958. Not until the eleventh ballot did the old man collect enough support to be elected. And when his unlikely name was announced to the world as the newest successor to the throne of St. Peter, it was widely predicted that he would be merely a caretaker of the church for a brief interim space between the significant pontificate which preceded him and the one which would follow him. Predictions were right on the brevity of his reign; he died after four and one-half years. But who would have guessed on that October day of his election in 1958 that in those short years the good-natured little caretaker would insist on throwing open the windows of the ancient structure he had inherited, on opening doors which no previous pope has cared or dared to open, sending through that old church fresh winds of change which are still blowing at near gale force? He was the first pope in centuries to celebrate Mass according to the Byzantine liturgy, and the first pope since the seventh century to authorize a change in the Latin Canon of the Mass. He reestablished direct contact between Rome and Canterbury for the first time in four hundred years, began a new era of relationships with Iron Curtain countries, and appointed the first native African Negro, Japanese, and Philippine cardinals. Two encyclicals—*Mater et Magister* and *Pacem in Terris*—had a profound impact on men of goodwill of all faiths. Says one historian, "No pope ever made such an impression on world opinion as did this octogenarian pontiff." As a crowning achievement, he convened the Second Vatican Council in 1962, whose transforming energies and consequences are a source of continuing surprise to this very hour, shocking those both in and out of the church who had preferred to think of its posture as fixed. It is unimportant that, looking back, it becomes clear that the church was ready for John XXIII, that *aggiornamento* was an idea whose time had come. For that judgment comes *after* the surprising, unpredictable event, not before it.

Or who could have believed that a modest, obscure black man, who cared deeply about where other black men sat in the buses of Montgomery, Alabama, would become the acknowledged leader of a world movement for nonviolent liberation? It was not Martin Luther King's end which was unpredictable but his beginning. Everything about it was unlikely. Never before him had his race succeeded in raising up a genuine national leader; how, then, a world figure? In this most violent of centuries, nonviolence was nothing if not unpromising as a social strategy. The expectation that a race of people, who had been ground into the dust for centuries, could be captured by that strategy once power was grudgingly ceded to them was perhaps most unlikely of all. It is unimportant that Dr. King is now being hailed as an original philosopher and theologian, and that his strategy, apart from its moral character, is now seen simply as the only one that could have worked. All that comes *after* the surprising, unpredictable event, not before it.

These are not, I am bound to believe, simply oddities in the human record. Rather they disclose a hope in history which physicist Dr. William Pollard has put in these striking words:

> The great thing about history is that it seems to have a way of selecting the most improbable things to make it up, rather than the probable ones; or at least what seem to be the most significant turning points in history are of this character. They are always the most improbable. And yet all you can say scientifically is that it was possible.[5]

History as the source of surprise, the realm within which the improbable becomes the possible: I find great hope in that.

THE EMERGENCE OF THE UNINTENDED

There is a second hope in history, intimately related to this first but worth our separate attention. I dare say that many of our contemporaries think of historical events as the realm of the power play, moved only by the application of overwhelming force and indomitable will. In such a world, historical influence can be wielded only by certain giant figures and disciplined movements which have set about to shape a future with deliberate forethought and intent. I call this the titanic view of history, since it assumes that the makers and shakers must be almost larger than life to have any effect at all.

Then in a world where the concentrations of power are greater than they have ever been before, it is no wonder that hopelessness grows among us. We have had good reason to distrust the powerful, even when they profess a certain benevolent intent, and we fear for the future of a world shaped by their hands. More than that, the titanic view of history simply leaves most of us out. We are not titans, and we know it! Measured by contemporary dimensions, we are powerless and therefore must consider ourselves irrelevant. And there is no one more hopeless than the man who is persuaded of his own utter irrelevance to the world, his inability to make any impact at all.

Then I want to dispute the titanic view. For one thing, I am persuaded that the effectiveness of power is vastly overrated, especially by those who possess little of it themselves. There are weaknesses and vulnerabilities in power which are not adequately understood in a world fixated by force. Not long after the Pueblo incident in the waters off North Korea, humorist Arthur Hoppe wrote a fanciful piece in which the president of the United States called in his advisers and asked them to suggest an appropriate response to the North Korean seizure of the American ship. One by one their suggestions—to send in a liberating force, to declare war, to drop a few hydrogen bombs—were rejected because they would turn the rest of the world against us and get us into an even stickier mess.

American frustration mounted and mounted. But worse was to come. Peru swiped an American crab boat. Lower Volta copped a C.I.A. canoe on the upper Zambezi. And Fidel Castro kidnapped Mrs. Jacqueline Kennedy, who had water skied too far out from shore.

In each case, the President sent a stern diplomatic note. In each case, he received an undiplomatic one in return saying, "Yanh, yanh, go climb a sapling."

The end came when the Ambassador from Phyknia stole a Presidential ash tray at a White House reception and coolly demanded to know what the President was going to do about it.

The President did the only possible thing. He called a Convention of the States; the Articles of Confederation were repealed; and America became 50 sovereign nations—each small enough so that no one dared push it around.

And everybody lived happily ever after.

In his retirement in the Republic of Texas, the President was visited in his declining years by a young historian who said, "There's just one thing I don't understand, Sir. How could this have happened to America? It was the mightiest nation on earth."

"Yep," agreed the President sadly. "Our other problems we could've licked."[6]

And that, I suggest, is not so fanciful at all. It is, rather, a truth about the exercise of power which we shall fail to learn at our peril.

But there is an even more important objection to the titanic view. In its fascination with heavy-handedness in history, it fails to detect the astonishing influence of the light touch. *History is not only a source of surprise; it is also the place of the serendipitous.* Serendipity is the term which refers to the accidental and unanticipated things one discovers when he is actually looking for something else. So history confronts us not only with the appearance of the unpredictable, but also with the emergence of the unintended.

Indeed, some of the most striking events of our past were the unintended and unanticipated effects of causes no one at the time would have considered particularly promising. The Protestant Reformation was such an event. There was nothing daring or dramatic in the nailing of the Ninety-five Theses to the door of the Wittenberg Church by an obscure Augustinian monk named Luther. To begin with, they were written in Latin and could not even be read by most of those who passed through that portal. More than that, the theses were mostly technical propositions of scholastic theology. Finally, nailing them on the church door was simply the accepted way of announcing an academic debate. The door was much used as a kind of bulletin board for such affairs. And from this insignificant and unpromising act came the unintended results: the power of the Roman Church permanently shattered beyond repair, new economic and political institutions spawned, a fresh moral and intellectual movement begun, with patterns of faith and practice which shape our own time 450 years later.

One of the most significant developments of this present century is the ecumenical movement, the growing fellowship of Christians of all persuasions around the world. The ecumenical movement is a serendipitous event, the effect of causes which never directly envisaged or intended it. So the late Archbishop William Temple described it in these words:

As though in preparation for such a time as this, God has been building up a Christian fellowship which now extends into almost every nation, and binds citizens of them all together in true unity and mutual love. No human agency planned this. It is the result of the great missionary enterprise of the last hundred and fifty years. Neither the missionaries nor those who sent them out were aiming at the creation of a world-wide fellowship interpenetrating the nations, bridging the gulfs between them, and supplying the promise of a check to their rivalries. The aim for nearly the whole period was to preach the Gospel to as many individuals as could be reached so that those who were won to discipleship should be put in the way of eternal salvation. Almost incidentally the great world fellowship has arisen; it is the great new fact of our era. . . .[7]

And I dare to suggest that the modest missionaries who, all unintended, gave us religious ecumenism also, with equal innocence of intent, created the world-awareness and the human linkages which have made possible such political ecumenism as is represented in the United Nations.

To be sure, the influence of the serendipitous is not always benign—which suggests that we ought to maintain a healthy respect for the mystery and ambiguity of the historical process. I suspect that the scientist who first made cellulose soluble in the laboratory thought he was making a discovery of pure science. What would he have thought if he could have foreseen the unintended influence of that apparently innocent discovery on a tragic future? For when the solubility of cellulose was given industrial application, it made possible the production of the first modern synthetic fiber, rayon. And as rayon came more and more into use, it seriously depressed the Japanese silk market. Financial crisis in Japan led to territorial expansion and military adventurism, and adventurism led eventually to the attack on Pearl Harbor and the sad warfare of our own generation.[8]

It is perhaps dangerous to point to any serendipitous effect while it is still in process and before the unintended result finally and fully appears, but I shall hazard it. It is entirely possible that the vigorous antireligious policies of the Soviet government may, in the end, succeed in creating a new generation of religious interest and conviction where it has not previously existed, for a part of the Soviet propaganda campaign against religion has been the publication of religious writings so that they can be subjected to official criticism and ridicule. But the effect of this policy, in spite of the ridicule, may just be to give wider circulation to Christian literature than Christians themselves could possibly do, to create a new public for it beyond any public Christians could command, and thus to strengthen and perpetuate the very thing it intended to destroy.

More of history's striking occurrences than we realize are the result, not of titanic forces with overwhelming influence and indomitable will, but of the serendipitous—innocent, modest, unintended, and unanticipated. Cambridge professor of modern history Herbert Butterfield confirms this observation:

> A very considerable part of the attention of historians is concentrated in fact upon that kind of history-making which goes on so to speak over our heads, now deflecting the results of our actions, now taking our purposes out of our hands, and now turning our endeavors to ends not realised. . . . Ranke, one of the greatest analysts of the historical process, more than once called attention to something subtle in history which remained at the finish as a sort of residuum, unexplained. He said that it felt sometimes as though an occult force were at work in the midst of the apparent confusion.[9]

The truth is that even the most sophisticated intelligence never knows enough to know fully what the world is ready for. We possess insufficient wisdom to determine in advance which are the ideas whose time has come, nor indeed which are the ideas whose time has expired. Only hindsight tells us that. English historian R. G. Collingwood once remarked that "Civilizations die as they are born, not with the waving of flags and the rattle of machine guns in the streets, but in the dark, in the stillness, when no one is aware of it. Looking back, one sees that it has happened."

So the serendipitous may bring down the titanic. I find great hope in that.

"AND LOVE IS VERY LONG"

I want to suggest still another thing about the hope history offers. It has to do with the particular form the serendipitous often takes, and it is suggested by the closing lines in one of the "Naylor Sonnets" by Kenneth Boulding. These are the lines:

> Know this: though love is weak and hate is strong,
> Yet hate is short, and love is very long.[10]

If only we might believe that, then this world would seem a very different place and each of us a different person. Can we not believe it? Can we find the same kind of historical evidence for the toughness of tenderness that we have found for history's other hopes? I was not at all sure of that when I first began to reflect on these matters. Now I am sure. Look into the human record and ask: Who are the persons who have become, as it were, the permanent human models to whom generation after generation of men and women turn for inspiration and example? Who are the persons in history who have been universalized, broken out of their own time and culture to become contemporary in every age and place? Who are the persons who have given us not their systems but themselves, whose influence is not in ideas only but in incarnations? Who are they? Not Alexander the Great, but Socrates and Gautama Buddha. Not the Emperor Nero, but Jesus of Nazareth. Not Attila the Hun, but Augustine of Hippo. Not Genghis Khan, but Francis of Assisi. Not Niccolò Machiavelli, but Martin Luther. Not Friedrich Nietzsche, but Abraham Lincoln. Not Benito Mussolini, but Mohandas Gandhi. Not Adolf Hitler, but Dietrich Bonhoeffer.

Who indeed are the persons in your own more intimate history whose claim on your existence has been most durable and indelible? Are they not those who have had a talent for love? Then perhaps Paul was right after all: Love lasts! I find great hope in that.

THE SOVEREIGNTY OF LOVE

Yet hope is not restricted to history for its resource. In the end, the possibilities for our human and bewildered kind are not limited by our individual capacities for self-love and for neighbor-love, admirable and even astonishing as those nevertheless flawed talents are. For there is something else at work. *If love lasts, that is not merely because it displays a dogged persistence but because it discloses a radical sovereignty.* In chapter nine I undertook a definition of love and concluded with the conviction that "love is the *destiny* for which man is made." It remains now to say what that may signify.

The word "love," in its broadest and deepest meaning, points to all of the influences which enable us to be human. To affirm that "love is the destiny for which man is made" is to assert that those influences extend far beyond our willing them, or even our wanting them, far beyond any historical achievement; that, rather than the process of nature intending to kill man, the creative power of humanness is precisely a primordial purpose to which we may respond but which we neither initiate nor ultimately frustrate. We have our individual beings in that power, but its being is not exhausted by what we are. It is the transhistorical source of our existence in history—hope, as it were, "over our heads."

This is, in fact, the single theme in all that I have written in this book, as we may now see in a retrospective and summary moment. To be a man is to have a history, I asserted. There is a "givenness" in life to which we are fated and which, if we are to be fully human, we must learn to affirm. To say this is really to say that every human existence is supported by structures outside of itself, in the very nature of things, which both shape life and sustain it— prevenient structures which are always there before there is a human being to need them and without which the human could neither emerge nor persist. Biological structures, psychological structures, physical structures, social structures—"orders of creation," Emil Brunner called them. *Loving* orders of creation, I would add, which enable us to be human.

To be human is to be free, I have insisted. There is in each of us an inner imperative to be human and to take full responsibility for our own humanness. "Freedom," Daniel Day Williams wrote, "means the opportunity to decide how one's life shall enter into the continuum of conditions and consequences. We have no freedom to decide whether we shall 'give our lives away' in the continuing social process. We are always giving them away either constructively or destructively."[11] We are, insofar, "condemned" to be free, as Sartre would say, by a structure within the self which will not permit us to renounce our humanity but requires us instead to take a position in respect of it. A *loving* condemnation, I would add, which enables us to be human.

To be human is to be in relation, I have persisted. Life is not possessed but is, rather, a gift to be received and given. Man is built for "response-ability." So, as Bernard Loomer once wrote: "Wherever human communities are found, there is language, the instrument and organ of communication. . . . Sex is a built-in mechanism driving us to relatedness. . . . Suffering, likewise, is a psychic reaction or mechanism which also propels us toward each other in times of loss."[12] So we live out the mystery of relation without ever exhausting it. A *loving* mystery, I would add, which enables us to be human.

To be human, then, finally and ultimately, is to live within a providence: a will which knew me and intended me before I was, which created the prevenient structures which are both the source and center of my being, and in which that being will not be forgotten when it has dissolved. A *loving* will, I would add, which enables me to be human. In Christian terms, providence means that the One who surprises us in the resurrection of Jesus Christ from the dead meets us also in the surprising turns of our nearer history. Providence means believing that what is unintended from the point of view of human will bears the imprint of a divine intent. Providence means confidence that the human loves which hearten us are clues to a larger love which lives at the heart of the universe itself. *Providence means grace within the structures.*

You may wonder why I have left this for the last word. Principally because I think we Christians have often been lacking in a proper modesty. We have claimed at one time or another to know too much about God's detailed intention for history, have been far too eager to declare this or that event to be identical with God's work in the world. Providence means that there are limits to the ways in which we can deliberately attempt to bend history and that there are limits to what we can confidently claim to know.

So providence is not a matter of demonstration but of confession. The hope our generation needs cannot, at the last, be proved but only pointed to; it cannot be shouted but only listened for. Standing in the presence of history's surprises and serendipities, and touched by history's incredibly persistent lovers and loving structures, the vocation of the Christian is to point to the One who demonstrated his lordship over history in the astonishing event of Jesus Christ, in the confidence that others may hear, as we have sometimes heard, his words: "Behold, I am doing a new thing!"

Such faith may make it possible, in this century of our discontent, to earn—as earn we must—the accolade which I have seen inscribed over the entrance to a church in the English countryside at Staunton Herald. It reads:

In the yeare: 1653
When all thinges sacred where throughout ye nation
Either demolisht or profaned
Sr Robert Shirley Baronnet
Founded this Church
Whose singular praise it is
to have done the best thinges in ye worst times
And
hoped them in the most callamitous
The righteous shall be had in everlasting remembrance

Notes

CHAPTER ONE: A PROBLEMATIC AMBIENCE

[1] Kenneth Boulding, *The Meaning of the Twentieth Century* (New York: Harper & Row, Publishers, 1964), p. 192.

[2] Eric Sevareid, "The World Still Moves Our Way," *Look* (July 9, 1968), p. 28.

[3] George Morgan, *The Human Predicament* (Providence, R.I.: Brown University Press, 1968), p. 17.

[4] Quoted in Archibald MacLeish, "The Revolt of the Diminished Man," *Saturday Review* (June 7, 1969), p. 17.

[5] *Ibid.*, p. 61.

CHAPTER TWO: HISTORICITY AND HUMANHOOD

[1] Archibald MacLeish, "The Revolt of the Diminished Man," *Saturday Review* (June 7, 1969), pp. 18-19.

[2] C. F. von Weizsäcker, *The History of Nature* (Chicago: University of Chicago Press, 1949), pp. 8-9.

[3] *Ibid.*, p. 9 (emphasis added).

[4] Ellis Arnall, *The Shore Dimly Seen* (Philadelphia: J. B. Lippincott Company, 1946), p. 128.

[5] Peter Berger, *Invitation to Sociology: A Humanistic Perspective* (New York: Doubleday & Company, Inc., 1963), p. 57.

[6] Reinhold Niebuhr, *The Nature and Destiny of Man* (New York: Charles Scribner's Sons, 1941), vol. 1, p. 156.

[7] *Ibid.*, p. 158.

CHAPTER THREE: AN AUTOBIOGRAPHICAL EXCURSUS: *APOLOGIA PRO VITA MEA*

[1] Roger Hazelton, "Truth in Theology," *Christian Century* (June 23, 1971), p. 774.

[2] Quoted in Henry Brandon, "A New Tranquility on the U.S. Campus," *Washington Post* (June 17, 1971), p. A18.

[3] Quoted in Roger L. Shinn, "Human Freedom and the SST," *Christianity and Crisis* (February 8, 1971), p. 2.

[4] Lloyd J. Averill, *American Theology in the Liberal Tradition* (Philadelphia: The Westminster Press, 1967).

[5] Jack Newfield, "The Death of Liberalism," *Playboy* (April, 1971), p. 99.

[6] Herbert Butterfield, *Christianity and History* (New York: Charles Scribner's Sons, 1950), p. 146.

[7] Michael Novak, "God in the Colleges," *Harper's Magazine* (October, 1961), p. 178.

[8] *Ibid.*

[9] Learned Hand, in an address to the Board of Regents, University of the State of New York, October 24, 1952.

CHAPTER FOUR: HOW "NEW" IS MODERN MAN?

[1] James Russell Lowell, lines from "The Present Crisis."

[2] Alfred Lord Tennyson, lines from "In Memoriam."

[3] Fred Hoyle, *The Nature of the Universe* (New York: Harper & Row, Publishers, 1950), pp. 138-139.

[4] *Ibid.*, pp. 123-124.

[5] Fred Hoyle, *The Nature of the Universe*, rev. ed. (New York: Harper & Row, Publishers, 1960), pp. 123-124.

[6] *Ibid.*, p. 122.

[7] John A. T. Robinson, *Exploration into God* (Stanford, Calif.: Stanford University Press, 1967), esp. chapter 5.

[8] Ronald W. Hepburn, "A Critique of Humanist Theology," in H. J. Blackham, ed., *Objections to Humanism* (Philadelphia: J.B. Lippincott Company, 1963), pp. 32, 53.

[9] *Ibid.*, pp. 50-51.

[10] *Ibid.*, p. 50

[11] Julian Huxley, *Religion Without Revelation* (New York: New American Library, Inc., 1957), p. 182.

[12] Max C. Otto, *The Human Enterprise* (New York: F. S. Crofts & Co., 1941), p. 342.

CHAPTER FIVE: REVOLUTIONARIES AND OTHER ROMANTICS: THE ESCAPE FROM FATE

[1] Sidney Hook, "Barbarism, Virtue, and the University," *The Public Interest* (Spring, 1969), p. 24.

[2] Nat Hentoff, "Dehumanized Radicalism," *Mademoiselle* (May, 1969), p. 16.

[3] Quoted in Hook, *op. cit.*, p. 36.

[4] Quoted in Hentoff, *op. cit.*, p. 22.

[5] Shailer Mathews, *The Church and the Changing Order* (New York: The Macmillan Company, 1907), p. 166.

[6] George F. Kennan, *Democracy and the Student Left* (Boston: Little, Brown and Company, 1968), pp. 9-10.

[7] Paul Jacobs and Saul Landau, *The New Radicals* (New York: Vintage Books, 1966), p. 4.

[8] Renata Adler, "How Movies Speak to Young Rebels," *The New York Times* (May 19, 1968), Section 2, p. 1.

[9] Jack Newfield, "The Death of Liberalism," *Playboy* (April, 1971), p. 99.

[10] *Ibid.*

[11] Henry B. Parkes, *The American Experience* (New York: Vintage Books, 1956), p. 3.

[12] *Ibid.*, pp. 351-352.

[13] Denis W. Brogan, *The American Character* (Time, Inc., 1962), pp. 228-229.

[14] Seymour L. Halleck, "Why They'd Rather Do Their Own Thing," *This Week Magazine* (March 16, 1969), p. 7.

[15] Kennan, *op. cit.*, p. 14.

[16] Robert Kaiser, "Letting Go," *Playboy* (July, 1969), p. 84.

[17] *Ibid.*

[18] *Ibid.*

[19] Charles A. Reich, *The Greening of America* (New York: Random House, 1970), p. 261.

[20] *Ibid.*

[21] Lionel Trilling, "Commitment to the Modern," *Harvard Today* (Autumn, 1962), as reprinted by the Division of College and University Work, National Lutheran Council, and United Campus Christian Fellowship Publications Office, n.p.

CHAPTER SIX: THE COORDINATES OF MAN

[1] Blaise Pascal, *Pensées,* trans. W. F. Trotter (New York: E. P. Dutton & Co., Inc., 1948), Fragment 72, pp. 17-18.

[2] Horace Bushnell, "Nature and the Supernatural," excerpted in H. S. Smith, ed., *Horace Bushnell* (New York: Oxford University Press, 1965), p. 147.

[3] *Ibid.*

[4] Albert Camus, *The Stranger,* trans. Stuart Gilbert (New York: Alfred A. Knopf, Publisher, 1970).

[5] Germaine Bree, *Camus,* rev. ed. (New Brunswick: Rutgers University Press, 1964), p. 114.

[6] Austin Des Lauriers, *The Experience of Reality in Childhood Schizophrenia* (New York: International Universities Press, 1962), p. 27.

[7] Pascal, *op. cit.,* Fragment 347, p. 97.

[8] Quoted in Reinhold Niebuhr, *The Nature and Destiny of Man,* vol. 1 (New York: Charles Scribner's Sons, 1964), p. 155.

[9] Erich Fromm in Suzuki, Fromm, and DeMartino, *Zen Buddhism and Psychoanalysis* (New York: Harper & Row, Publishers, 1960), p. 93.

[10] *Ibid.*, p. 88.

[11] *Ibid.*

[12] Sherwood Anderson, *Winesburg, Ohio* (New York: The Modern Library, 1947), pp. 286-287.

[13] *Ibid.*, pp. 287-288.

[14] Fromm, *op. cit.,* p. 91.

[15] Alberto Moravia, *Woman of Rome,* trans. Lydia Holland (New York: Farrar, Straus & Giroux, Inc., 1949), pp. 179-180.

[16] Des Lauriers, *op. cit.,* p. 51.

[17] Niebuhr, *op. cit.,* p. 156.

[18] *Ibid.*, p. 183.

[19] *Ibid.*, p. 185.

[20] *Ibid.*

[21] William Hamilton in Thomas J. J. Altizer and William Hamilton, *Radical Theology and the Death of God* (New York: The Bobbs-Merrill Company, Inc., 1966), pp. 159, 164.

[22] H. Richard Niebuhr, *The Responsible Self* (New York: Harper & Row, Publishers, 1963).

[23] *Ibid.*, p. 61.

[24] *Ibid.*, p. 63.

[25] *Ibid.*, p. 61.

[26] *Ibid.*, p. 64.

[27] *Ibid.*, p. 71.

[28] *Ibid.*, pp. 70, 71.

CHAPTER SEVEN: POLITICAL FUNDAMENTALISTS AND OTHER REACTIONARIES: THE ESCAPE FROM FREEDOM

[1] Charlotte Perkins Stetson Gilman, "A Conservative," *In This Our World* (Boston: Small, Maynard & Co., 1899), pp. 100-101.

[2] Phyllis Schlafly, *A Choice Not an Echo* (Alton, Ill.: Pere Marquette Press, 1964), pp. 89-91.

[3] *Ibid.*, p. 93.

[4] Robert F. Kennedy, "Thirteen Days: The Story About How the World Almost Ended," *McCall's* (November, 1968), pp. 9, 149.

[5] *Ibid.*, p. 149.

[6] E. Merrill Root, "The Quicksands of the Mind," an address before the Sons of the American Revolution, February, 1960. Root was then professor of English in Earlham College. *Christian Economics* (July 19, 1961), p. 3.

[7] *Ibid.*

[8] From a personal letter to the author.

[9] *Ibid.*

[10] John C. Bennett, quoted in *Interchurch News*, a periodical of the National Council of the Churches of Christ in the U.S.A.

[11] Reinhold Niebuhr, *The Children of Light and the Children of Darkness* (New York: Charles Scribner's Sons, 1944), p. xi.

[12] Reinhold Niebuhr, "How Liberal Is the New Pope?" *New Leader* (July 22, 1963), p. 10.

[13] William F. Buckley, Jr., "What George Wallace Means to Me," *Look* (October 29, 1968), pp. 101-102.

[14] William F. Buckley, Jr., "When Freedom Is Threatened," *Quillen* (February, 1963).

CHAPTER EIGHT: THE MATRIX OF MAN

[1] Hendrik Ibsen, "Peer Gynt," *Eleven Plays of Hendrik Ibsen* (New York: The Modern Library, n.d.), p. 397.

[2] *Ibid.*, pp. 481-482.

[3] H. Richard Niebuhr, *The Responsible Self* (New York: Harper & Row, Publishers, 1963), p. 71 (italics added).

[4] Martin Buber, *I and Thou*, trans. Ronald Gregor Smith (New York: Charles Scribner's Sons, 1958), p. 11.

[5] Details of the story of Anna and generalized conclusions attributed in my text to the "investigator" are taken from Kingsley Davis, "Extreme Social Isolation of a Child," *American Journal of Sociology*, vol. 45, no. 4 (January, 1940), pp. 554-565.

[6] Ferdinand Tönnies, *Fundamental Concepts of Sociology*, excerpted from A. McC. Lee, ed., *Readings in Sociology* (New York: Barnes & Noble Books, 1951), p. 82.

[7] Details of the story of Isabelle and generalized conclusions attributed in my text to the "investigator" are taken from Kingsley Davis, "Final Note on a Case of Extreme Isolation," *American Journal of Sociology*, vol. 52, no. 5 (March, 1947), pp. 432-437.

[8] *Ibid.*, p. 437.

[9] Davis, "Extreme Social Isolation of a Child," p. 565.

[10] Loren Eiseley, "An Evolutionist Looks at Modern Man," in Richard Thruelson and John Kobler, eds., *Adventures of the Mind* (New York: Alfred A. Knopf, Inc., Vintage Books, 1959), p. 7. Reprinted with permission from *The Saturday Evening Post* © 1958 by The Curtis Publishing Company.

[11] Erich Fromm in Suzuki, Fromm, and DeMartino, *Zen Buddhism and Psychoanalysis* (New York: Harper & Row, Publishers, 1960), p. 87.

[12] Eiseley, *op. cit.*, p. 7.

[13] *Ibid.*, pp. 7-8.

[14] George H. Mead, *Mind, Self and Society* (Chicago: University of Chicago Press, 1934), pp. 191-192.

[15] Alan Richardson, ed., *A Theological Word Book of the Bible* (New York: The Macmillan Company, 1950), p. 106.

[16] Albert Camus, *The Fall*, trans. Justin O'Brien (New York: The Modern Library, 1956), pp. 56, 57, 58, 102, 103.

[17] Viktor E. Frankl, "Beyond Self-Actualization and Self-Expression," *Psychotherapy and Existentialism* (New York: Clarion Books, 1968, imprint of Simon and Schuster, Inc.), p. 50.

[18] Patricia M. Greenfield and Jerome S. Bruner, "Learning and Language: Work with the Wolof," *Psychology Today* (July, 1971), p. 74. Reprinted from *The Relevance of Education* by Jerome S. Bruner, edited by Anita Gil. Copyright © 1971 by Jerome S. Bruner. W. W. Norton & Company, Inc., New York, N.Y.

[19] *Ibid.*

[20] *Ibid.*, p. 42.

[21] *Ibid.*, p. 79.

[22] *Ibid.*

[23] *Ibid.*, p. 78.

[24] *Ibid.*, p. 79.

[25] Peter Berger, *Invitation to Sociology: A Humanistic Perspective* (Garden City, N.Y.: Doubleday & Company, Inc., 1963), pp. 63-64.

[26] Ugo Betti, *Three Plays by Ugo Betti* (New York: Grove Press, Inc., 1958), p. 151.

[27] Philip Slater, *The Pursuit of Loneliness* (Boston: Beacon Press, 1970), p. 26.

CHAPTER NINE: CRISIS IN SEXUALITY: THE LOSS OF THE OTHER

[1] *The Random House Dictionary of the English Language,* unabridged edition (New York: Random House, Inc., 1966), p. 344.

[2] Paul Tillich, *The Eternal Now* (New York: Charles Scribner's Sons, 1963), pp. 16-17.

[3] Dietrich Bonhoeffer, *Letters and Papers from Prison* (New York: The Macmillan Company, 1962), p. 113.

[4] Walter Kerr, *The Decline of Pleasure* (New York: Simon & Schuster, Inc., 1962), p. 307.

[5] *Ibid.*, pp. 307-308.

[6] *Ibid.*, p. 308.

[7] *Ibid.*, p. 309.

[8] Bonhoeffer, *op. cit.*, p. 99.

[9] Lloyd J. Averill, *Between Faith and Unfaith* (Richmond, Va.: John Knox Press, 1968), pp. 25-26. Some of the language in the present discussion is drawn from the earlier passage cited here.

[10] Melvin Maddocks in a review of *I Want It Now* by Kingsley Amis, in *Life* (March 14, 1969), p. 8.

[11] Werner and Lotte Pelz, *God Is No More* (Philadelphia: J. B. Lippincott Company, 1963), p. 117.

[12] Paraphrase of Blaise Pascal, *Pensées*, trans. J. M. Cohen (Baltimore, Md.: Penguin Books, Inc., 1961), Fragment 335. The original passage refers to unbelievers, and Pascal wrote, ". . . our religion obliges us always to consider them, so long as they are alive, capable of being illuminated by grace, and to believe that in a short while they may be fuller of faith than we ourselves, while we, on the other hand, may fall into the blindness which is now theirs."

[13] William Hamilton, *Faith, Sex and Love* (National Student Council of the YMCA and YWCA, 1954), p. 19.

[14] Kahlil Gibran, *The Prophet* (New York: Alfred A. Knopf, Inc., 1946), pp. 19-20.

[15] I myself insisted on the distinction in *Between Faith and Unfaith* (p. 61), but I now believe it to be etymologically dubious and theologically unnecessary. For a discussion of the etymological problems, cf. Alan Richardson, ed., *A Theological Word Book of the Bible* (New York: The Macmillan Company, 1950), pp. 133-134.

[16] Dietrich Bonhoeffer, *Life Together* (New York: Harper & Row, Publishers, 1954), pp. 35-36. In this passage Bonhoeffer makes a distinction between "human love" and "spiritual love" which I am here calling into question, but Bonhoeffer's words cited in my text stand independently of that distinction.

[17] Paul Tillich, *op. cit.*, p. 24.

CHAPTER TEN: THE INEXPUGNABLY PERSONAL

[1] Calvin Hall, *A Primer of Freudian Psychology* (New York: New American Library, 1954), p. 27. Reprinted by permission of The World Publishing Company from *A Primer of Freudian Psychology* by Calvin S. Hall. Copyright © 1954 by The World Publishing Company.

[2] Walter Kerr, *The Decline of Pleasure* (New York: Simon & Schuster, Inc., 1962), p. 305.

[3] Albert Camus, *The Fall*, trans. Justin O'Brien (New York: Alfred A. Knopf, Inc., 1956), pp. 58, 104-105.

[4] *Ibid.*, p. 144.

[5] Quoted in Bertrand Russell, *A History of Western Philosophy* (New York: Simon & Schuster, Inc., 1945), p. 763.

[6] *Ibid.*, p. 766.

[7] *Ibid.*, p. 767.

[8] See Max Weber, *The Protestant Ethic and the Spirit of Capitalism*, trans. Talcott Parsons (New York: Charles Scribner's Sons, 1958).

[9] For representative sources and interpretations of the movement, see Gail Kennedy, ed., *Democracy and the Gospel of Wealth* (Lexington, Mass.: D. C. Heath & Company, 1949).

[10] Arthur Miller, *Death of a Salesman* (New York: The Viking Press, 1949), p. 23.

[11] Eric Hodgins, *Blandings' Way* (New York: Simon & Schuster, Inc., 1950), pp. 24-26.

[12] Lawrence J. Peter and Raymond Hull, *The Peter Principle* (New York: William Morrow & Co., Inc., 1969).

[13] Edgar Z. Friedenberg, *The Vanishing Adolescent* (Boston: Beacon Press, 1960), p. 17.

[14] Langdon Gilkey, *Naming the Whirlwind: The Renewal of God-Language* (New York: The Bobbs-Merrill Company, 1969), p. 340.

[15] Paul Tillich, *The Dynamics of Faith* (New York: Harper & Row, Publishers, 1957), p. 12.

[16] Viktor Frankl, *Man's Search for Meaning* (New York: Washington Square Press, 1963), p. 168.

[17] *Ibid.*, p. 169.

[18] For a more extensive discussion of the "will to meaning," see Frankl, *Man's Search for Meaning*, esp. pp. 151-214; also Frankl, *The Doctor and the Soul: An Introduction to Logotherapy* (New York: Alfred A. Knopf, Inc., 1961).

[19] Frankl, *op. cit.*, p. 172.

[20] H. Richard Niebuhr, *The Responsible Self* (New York: Harper & Row, Publishers, 1963), p. 119.

[21] *Ibid.*, p. 118.

[22] *Ibid.*

[23] *Ibid.*, p. 120 (italics added).

[24] Andras Angyal, *Neurosis and Treatment: A Holistic Theory*, ed. E. Hanfmann and R. M. Jones (New York: John Wiley & Sons, Inc., 1965), p. 100.

[25] Langdon Gilkey, *The God Is Dead Theology and the Possibility of God-Language* (Mimeographed, privately distributed), Part II, p. 19. This is an earlier statement of the argument in *Naming the Whirlwind*.

[26] Langdon Gilkey, *Naming the Whirlwind: The Renewal of God-Language*, p. 303.

[27] Peter Berger, *A Rumor of Angels* (Garden City, N.Y.: Doubleday & Company, Inc., 1969).

[28] Peter Berger, *The Sacred Canopy* (New York: Doubleday & Company, Inc., 1969), p. 23; also chapters 2 and 3.

[29] Albert Camus, *The Rebel* (New York: Vintage Books, 1960), p. 21.

[30] Berger, *A Rumor of Angels*, p. 52.

[31] *Ibid.*, p. 58.

[32] *Ibid.*, pp. 58-59.

[33] *Ibid.*, p. 65.

[34] *Ibid.*, p. 69.

[35] *Ibid.*

[36] *Ibid.*, p. 72.

[37] *Ibid.*, p. 74.

[38] *Ibid.*, p. 76.

[39] *Ibid.*, p. 84.

[40] *Ibid.*, p. 86.

[41] *Ibid.*, p. 87.

[42] *Ibid.*, p. 88.

[43] Harry Emerson Fosdick, *The Modern Use of the Bible* (New York: The Macmillan Company, 1958), p. 30.

[44] Frankl, *op. cit.*, p. 157.

[45] Reinhold Niebuhr, *The Nature and Destiny of Man* (New York: Charles Scribner's Sons, 1946), vol. 2, p. 16.

[46] Paul Tillich, *The Shaking of the Foundations* (New York: Charles Scribner's Sons, 1948), p. 46.

[47] Camus, *The Fall*, p. 39.

[48] Tillich, *The Shaking of the Foundations*, pp. 47-48.

[49] Paul Tillich, *The Eternal Now* (New York: Charles Scribner's Sons, 1963), p. 18.

CHAPTER ELEVEN: HISTORY OVER OUR HEADS: THE RECOVERY OF HOPE

[1] W. B. Yeats, *The Autobiography of William Butler Yeats* (New York: Collier Books, 1965), p. 130.

[2] Charles Dickens, *A Tale of Two Cities* (New York: The Macmillan Company, 1962), pp. 13-15.

[3] *Ibid.*

[4] Attributed to "Thompson"; more precise attribution not available.

[5] William Pollard in *Schools and Scholarship*, ed. Edmund Fuller (New Haven, Conn.: Yale University Press, 1962), p. 287.

[6] Arthur Hoppe, syndicated column in *San Francisco Chronicle*, February, 1968.

[7] William Temple, *The Church Looks Forward* (New York: The Macmillan Company, 1944), p. 2.

[8] These historical consequences which followed upon the solubility of cellulose were first noted many years ago by R. G. Gustavson of the University of Chicago in his Phi Delta Kappa lecture, "A Liberal Education as a Scientist Sees It."

[9] Herbert Butterfield, *Christianity and History* (New York: Charles Scribner's Sons, 1950), p. 94.

[10] Kenneth Boulding, *There Is a Spirit* (Nyack, N.Y.: Fellowship Publications, 1945), p. 3.

[11] Daniel D. Williams, *God's Grace and Man's Hope* (New York: Harper & Row, Publishers, 1949), pp. 116-117.

[12] Bernard M. Loomer, "The Nature of Man" (mimeographed, n.d.), p. 4.